# Climbing
# the
# Heights

# Also by Al Bryant

*Day by Day with C. H. Spurgeon* (compiler)

*New Every Morning* (compiler)

*Sourcebook of Poetry*

*Sermon Outlines on:*

> *the Attributes of God*
> *Bible Characters from the Old Testament*
> *Bible Characters from the New Testament*
> *the Cross of Christ*
> *the Death, Resurrection, and Return of Christ*
> *the Deeper Life*
> *Evangelistic Occasions*
> *Faith, Hope, and Love*
> *the Family and Home*
> *the Fruit of the Spirit*
> *[for] Funerals and Other Special Services*
> *the Grace of God*
> *the Holy Spirit and Spiritual Life*
> *[for] Lay Leaders*
> *the Life of Christ*
> *Prayer*
> *Prophetic Themes*
> *the Psalms*
> *Revival Themes*
> *Romans*
> *[for] Special Occasions*
> *[for] Worship Services*

# Climbing
## the
# Heights

## 366 DAILY DEVOTIONALS

Compiled by
# AL BRYANT

kregel
PUBLICATIONS

Grand Rapids, MI 49501

To my wife, Jeanne,
who still says that this book has blessed and
comforted her more than any other collection
to come from my labors.
She has been my anchor, my joy, and my best friend—
and the best is yet to be!

———————————————

*Climbing the Heights: 366 Daily Devotionals*

© 1956 by Al Bryant

Published in 1991 by Kregel Publications, a division of
Kregel, Inc., P.O. Box 2607, Grand Rapids, MI 49501.
Kregel Publications provides trusted, biblical publications
for Christian growth and service. Your comments and
suggestions are valued.

For more information about Kregel Publications, visit our
web site at: www.kregel.com

**Library of Congress Cataloging-in-Publication Data**
Climbing the heights: 366 daily devotions / [compiled by]
Al Bryant.
        p.       cm.
        Includes indexes.
1. Devotional calendars. I. Bryant, Al. II. Title.
BV4810.C536    1991    242'.2—dc20    91-24339

ISBN 0-8254-2068-7

2 3 4 / 04 03 02 01 00

*Printed in the United States of America*

# CONTENTS

# ACKNOWLEDGMENTS

The compiler wishes to express his deep appreciation to those authors and publishers who have graciously granted permission to use extracts from their copyrighted publications. Among those whose publications have been valuable in the compilation of this book of daily devotions and to whom grateful thanks are expressed are the following publishers and authors:

Evangelical Publishers, Toronto, Canada, for selections from books by Annie Johnson Flint and Robert Barr

The Christian Press, Sydney, Australia, for selections from books by John Ridley

Marshall, Morgan & Scott, Ltd., London, England, for selections from books by J. Sidlow Baxter

Fleming H. Revell Company, Westwood, New Jersey, for selections from S. D. Gordon

Vantage Press, New York, New York, for selections from books by Bernice Richtmeyer

Victory Press, London, England, for selections from books by Frederick L. Tatford

Beacon Hill Press, Kansas City, Missouri, for selections from books by Bertha Munro

In addition to the above, grateful appreciation is also expressed to many other men (and women) of God whose works were used in the compilation of this book and whose thoughts have influenced my own spiritual life.

# FOREWORD TO THE 35TH ANNIVERSARY EDITION

In 1991, I look back upon more than forty years as a Christian writer, compiler and editor. One of the most challenging and rewarding tasks of those forty years was the opportunity to compile the daily meditations that make up the contents of *Climbing the Heights*. The unsigned meditations came from my own pen, but I am deeply indebted to those thinkers and writers who have influenced and directed my spiritual life. Their names appear elsewhere in this book, but I want to publicly thank them, here and now, for their influence in my life.

The purpose of *Climbing the Heights* is to help provide God's people with spiritual foundation and basis for their day-by-day lives, to supply them with at least a part of their daily spiritual requirements for a healthy Christian life. I feel that I myself was spiritually blessed and strengthened as I worked on the compilation of these devotional thoughts from God's servants of today and yesterday.

The central theme of *Climbing the Heights* is beautifully illustrated in a thought from the pen of J.R. Miller: "Men do not fly up mountains; they go up slowly, step-by-step. True Christian life is always mountain-climbing. Heaven is above us and ever keeps above us. It never gets easy to go heavenward. It is a slow and painful process to grow better. No one leaps to sainthood at a bound. No one gets the victory once for all over his faults and sins. It is a struggle of years, and every day must have its victories if we are ever to be final and complete overcomers. Yet while we cannot expect to reach the radiant mountaintop at one bound, we certainly ought to be climbing at least step-by-step. We ought not to sit on the same little terrace, part way up the mountain day-by-day. Higher and higher should be our unresting aim."

These thoughts remind us that the Christian life is not to be static or stagnant. We do not reach a plateau of complacency and then sit there content with our progress. Rather, the Christian life must be a growing process. Sometimes as you read the meditations in this book, you may be in the valley looking up. But, thank God, you won't stay there! The next day you may be on a mountaintop looking across to another spiritual high place. The general trend of our lives will be upward as we wind our way toward the heavenly kingdom, always *Climbing the Heights*!

In His love and mine,

AL BRYANT

*Grand Rapids, Michigan*

# TRUST

I know not what the future holds,
Of good or ill for me and mine;
I only know that God enfolds
Me in His loving arms divine.

So I shall walk the earth in trust
That He who notes the sparrow's fall
Will help me bear whate'er I must
And lend an ear whene'er I call.

It matters not if dreams dissolve
Like mists beneath the morning sun,
For swiftly as the worlds revolve
So swiftly will life's race be run.

It matters not if hopes depart,
Or life be pressed with toil and care.
If love divine shall fill my heart
And all be sanctified with prayer.

Then let me learn submission sweet
In every thought, in each desire,
And humbly lay at His dear feet
A heart aglow with heavenly fire.

*In the beginning God . . .* —Genesis 1:1

By God's grace, dear friends, we are standing on t
threshold of a New Year. It is the "beginning" of a new
adventure with God. No matter what may greet us as we
journey this untrodden way, His grace will prove sufficient.
May we therefore this day rededicate ourselves and all that
we are and have to Him.

For all of us, before the year is well on its way, problems
will have to be faced, decisions made and plans affecting
every phase of our lives considered. All of these things will
require a wisdom above our own. If we place our
responsibilities before the Lord and sincerely seek His will
and guidance, we can rely on Him to direct our steps.

As we begin this year in an attitude of prayer and meditation
before the Lord, we should resolve to begin each day of the year
in His presence and in His will. Let this year be one not only of
*beginning* with God but *continuing* with Him day by day.

*I asked the New Year for some motto sweet,*
*Some rule of life with which to guide my feet;*
*I asked, and paused; he answered soft and low:*
*  "God's will to know."*

*"Will knowledge then suffice, New Year?" I cried;*
*And, ere the question into silence died,*
*The answer comes: "Nay, but remember, too,*
*  God's will to do."*

*Once more I asked, "Is there no more to tell?"*
*And once again the answer sweetly fell:*
*"Yes! this one thing, all other things above,*
*  God's will to love."*

*downsitting and mine uprising, thou un-*
*...ht afar off.* —Psalm 139:2

...ие is foreplanned. It seems hard for us to take
...really so. But that's the kind of a God our God is. A
...ple shepherd lad, years ago, tending sheep, found out that
the plan for his life was written down in a book beforehand —
God's own record book (Ps. 139:16). We may find this out,
too. God will foretell us His plan. May we not fail God, nor
His plan. —S. D. Gordon

Friend, if you don't know what you ought to do, stay where
you are until you do. I am convinced that God has important
work where you are; see it and enter into it zealously until
God clearly shows you the next move. —B. Charles Hostetter

*God hath not promised*
*Skies always blue,*
*Flower-strewn pathways*
*All our lives through;*
*God hath not promised*
*Sun without rain,*
*Joy without sorrow,*
*Peace without pain.*

*But God hath promised*
*Strength for the day,*
*Rest for the labor,*
*Light for the way,*
*Grace for the trials,*
*Help from above,*
*Unfailing sympathy,*
*Undying love.*
—Annie Johnson Flint

*And we know that all things work together for good to them that love God, to them who are the called according to his purpose.*
—Romans 8:28

All things work together for good. This must be so for three reasons. First, because all things are under the absolute control of the Governor of the Universe. Second, because God desires our good: and nothing but our good. Third, because even Satan himself cannot touch a hair of our heads without God's permission, and then only for our further good. Not all things are good in themselves, nor in their tendencies; but God makes all things work for our good. Nothing enters our life by blind chance: nor are there any accidents. Everything is, being moved by God, with this end in view, our good.

—*Arthur W. Pink*

Let us beware of passing hasty judgments on God's dealings with us. He cannot work out His fair design without some cross-stitches on this side of the canvas. The black clouds are only His water-cisterns, and on the other side they are bathed in sunshine. Do not look at your sorrows from the lowlands of your pilgrimage — but from the uplands of God's purpose. No chastening for the present is joyous but grievous, nevertheless, afterward . . . dwell on that afterward! If Jacob had not been led along this special path, he would never have come out on the shining tableland, where God Himself is Sun.

—*F. B. Meyer*

*Through His wise and loving purpose*
*Clearly now thou may'st not see,*
*Still believe, with faith unshaken,*
*All shall work for good to thee.*

*I am the God of Abraham, and the God of Isaac and the God of Jacob. God is not the God of the dead, but of the living.* —Matthew 22:32

In this text Christ powerfully shows the resurrection of the dead; for if there were no hope of the resurrection of the dead, nor of another and better world after this short and miserable life, wherefore does God offer to be our God, to give us all that is necessary and healthful for us, and in the end to deliver us out of all trouble, both temporal and spiritual? To what purpose is it that we heed His Word and believe in Him? What does it serve us that we sigh and cry to Him in our anguish and need, that we wait with patience for His comfort and salvation, for His grace and benefits which He shows us in Christ? Why do we praise and thank Him for the same? Why are we daily in danger, and suffer ourselves to be persecuted and slain for the sake of Christ's Word, which we teach and hold for our greatest treasure? Because through His Word the everlasting and merciful God talks and deals with us concerning our future life, where we shall be when we depart from this life, and He gives unto us His Son, our Savior, who delivers us from sin and death, and has purchased for us everlasting righteousness, life and salvation. Therefore we are sure that we do not die like the beasts that have no understanding; but that all who die in Christ shall through Him be raised again to everlasting life. —*Martin Luther*

*He lives and grants me daily breath;*
*He lives, and I shall conquer death;*
*He lives, my mansion to prepare;*
*He lives to bring me safely there.*

*. . . and God shall wipe away all tears from t*
        —Reve

Long will be eternity but not longer than the joys of eternity. Long will be the eternal years, but not longer than the companionship we shall enjoy with the redeemed, in fellowship with those who are "arrayed in white . . ." (Rev. 7:13) and who "came out of great tribulation, and have washed their robes, and made them white in the blood of the Lamb" (Rev. 7:14). And there, in the land of eternal day, where no grave digger plies his spade and where no roll of hearse wheel is ever heard, where no tears be-dim the eyes and no fears beset the heart, "they shall hunger no more, neither thirst any more" (Rev. 7:6). "The Lamb which is in the midst of the throne shall feed them, and shall lead them unto the living fountains of waters: and God shall wipe away all tears from their eyes" (Rev. 7:17).       —*R. G. Lee*

*God is in every tomorrow,*
 *Therefore I live for today;*
*Certain of finding at sunrise*
 *Guidance and strength for the day,*
*Power for each moment of weakness,*
 *Hope for each moment of pain*
*Comfort for every sorrow,*
 *Sunshine and joy after rain.*

*God is in every tomorrow,*
 *Planning for you and for me,*
*E'en in the dark I will follow,*
 *Trust where my eyes cannot see,*
*Stilled by His promise of blessing,*
 *Soothed by the touch of His hand,*
*Confident in His protection,*
 *Knowing my life-path is planned.*

*So shall my word be that goeth forth out of my mouth: it shall not return unto me void, but it shall accomplish that which I please, and it shall prosper in the thing whereto I send it.* —Isaiah 55:11

Who is there so accustomed to the difficulties and perplexities of life's journey; so experienced in the snares and wiles of the enemy; so reliant upon his own wisdom, as to be no longer in need of guidance? Looking out upon the mazy pathways of life, with advancing experience of the dangers that surround us, and the utter weakness and insufficiency that characterize us, the consciousness of our need of guidance deepens and grows upon us, until at last we find that as "the only real abiding strength of any man is to lean," so the only real prevailing wisdom of any man is to be willing to be guided, and from the depths of our hearts the cry continually ascends, "For Thy name's sake lead me and guide me."

— *E. W. Moore*

*Take my hand, O blessed Master,*
*Lead me by the waters still,*
*Lead me, Savior, by the river,*
*Lead me ever in Thy will.*

*Take my hand, yea, in the valley*
*Through the shadow, lead me, Lord,*
*Through the vale and through the darkness,*
*Let Thy blessing be outpoured.*

*O'er life's journey, through its trial,*
*Take my hand, O Lord, I pray,*
*Lead me gently, lead me sweetly*
*To Thy home. Lead all the way.*
—Connie Calenberg

*Pray without ceasing.* —1 Thessalonians 5:17

Praying men mean much more than men who say prayers; much more than men who pray by habit. It means men with whom prayer is a mighty force, an energy that moves heaven and pours untold treasures of good on earth. The number and efficiency of the laborers in God's vineyard in all lands is dependent on the men of prayer. The mightiness of these men of prayer increases, by the divinely arranged process, the number and success of the consecrated labors. Prayer opens wide their doors of access, gives holy aptness to enter, and holy boldness, firmness, and fruitage. Praying men are needed in all fields of spiritual labor.  —*E. M. Bounds*

God does not always allow us to get the things for which we ask, the first time that we ask for them. He would train us to be strong in faith. The best training for our faith is to be compelled to ask again and again for the things we, or others need. We may have to ask for a long period of years for some things.  —*Benjamin H. Spalink*

*Art Thou not weary of our selfish prayers,*
   *Forever crying, "Help me, save me, Lord"?*
*We stay fenced in by petty fears and cares,*
   *Nor heed the song outside, nor join its vast accord.*

*Still are we saying, "Teach us how to pray."*
   *Oh, teach us how to love, and then our prayer*
*Through other lives will find its upward way,*
   *As plants together seek and find sweet light and air.*

# JANUARY 8

*Truly my soul waiteth upon God: From him cometh my
salvation.* —Psalm 62:1

If salvation indeed comes from God, and is entirely His work, just as our creation was, it follows, as a matter of course, that our first and highest duty is to wait on Him to do that work as pleases Him. Waiting becomes then the only way to the experience of a full salvation. All the difficulties that are brought forward as keeping us back from full salvation, have their cause in this one thing: the defective knowledge and practice of waiting upon God. All that the Church and its members need for the manifestation of the mighty power of God in the world, is the return to our true place, the place that belongs to us, both in creation and redemption, the place of absolute and unceasing dependence upon God.

"Truly my soul waiteth upon God; from Him cometh my salvation." First we wait on God for salvation. Then we learn that salvation is only to bring us to God, and teach us to wait on Him. Then we find what is better still, that waiting on God is itself the highest salvation. It is the ascribing to Him the glory of being All; it is the experiencing that He is All to us. May God teach us the blessedness of waiting on Him.

—*Andrew Murray*

*Be still, my soul: thy God doth undertake
To guide the future as He has the past.
Thy hope, thy confidence let nothing shake;
All now mysterious shall be bright at last.
Be still my soul: the waves and winds still know
His voice who ruled them while He dwelt below.*
—Katharina Von Schlegel

*Wherefore the rather, brethren, give diligence to make your calling and election sure: for if ye do these things, ye shall never fall.*
—2 Peter 1:10

In order to fulfill God's purpose, one must be willing to abandon one's own designs and desires and leave all to follow Christ. Nothing should stand in the way. Just as a soldier of the state disentangles himself from all civil and personal pursuits, even so the soldier of the Cross must sever all ties that could in any wise hinder a full obedience to the commands of the Captain of the Lord's hosts. —*S. Franklin Logsdon*

Surrender is not simply making a promise to God to forsake sin and always to do His will. Surrender is just turning over to God all that we are and have, for Him to do with us whatever He wishes.

It is not our surrender that gives us the victory. It is not even our faith! It is Christ Himself—the Faithful One.

Surrender and trust, and Christ will never fail you.

*The winds blow hard? What then?*
*He holds them in the hollow of His hand;*
*The furious blasts will sink when His command*
    *Bids them be calm again.*

*The night is dark? What then?*
*To Him the darkness is as bright as day.*
*At His command the shades will flee away,*
    *And all be light again.*

*The wave is deep? What then?*
*For Israel's host the waters upright stood.*
*And He whose power controlled that raging flood*
    *Still succors helpless men.*

# JANUARY 10

*Behold, I shew you a mystery; We shall not all sleep, but we shall all be changed.* — 1 Corinthians 15:51

For those who, conscious of their need, are seeking and would enter the way of perennial victory, it will be a great help to realize that they are not seeking something which they do not already have. That is to say, if they have named the name of Jesus in true faith and have surrendered to Him, crowning Him Lord of their lives, as Christians they have been made kings and priests unto God (Rev. 1:6), and as such they have a right to reign. If they fail to reign, they are simply not exercising their rights. It cannot be too earnestly stressed that all Christians come into the same glorious inheritance. They have received Christ, and all things are theirs for they are Christ's. In Him they are complete. —*F. J. Huegel*

There is no true Christian victory in simply resigning one's self to the acts of Providence. The secret of victorious living is found in a human cooperation with the divine will that brings victory out of failure and joy out of deepest sorrow. It is the secret of being able to rejoice in all the situations which befall us, knowing that God does not work simply to disappoint our hopes but rather to build our souls. — *Jack Shuler*

*The hills of difficulty are no longer,*
*The mountains of despair are ironed smooth;*
*When high and looking down upon your problems,*
*The deep and darker valley seems a groove.*

*"It's safer flying high," says the apostle,*
*The world beneath, and God's own blue above;*
*Remember Christ is seated in the heavenlies,*
*And you are with Him there — climax of love.*
—Will H. Houghton

*For we have not an high priest which cannot be touched
with the feeling of our infirmities; but was in all points tempted
like as we are, yet without sin. Let us therefore come boldly
unto the throne of grace, that we may obtain mercy, and find
grace to help in time of need.* —Hebrews 4:15, 16

As we ponder these wonderful verses, we notice that Christ
as our High Priest has obtained for us access to and acceptance
with God, and on this account we may and must be courageous
in our confession. But He also possesses sympathy, and on
this account we must and should have confidence in approaching
Him. His greatness inspires our courage, and His sympathy
elicits our confidence.           —*W. H. Griffith-Thomas*

*Lord, what a change within us one short hour
    Spent in Thy presence will avail to make!
    What heavy burdens from our bosoms take!
    What parched grounds refresh as with a
    shower!
We kneel, and all around us seem to lower;
    We rise, and all, the distant and the near,
    Stands forth in sunny outline, brave and clear;
We kneel, how weak; we rise, how full of power!
Why, therefore, should we do ourselves this wrong,
Or others — that we are not always strong —
    That we are sometimes overborne with care —
    That we should ever weak or heartless be,
Anxious or troubled — when with us is prayer,
    And joy and strength and courage are with
    Thee!*

—Richard Chenevix Trench

# JANUARY 12

*And my people shall dwell in a peaceable habitation, and in sure dwellings, and in quiet resting places.* —Isaiah 32:18

When we get into that beautiful quiet resting place which God hath prepared for His people, we can serve Him there. The Book teaches us that we shall see His face and His servants shall serve Him, and there shall be service without complaint or weariness, and service without ending and service without thought of self-glory. Resting from their earthly labors, God's people enter upon labors more glorious, more magnificent: glorifying God, serving Him. God's people will *constantly* see Him. They will constantly see Him, and bear His name in their forehead.

Let this rest on your heart. Study to be quiet. And the work of righteousness shall be peace, and the effect of righteousness quietness and assurance forever. For a Christian to go home to God is like a soldier coming home from hard warfare, from the whine of bullets and the boom of cannons to the home of loving voices. For a Christian to go home is like a sailor home from a stormy sea, to know the quiet of a peaceful harbor.

—*Robert G. Lee*

*Hidden in the hollow of His blessed hand,*
*Never foe can follow, never traitor stand;*
*Not a surge of worry, not a shade of care,*
*Not a blast of hurry moves the spirit there.*

*Now the God of hope fill you with all joy and peace in believing, that ye may abound in hope, through the power of the Holy Ghost.* —Romans 15:13

Peace comes by belief; not by ourselves or our own strength, but by being held in the hand of Him who saved us, do these disturbed natures of ours come to their true selves and work harmoniously and to their best results. Doubt finds its only rest in personal confidence. Self-conceit, which is the most peace-destroying thing in all the world, is overwhelmed in consecration to the Master. — *Phillips Brooks*

The indwelling of God in the believer by the Holy Ghost, which makes man God's habitation, temple, holy of holies! There are two ways in which a man shows himself to be the owner of a house: First, by purchase; second, by occupation. He buys the dwelling, and then he enters into it and lives in it. And these are the two ways in which God is represented as making the believer His special dwelling place: First, you are bought with a price; second, the Spirit of God dwells in you. There can be no separation more unmistakable than this. We have been purchased by redeeming blood for the habitation of God through the Spirit, and through the Spirit God actually does indwell in every true believer. —*A. T. Pierson*

*Walk beside me, O, my Savior,*
*Through this darkening vale of tears,*
*For if Thou art close beside me*
*My faint heart can keep no fears:*
*When at last the morning breaketh*
*In the land of endless day,*
*Still my prayer shall be, dear Savior,*
*Walk beside me all the way.*
—L. P. Lehman, Jr.

# JANUARY 14

*I am crucified with Christ: nevertheless I live; yet not I, but Christ liveth in me: and the life which I now live in the flesh I live by the faith of the Son of God, who loved me, and gave himself for me.* — Galatians 2:20

A young man appealed for spiritual help to Dr. A. B. Simpson who, over a period of months, displayed a fatherly interest in him. One day the young man said, "Dr. Simpson, I am all right when I am with you, but when I get away from you, I do not seem to have the strength to resist temptation."

Whereupon the beloved teacher said, "Suppose it were possible for me to get inside of you and live my life in you and through you. Do you think that would solve your problem?"

"Most assuredly," replied the young man.

"But," said Dr. Simpson, "you must believe that the Scriptures teach that you have a greater than I living in you, for every believer has Jesus Christ abiding in his heart. He is your life. It is your privilege and duty to let Him live His life in and through you." —*Howard W. Ferrin*

*Compared with Christ, in all beside*
*No comeliness I see;*
*The one thing needful, dearest Lord,*
*Is to be one with Thee.*

*The sense of Thy expiring love*
*Into my soul convey;*
*Thyself bestow; for Thee alone*
*I absolutely pray.*

*Whatever else Thy will withholds,*
*Here grant me to succeed:*
*O let Thyself my portion be,*
*And I am blest indeed!*
—Toplady

*The peace of God, which passeth all understanding, shall keep your hearts and minds through Christ Jesus.*
—Philippians 4:7

Peace is the most precious of all the gifts and graces of the Spirit; so precious indeed is peace that it was the one legacy left us by our departing Lord. "Peace I leave with you, My peace I give unto you: not as the world giveth give I unto you. Let not your heart be troubled, neither let it be afraid." Joy may be more exciting but peace is more sustaining.

It is the "peace of God." It is not peace with God which comes to us with forgiveness and salvation, but is the very peace of God Himself, His own calm, restful heart possessing ours and filling us with His divine stillness.

It is a "peace which passeth all understanding." There is no rational explanation for it. It does not come to us by reasoning things out and seeing our way clear, but it is often most profound when all the circumstances of our life are most perplexing and distressing. It contradicts all conditions and constantly proves its heavenly origin and its supernatural birth.

It is the peace that saves us from anxious care. Its watchword is "Be careful for nothing." It simply crowds out all our corroding anxieties and fills us with such satisfaction that there is really nothing that we can fear.

It is a peace that fills the heart with constant thankfulness and the lips with praise. A life of peace leads to a life of praise, and a life of praise in turn leads to a life of peace.

—*A. B. Simpson*

*There is a life deep hid in God*
*Where all is calm and still,*
*Where, listening to His holy Word,*
*One learns to trust, until*
*All anxious care is put away*
*And there is peace, profound, alway;*
  *Grant us Thy Peace, O God!*
—Henry W. Frost

# JANUARY 16

*But thou, when thou prayest, enter into thy closet, and when thou hast shut thy door, pray to thy Father which is in secret; and thy Father which seeth in secret shall reward thee openly.* —Matthew 6:6

Prayer has as much power today, when men and women are themselves on praying ground and meeting the conditions of prevailing prayer, as it ever has had. God has not changed; and His ear is just as quick to hear the voice of real prayer, and His hand is just as long and strong to save, as it ever was. "Behold, the Lord's hand is not shortened, that it cannot save: neither his ear heavy, that it cannot hear." But "our iniquities" may "have separated between us and our God, and our Sins," may "have hid his face from us, that he will not hear." (Isaiah 59:1, 2.) Prayer is the key that unlocks all the storehouses of God's infinite grace and power. All that God is, and that God has, is at the disposal of prayer. But we must use the key.

—R. A. Torrey

*To know Thy will, Lord of the seeking mind,*
*To learn Thy way for me, Thy purpose kind,*
*Thy path to follow and Thy guide find—*
    *For this I pray.*

*To do Thy will, Lord of the eager soul,*
*To bring my restlessness 'neath Thy control,*
*To give Thee, not a part, but all—the whole—*
    *For this I pray.*

*To love Thy will, Lord of the ardent heart,*
*To bid all selfishness, all sloth depart,*
*To share with gladness all Thou dost and art—*
    *For this I pray.*

—Alice M. Kyle

*Henceforth there is laid up for me a crown of righteousness, which the Lord, the righteous judge, shall give me at that day: and not to me only, but unto all them also that love his appearing.* — 2 Timothy 4:8

It will always give a Christian the greatest calm, quiet, ease and peace, to think of the perfect righteousness of Christ. How often are the saints of God downcast and sad! I do not think they ought to be. I do not think they would if they could always see their perfection in Christ.

When the believer says, "I live on Christ alone; I rest on him solely for salvation; and I believe that, however unworthy, I am still saved in Jesus"; then there rises up as a motive of gratitude this thought—"Shall I not live to Christ? Shall I not love Him and serve Him, seeing that I am saved by His merits?" "The love of Christ constraineth us," "that they which live should not henceforth live unto themselves, but unto Him which died for them." If saved by imputed righteousness, we shall greatly value imparted righteousness.

—*C. H. Spurgeon*

*In Christ, I find the greatest human treasures,*
*The washing-white from sin, salvation free.*
*In Him is found a joy that knows no measure,*
*The Gift of One, who gave His all for me!*
*In Christ I find all love, all joy, all blessing,*
*I find the peace, that shares with doubt, no part.*
*In Christ I find the gate to heaven's glory!*
*"In Christ," the Christ who dwells within my heart!*
—Connie Calenberg

# JANUARY 18

*Through the tender mercy of our God; whereby the day-spring from on high hath visited us.* — Luke 1:78

What would we ever have done if God had not been merciful? There could never have been a soul saved in this world. There is a story of a man who dreams that he is out in an open field in a fierce driving storm. He is wildly seeking a refuge. He sees one gate over which "Holiness" is written. There seems to be shelter inside, and he knocks. The door is opened by one in white garments; but none save the holy can be admitted, and he is not holy. So he hurries on to seek shelter elsewhere. He sees another gate, and tries that; but "Truth" is inscribed above it, and he is not fit to enter. He hastens to a third, which is the palace of Justice; but armed sentinels keep the door and only the righteous can be received. At last, when he is almost in despair, he sees a light shining some distance away, and hastens toward it The door stands wide open, and beautiful angels meet him with welcomes of joy. It is the house of Mercy, and he is taken in and finds refuge from the storm, and is hospitably entertained.

Not one of us can ever find a refuge at any door save the door of Mercy. But here the vilest sinner can find eternal shelter; and not mere cold shelter only, for God's mercy is "tender." We flee for refuge, and find it. Strong walls shut out all pursuing enemies, and cover us from all storms. Then, as we begin to rejoice in our assurance, we learn that we are inside a sweet home, and not merely a secure shelter. Our refuge is in the very heart of God; and no mother's bosom was ever so warm a nest for her own child as is the Divine mercy for all who find refuge in it. —*J. R. Miller*

*The Lord is my shepherd; I shall not want.* —Psalm 23:1

David, the Psalmist, was content because as a sheep, constrained to live with other sheep in the fold, his peace of mind was determined not by the whims, moods and caprice of the other sheep, but by the Shepherd Himself. His relationship was primarily with the Shepherd, and after that with the other sheep. So with David, the weather of his soul from day to day was determined not by human nature but by divine nature. "The Lord is my shepherd" and because of this I refuse to have my peace of mind disturbed by the uncertain and mercurial conduct of the other sheep. David has given us a golden key to spiritual contentment. When we allow the music of our daily life to be determined by people round about us, it becomes a story of discord and disharmony. Peter knew this. On one occasion at the lakeshore, disturbed by something John was doing or not doing, he said to Jesus, "Lord, and what shall this man do?" Jesus said unto him, "What is that to thee? Follow thou me." In other words Peter had to keep his eyes fixed upon Jesus, as we all must if we would have that content of mind and soul that David had, and that Paul had. In all things Christ must have the pre-eminence. Then we shall be able to say with David, "The Lord is my shepherd, I shall not want." —*Robert Barr*

*Rest, spirit free!*
*In the green pastures of the heavenly shore,*
*Where sin and sorrow can approach no more,*
*With all the flock by the Good Shepherd fed,*
*Beside the streams of life eternal led,*
*Forever with thy God and Savior blest,*
*Rest, sweetly rest!*

# JANUARY 20

*From the end of the earth will I cry unto thee, when my heart is overwhelmed: lead me to the rock that is higher than I.*
　　　　　　　　　　　　　　　　　　—Psalm 61:2

Most of us know, dear reader, what it means to be overwhelmed in heart. Disappointments and heartbreaks will overwhelm us as wave after wave rolls over us as if we were a foundered ship being beaten to pieces against a reef.

Thanks be to our God, however, that at such times we are not without solace, for our God is a harbor for wind-beaten ships. How much higher is He than we, His mercy greater than our sins, His love higher than our most soaring thoughts!

Why is it then that men will put their trust in something lower than themselves, rather than fixing their confidence upon an exceedingly great Lord? Our Lord is a Rock that changes not, a high Rock that cannot be overwhelmed nor disturbed by rolling waves. Under the shelter of this Rock we may defy the rushing hurricane of trouble secure in the calm rest that only He can give.

We cannot find this shelter by ourselves. That is why we should join the Psalmist in praying this heartfelt prayer.

*Soul of mine, why choosest thou*
*To worry for thy daily need?*
*Thy Heavenly Father taketh heed*
*Of all the future's changing scenes*
*And watcheth over thee.*

*Soul of Mine, trust all to Him*
*Who follows e'en the sparrow's flight;*
*Along with thee the darkest night*
*He fain would go and light the way*
*By His approving smile.*
　　　　　　　　　—Vera Melville Biddle

*If ye then, being evil, know how to give good gifts unto your children: how much more shall your heavenly Father give the Holy Spirit to them that ask him?* —Luke 11:13

The believer is complete in Christ; that is, when he accepts Christ he receives the right and the title to all of his spiritual inheritance. He does not, however, necessarily and automatically come into the full possession of his inheritance. One may possess something he has no title to and he may have a title to something he does not possess. The Christian has a title to all the riches of grace in Christ Jesus, but he does not come into the possession of these blessings until he surrenders to Christ, lays hold of the promises of God and claims the blessings by faith. The supreme blessing which God has for His children is the infilling of the Holy Spirit for life and for service. —*J. B. Lawrence*

The power of God is demonstrated when the individual believer completely yields to the Holy Spirit. When the Holy Spirit takes hold of all the areas of that individual's life he will find a new day dawning in his life. —*Richard A. Elvee*

*Well content am I if only*
   *Thou wilt deign to dwell with me;*
*With Thee I am never lonely,*
   *Never comfortless with Thee.*
*Thine forever make me now,*
   *And to Thee, my Lord, I vow*
*Here and yonder to employ*
   *Every power for Thee with joy.*
      —Paul Gerhardt

# JANUARY 22

*Pray without ceasing.* —1 Thessalonians 5:17

Prayer is the most important spiritual exercise that a Christian can have. If you are to live a happy, yielded and victorious life, prayer is absolutely essential daily.

The Bible makes it clear that you can pray at any time, for God never sleeps, and His ear is ever open to your cry.

Pray harder when it is hardest to pray.

Prayer is the key of the morning and the bolt of the night.

One with God is a majority. —*Billy Graham*

*In the morning, prayer is the key that opens
to us the treasures of God's mercies and blessings;
in the evening, it is the key that shuts
us up under His protection and safeguard*
—Anonymous

*Perhaps the day would not have been so long,
The skies would not have seemed so gray,
If on my knees in humble prayer
I had begun the day.*

*Perhaps the fight would not have been so hard,
Prepared, I might have faced the fray,
If I had been alone with Him
Upon my knees, to pray.*

*Perhaps I might have cheered a broken heart
Or helped a wand'rer on the way,
If I had asked to be a light
To some dark soul today.*

*I would remember just the pleasant things;
The harsh words that I meant to say
I would forget, if I had prayed
When I began the day.*

*But if we hope for that we see not, then do we with patience
wait for it.* — Romans 8:25

I know very well how hopeless it seems that you might ever
conquer where you have so often failed. Your own energy and
natural force can never overcome the problem at hand; but
this is the province of the Savior. The whole need not the
physician, but they that are sick; and He comes to make the
sick whole. Believe that in Him is the answer to your need;
that He does more than heal, because He can make what
used to be your weakness, your strength; and what had been
your perpetual failure, the most noticeable grace in your
character. It seems impossible, but to God all things are
possible.
*—F. B. Meyer*

The Christian should be unaffected by the variations in
emotional temperature which occur around him. With a faith
which is constant and unchanging, he walks serene amid the
change and chaos of the world around. He maintains an inward
peace however noisy the tumult and bloody the war which
shakes the earth around him. When others are afraid he
maintains the same restful attitude of trust which he felt when
outward conditions were settled and quiet. His faith is fixed in
a God who is eternal; his feet are set on the Rock of Ages.
*—Bob Jones, Jr.*

*He giveth more grace when the burdens grow greater,
   He sendeth more strength when the labors increase;
To added affliction He addeth His mercy,
   To multiplied trials, His multiplied peace.*

*His love has no limit, His grace has no measure,
   His power no boundary known unto men;
For out of His infinite riches in Jesus
   He giveth and giveth, and giveth again.*
*—Annie Johnson Flint*

*But when he saw the multitudes, he was moved with compassion on them, because they fainted, and were scattered abroad, as sheep having no shepherd.* — Matthew 9:36

We see the loveliness of Christ in His sympathy. Perhaps in this respect His loveliness stands out most glowingly. He is never more lovely than when His face is turned in compassion toward those who looked to Him for help. He is always being touched with compassion. Human suffering made deep furrows in His face and still deeper ones in His heart. The multitude without a shepherd, the sorrowing widow of Nain, the little dead child of the ruler, the demoniac of Gadara, the hungry multitudes — wherever suffering touched Him, His heart went out in full sympathy. He need not have touched the leper, but He did. Why? Because for years that poor wretch had been an outcast, counted as the offscouring of the earth. He had almost lost the sense of being a man. It was defilement even to come near him and, horror of horrors — no one would ever think of touching him! But that is exactly why Jesus did touch him, and that touch made him not only whole, but human again.

So the compassion of Jesus continues to make Him lovely as His love is displayed in the lives of those who have come under the influence of this compassionate Christ.

—*Howard W. Ferrin*

*Oh, break my life if need must be,*
*No longer mine, I give it Thee.*
*Oh, break my will; the off'ring take.*
*For blessing comes when Thou dost break.*

> *Now before the feast of the passover, when Jesus knew that his hour was come that he should depart out of this world unto the Father, having loved his own which were in the world, he loved them unto the end.* —John 13:1

Having loved His own, He loved them unto the end (John 13:1). What a love that was, the love that went to Calvary for you and me. Time cannot wither it, circumstances cannot weaken it. Little wonder the human heart should long to possess this LOVE, and cry,

> *Love Divine all loves excelling,*
> *Joy of heaven to earth come down,*
> *Fix in us Thy humble dwelling,*
> *All Thy tender mercies crown.*

When His love comes flooding into the surrendered heart, then there is an outgoing of that love to all through the same, surrendered heart. When I think of the love of Jesus, when I think of how He brings an eternal springtime to the human heart, my heart cries out for a portion of that love.

—*Robert Barr*

> *I love Thee, Lord, for blood Thou shed for sinners,*
> *For Calv'ry's cross, O rugged crimson tree,*
> *I love Thee for the grave which lieth open —*
> *For giving all, that I might sinless be.*
>
> *I love Thee, Lord, beyond all human loving,*
> *Beyond all love which earth may have in store,*
> *I love Thee as the Christ, who died to save me,*
> *The Lover of my soul for evermore!*
>
> —Connie Calenberg

# JANUARY 26

*That I may know him, and the power of his resurrection,*
*and the fellowship of his sufferings, being made conformable*
*unto his death.* —Philippians 3:10

If we look on sufferings as something to be avoided at all costs we will take no more of it than is forced upon us by our circumstances. In that case we will miss everything that is best in life. But if we take it as one of God's gifts, as a means of equipping us for the ministry of service to others, as one of the means by which He is imprinting His image on our characters, and above all as a means by which other souls might be brought into right relationship with Him, we can more readily understand how suffering may be working out His purpose for our good, and so join with the Apostle in the prayer that we might be brought into the fellowship of the suffering of the Captain of our Salvation, who was Himself made perfect through suffering. — W. J. Tunley

*It is not death to die;*
    *To leave this weary road,*
*And 'midst the brotherhood on high*
    *To be at home with God.*

*It is not death to fling*
    *Aside this sinful dust,*
*And rise, on strong exulting wing,*
    *To live among the just.*

*Jesus, Thou Prince of Life!*
    *Thy chosen cannot die;*
*Like Thee, they conquer in the strife,*
    *To reign with Thee on high.*
                    —H. Malan

*As newborn babes, desire the sincere milk of the word, that*
*ye may grow thereby.* —1 Peter 2:2

See what a charming parable the Lord has given us here in the mother's milk. Out of her own life does the mother yield food and life to her child. The feeding of the child is the work of the tenderest love, in which the child is pressed to the breast, and is held in the closest fellowship with the mother. And the milk is just what the weak child requires, food gentle and yet strong.

Even so is there in the Word of God the very life and power of God. His tender love will through the Word receive us into the gentlest and most intimate fellowship with Himself. His love will give us out of the Word what is, like warm soft milk, just fitted for our weakness. Let no one suppose that the Word is too high or too hard for him. For the disciple who receives the Word, and trustfully relies on Jesus to teach him by the Spirit, the Word of God shall practically prove to be gentle milk for newborn infants. —*Andrew Murray*

*The easy roads are crowded, and*
*The level roads are jammed.*
*The pleasant little rivers*
*With the drifting folks are crammed.*
*But off yonder where it's rocky,*
*Where you get the better view,*
*You will find the ranks are thinning,*
*And the travelers are few.*

*Be careful for nothing; but in every thing by prayer and supplication with thanksgiving let your requests be made known unto God.*            —Philippians 4:6

Although we often sing about the privilege of carrying everything to God in prayer, must we not confess that familiarity of approach has the tendency to make us forget that prayer is a privilege? Who are we, that we should be able to take God's name upon our lips and tell Him all about our hearts? He is high and holy, the Lord God Almighty, yet here are we, mere worms of earth, with authority to come before God at any time, in any place, and commune with Him! How different with ourselves! We have not to wait upon any whim or movement of God nor for the office of any human intermediary priest. No matter who we are, or where we are, by grace we have the right to come immediately into the presence of Him who bids His children ask and receive.

Our common tragedy is that of failure to take advantage of such a priceless privilege. We are not victorious in life and fruitful in service all because the communication line with Heaven is not in constant use. Privileged with daily opportunities of dwelling with the King and appropriating all His wealth of power and wisdom, we yet live as those who delight in penury.            —Herbert Lockyer

*Christian, seek not yet repose,*
    *Cast thy dreams of ease away;*
*Thou art in the midst of foes;*
    *Watch and pray.*
            —Charlotte Elliott

*The heavens declare the glory of God; and the firmament*
*sheweth his handiwork.*
—Psalm 19:1

In this world of wondrous beauty God is speaking. The glory-telling heavens, the winsome coloring of trees and all growing things, the soft round hills, the sublime mountains, the sea with its ever-changing mood but never-changing beneficence on the life of the whole earth, the great blue and gray above, the soothing green below, the brighter colors in their artistic proportion, the wondrous blendings — surely every bush and other green thing, every bright twinkler in the blue, everything is aflame with the Presence that burns but in great love consumes not.

But God comes closer yet in His wooing. The web of life's daily run, with its strange mixing and blending, shadings and tints, is of His weaving. He sits at life's loom ever watching and weaving. Were He but recognized oftener and His hand allowed to guide the skein, how different the weaving!

But chiefly in Jesus God came. Jesus is God going out in the cold black night, over the mountains, down the ravines and gullies, eagerly hunting for His lost man, getting hands and face torn on the brambly thorn bushes, and losing His life in the darkness on a tree thrust in His path, but saving the man.
— S. D. Gordon

*Time hath no aimless strands,*
  *God's warp and woof combines;*
*Life's loom is in His holy hands,*
  *His shuttles know their lines.*

# January 30

*Casting all your care upon him; for he careth for you.*
—1 Peter 5:7

No greater secret of longevity can be named as any physician will tell us, than a tranquil spirit. The carking cares and worries of life are far more trying to the bodily frame than the severest labors. A happy, calm, contented spirit is like oil upon the wheels of life, making them revolve swiftly and easily in the performance of their daily tasks. Such a peaceful, placid temperament is the privilege of every child of God to know. "Thou wilt keep him in perfect peace whose mind is stayed on thee, because he trusteth in thee" (Isa. 26:3). "Be careful for nothing" (Phil. 4:6) is not only counsel, it is a positive command, as real and as binding as "Thou shalt not steal." The willful infringement of this blessed heart-enlightening "Law of the House" is the cause of many a declining experience and backsliding step. Peace, peace, rest of heart as well as conscience, God's own peace — keeping ward and watch within, and holding all invaders at bay; glorious and unspeakable as the privilege is, nothing less is promised, nothing less should content us. It is the peace which Jesus Himself maintains as King. If we would have His peace, we must be submissive to His sway; the one can never be severed from the other, for the one is the effect of the other. It is not merely the peace that Christ has made with His blood that we are here speaking of (Col. 1:20), rather is it the peace that He maintains by His power. Rebel thoughts and proud uprisings His mighty hand puts down, and as He reigns the righteous flourish, yea, and "abundance of peace" is theirs as long as the moon endureth (2 Cor. 10:5, and Ps. 72:7).     —*E. W. Moore*

*That Christ may dwell in your hearts by faith . . .*
—Ephesians 3:17

Jesus Christ wants to reign in your life and in mine, and how blessed it is to be able to commit our way unto One who knows the end from the beginning, the One to whom all of our tomorrows are already known and who has said, "I will guide thee with Mine eye"; who has promised to go with us even unto the end of the way; who has promised that He will not leave us nor forsake us; whose strength is made perfect in weakness and whose grace is sufficient for every need. How wonderful it is to be able to commit our hearts, our homes, our businesses, our lives to Jesus Christ and acknowledge Him as King of kings and Lord of lords. Then He will dwell in our hearts in all of His fullness. He will make our hearts His home. When we commit ourselves to the sovereign will of our Savior, He lays a loving hand upon our hearts and lives and leads us in paths of righteousness, in ways of peace.

A friend told me a story recently which is simple but illustrates this thought. A ship at sea was in the midst of an awful storm. It seemed that inevitably it would go beneath the waves. The winds were fierce, and the waves were high, and the passengers on board were filled with fright. But there was one little girl who went about the ship in an attitude of confidence and with a smile on her face. No matter how rough it was, she was still smiling or humming a little song. As her attitude made its impression upon the passengers, one said to her, "You do not seem to be afraid of the storm."

She answered, "No, why should I be? My father is captain of this ship, and he will bring us safe to shore."  —*Larry Love*

It is never a question with any of us of faith or no faith; the question always is, "In what or in whom do we put our faith?"
—*Anonymous*

# FEBRUARY 1

*When Christ, who is our life, shall appear, then shall ye also appear with him in glory.* — Colossians 3:4

One question that rises in every mind is this: "How can I live that life of perfect trust in God?" Many do not know the right answer, or the full answer. It is this: "Christ must live it in me." That is why He became man; as a man to live a life of trust in God, and so to show to us how we ought to live. When He had done that upon earth, He went to heaven, that He might do more than show us, might give us, and live in us that life of trust. It is as we understand what the life of Christ is and how it becomes ours, that we shall be prepared to desire and to ask of Him that He would live it Himself in us.

Jesus got this divine life by depending absolutely upon the Father all His life long, depending upon Him even down into death. Jesus got that life in the full glory of the Spirit to be poured out, by giving Himself up in obedience and surrender to God alone, and leaving God even in the grave to work out His mighty power; and that very Christ will live out His life in you and me.

God keep us from being anything. God teach us to wait on Him, that He may work in us all He wrought in His Son, till Christ Jesus may live out His life in us! For this may God help us. —*Andrew Murray*

*To the cleft of the Rock! to the wounds of my Lord*
*From storms fierce within I would flee,*
*And in the blest haven for souls in distress*
*Find safety forever in Thee.*
—Grace W. Haight

*For there is one God, and one mediator between God and men, the man Christ Jesus.* —1 Timothy 2:5

One God—just one! And one Mediator—just one! But the beauty of it is that one is enough. One is often an abundance. It is only in the minor matters of human experience that we crave the privilege of picking and choosing; in the really vital things of life we are content with satisfaction. When the appetite is satisfied, and food is a matter of indifference, we like to be invited to choose from an array of tempting viands; but when a man is ravenous he ceases to be fastidious. Set food before him and he is content. The hiker, walking for pleasure, likes to choose between several intriguing trails; the pilgrim desires only the road that leads home. The globe-trotter lingers over the various shipping lists; the castaway longs but to sight a single sail. In the hour of our desperate need, satisfaction lies in simplicity.

No man, yearning after God as the hart pants after the water brooks, will resent the statement that there is but one God and but one Mediator. He feels that he does not need a host of gods if he has the God of Hosts. The man who, weighted with his consciousness of spiritual need, hungrily desires salvation, is glad that there is but one God and but one Mediator. — *F. W. Boreham*

*He is a path, if any be misled;*
*He is a robe, if any naked be;*
*If any chance to hunger, He is bread;*
*If any be a bondman, He is free;*
*If any be but weak, how strong is He!*
*To dead men life He is, to sick men health;*
*To blind men sight, and to the needy wealth;*
*A pleasure without loss, a treasure without stealth.*
—Giles Fletcher

# FEBRUARY 3

*Jesus said unto him, If thou wilt be perfect, go and sell that thou hast, and give to the poor, and thou shalt have treasure in heaven; and come and follow me.* —Matthew 19:21

The plan of our Lord is not the same for every life. "Follow thou Me!" The only thing God asks of His children is to be willing day by day to do His will. God does not ask the Christian to be a successful man or a brilliant one. God simply asks him to do daily, joyfully and obediently the thing which he gives him to do that day. Obedience is better than sacrifice, and the man who will be a great success in the will of God twenty years from now, is the man who today is obedient to God's will for his life in little things. —*Bob Jones, Jr.*

It is very remarkable how God guides us by circumstances. At one moment the way may seem utterly blocked, and then shortly afterwards some trivial incident occurs, which might not seem much to others, but which to the keen eye of faith speaks volumes.

We often make a great mistake, thinking that God is not guiding us at all, because we cannot see far in front. But this is not His method. He only undertakes that the steps of a good man should be ordered by the Lord. Not next year, but tomorrow. Not the next mile, but the next yard. Not the whole pattern, but the next stitch in the canvas.

*Bend not thine arms for tomorrow's load*
*Thou mayest leave that to thy gracious God.*
*"Daily," only He saith to thee,*
*"Take up thy cross and follow Me."*

*And when he putteth forth his own sheep, he goeth before them, and the sheep follow him: for they know his voice.*
—John 10:4

Do you need guidance as to your path? Look unto Jesus; it is always possible to discern His form, though partially veiled in mist; and when it is lost, be sure to stand still until He comes back to find and reestablish the blessed connection. Do not look to impressions which often contradict one another, which rise and fall with variable fickleness, and are like eddies upon a flowing current; do not seek for guidance from friends who will differ from each other, and no two of which will give the same advice on the same grounds, but look away to Christ; throw on Him the responsibility of making you know the way you are to take; leave it to Him to make it so abundantly clear that you cannot do other than follow; even tell Him that you will stand still until He puts His arms under you, and carries you where He would have you be. Do not get anxious or flurried. Put the government of your life upon His shoulder, and leave Him to execute His plan. —*F. B. Meyer*

Christ is the only way to God, the only door into the Father's house. Christ comes to us as the one Mediator, the Son of God, the Divine Savior; and we have only to receive Him, to accept Him with our hearts, and commit ourselves to Him.

*Thy piloting, how sure, how safe,*
*Until, all breakers passed,*
*We triumph o'er each hurricane,*
*And anchor, Home at last!*
—Louis A. Waterman

# FEBRUARY 5

*Thou hast made known to me the ways of life; thou shalt make me full of joy with thy countenance.*   —Acts 2:28

It is difficult to read the book of Acts and entirely miss the impression that first generation Christians were "absurdly happy." Their lives were radiant and their witness bold and contagious.

This element of joy that accompanies the presence of God in the soul is also not foreign to the Old Testament scriptures. The Psalmist wrote: "When the Lord turned again the captivity of Zion, we were like them that dream. Then was our mouth filled with laughter, and our tongue with singing" (Ps. 126:1, 2).

Nehemiah felt it in his day when, bidding the people dispel their sorrow, he said, "For the joy of the Lord is your strength."

The first century Christians believed in rejoicing always; they knew that giving thanks in all things was God's will for them (1 Thess. 5:16, 18). Their Lord had told of a coming day when no man could take their joy away, and they believed that day had now arrived. Through faith they rejoiced "with joy unspeakable and full of glory." They were radiant, irrepressible Christians. *May God's Spirit give me strength today to carry on their radiant message and bold witness.*

— *Samuel Young*

Joy is distinctly a Christian word and a Christian thing. It is the reverse of happiness. Happiness is the result of what happens of an agreeable sort. Joy has its springs deep down inside. And that spring never runs dry, no matter what happens. Only Jesus gives that joy. He had joy, singing its music within, even under the shadow of the cross. It is an unknown word and thing except as He has sway within.   —*S. D. Gordon*

*For there is no difference between the Jew and the Greek: for the same Lord over all is rich unto all that call upon him.*
—Romans 10:12

This is a new expression. The Apostle might have said, as we read in Joel 2:13: "He is gracious and merciful, slow to anger, and of great kindness, and repenteth him of the evil." But the Apostle means to emphasize the fact that God gives exceedingly abundantly above all that we ask or think, as we read in Ephesians 3:20, so that compared with His gifts, the prayers of those who call upon Him seem poor and modest. Those who call upon Him could make "all grace abound toward you." He therefore is rich when He gives; we are poor when we pray. He is mighty when He grants us our petitions; we are timid and weak when we ask. We do not pray for as much as He can and will give, for we do not pray according to His ability (to give), but far short of His ability, according to our weakness. But He can give only according to His might; therefore He always gives more than we ask for.

— *Martin Luther*

*O what treasure God has given,*
*Riches hid in His dear Son,*
*He reveals to all who seek Him,*
*Jewels rare for everyone.*
*O how rich we are in Jesus,*
*All the wealth of grace untold.*
*Things eternal, rare and precious,*
*Greater than the world can hold.*
—Jessie Bell Thabes

*For the which cause I also suffer these things: nevertheless I am not ashamed: for I know whom I have believed, and am persuaded that he is able to keep that which I have committed unto him against that day.* —2 Timothy 1:12

Learn from Paul to set your confidence only on the power of Jesus. I am persuaded that He is able to keep my pledge. You have an almighty Jesus to keep you. Faith keeps itself occupied only with His Omnipotence. Let your faith especially be strengthened in what God is able to do for you. Expect with certainty from Him that He will do for you great and glorious things, entirely above your own strength. See in the Holy Scriptures how constantly the power of God was the ground of the trust of His people. Take these words and hide them in your heart. Let the power of Jesus fill your soul. Ask only: "What is my Jesus able to do?" What you really trust Him with, He is able to keep.

And learn also from Paul where he obtained the assurance that this power would keep his pledge: it was in his knowledge of Jesus: "I know Him whom I have believed." Therefore I am assured. You can trust the power of Jesus, if you know that He is yours, if you hold converse with Him as your Friend. Then you can say: "I know whom I have believed: I know that he holds me very dear: I know and am assured that He is able to keep my pledge."

So runs the way to the full assurance of faith. Deposit your pledge with Jesus; give yourself wholly, give everything, into His hands; think much on His might, and reckon upon Him; and live with Him so that you may always know who He is in whom you have believed. —*Andrew Murray*

*Faith of our fathers, holy faith,*
*We will be true to Thee till death.*
                    —F. W. Faber

*I am crucified with Christ: nevertheless I live; yet not I but Christ liveth in me: and the life which I now live in the flesh I live by the faith of the Son of God, who loved me, and gave himself for me.*
—Galatians 2:20

Victory in the Christian experience is not gained by trying and conquering; it is obtained by trusting and surrendering. Christ is the Victor, and Satan is already a defeated foe through Calvary! It is in the Lord Jesus that we find our triumph, being made "more than conquerors through Him that loved us." Positionally, that is, in the reckoning of God, it is a fact, that the old man was crucified with Christ, that henceforth sin should no longer be served. Likewise it is also positionally true that the Christian is risen with Christ through faith, dead to sin and alive unto Christ.

These are theological facts—but how may they be made real and effectual in our day-by-day experience? By putting off the old man, as we would discard an old suit of clothes, being renewed in the Spirit, and by putting on the new man, who is Christ living in us. It is not I, but Christ. Here is the secret: there must no longer be any self effort, but an acceptance by faith of all that God has done, and a whole-souled surrender, a complete abandonment to the Lord Jesus Christ. Let Him who lives in my heart reign in my heart! Let the Spirit of Him who dwells within me, fill me! Then filled to overflowing with all the fullness of God, let me live out the inliving Christ.

"Not I, but Christ." "Not my will, but Thine be done." Not my desires, not my success, not my plans, not my ambitions, not my popularity, not my comfort, not my service — use me as Thine instrument that Thy will may be done, and Christ glorified.
—*E. Schuyler English*

# FEBRUARY 9

*This Child is set for the . . . rising again of many.*—Luke 2:34

You can rise with Christ, particularly when your hopes are lowest and when you understand His ways, though not your ways, are always the best. Sir Henry M. Stanley, searching for Livingstone in the heart of Africa, had to be led through a siege of tropical fevers that kept his temperature constantly at 105 degrees before his hardened attitude toward life turned to the joy of his salvation. His sick-bed became his school for Christ, and having read the warnings and promises of Scripture, he wrote. "I flung myself on my knees and poured out my soul utterly in secret prayer to Him from whom I had been so long estranged, to Him who had led me here mysteriously into Africa, there to reveal Himself and His will." Perhaps God has been leading some of you through the jungles of life, through the wastes of illness and loneliness, to have you find Christ and with Him this uplifting grace which Simeon proclaimed as his voice rang through the Temple, "This Child is set for the . . . rising again of many." —*Walter A. Maier*

*Lonely! The very word can start the tears*
 *And chill the heart as with the sun's eclipse;*
*It used to fall so sadly from my lips,*
 *It used to sound so mournful to my ears.*

*Lonely? The knell fades on the brightening air,*
 *And melts into a happy carillon.*
*Is the road rough? I have a Friend to share*
 *Its brave adventure till the journey's done.*
*Come, lonely heart, will you not join us there?*
 *Who walk with Christ can never walk alone.*
              —Ruby Weyburn Tobias

*And a crown was given to him: and he went forth conquering, and to conquer.*
—Revelation 6:2

The secret of victory in the Christian life is found in surrender. To the extent that we, dear fellow Christian, abandon ourselves to Christ, to that extent we will find ourselves victorious in Christ in day-by-day living.

As we yield ourselves to His Spirit, we find ourselves led of Him. We discover, in our prayer life, that our praying is guided by His hand. We are even given the words to say! Our prayer burdens are given at His command!

We will be startled to discover new force and vitality in our prayer life. We will find our hearts singing in spite of trial and temptation, in spite of testing from without. We will find ourselves girded with His might in the midst of temptation. We will discover that we are more than *conquerors* in Him.

This is the Word of God for us today. We must commit all into His hand. If, after this committal on our part, we continue to doubt — then we are doubting God! Rather, we should realize that ours is a spirit of power that the enemy dreads and fears. In an effort to neutralize that power Satan tries by clever ruses to trick us into forgetting its potency and might. The secret of victory, then, lies in complete recognition of God's power and might at the disposal of His child. Oh, that today we might realize the tremendous dynamic of faith that we are neglecting — that we might resolve this very day to, first of all, yield ourselves to Him, and secondly, take and use the conquering power He has placed at our command.

> *Faith came singing into my room,*
> *And other guests took flight;*
> *Fear and Anxiety, Grief and Gloom*
> *Sped out into the night;*
> *I wondered that such peace could be,*
> *But Faith said gently, "Don't you see?*
> *They really cannot live with me."*
> —Elizabeth Cheney

# FEBRUARY 11

*Rest in the Lord, and wait patiently for him.* —Psalm 37:7

I remember a saint whom it was my privilege to visit in the beginning of my life as a minister. Though poor and uneducated, she was a person of very unusual natural powers; her ideas were singularly original, and she had a charming pleasantness of wit. Though not very old, she knew that she was doomed to die; and the disease from which she was suffering was one of the most painful to humanity. Often, I remember, she would tell me, that, when the torture was at the worst, she lay thinking of the sufferings of the Savior, and said to herself that the shooting pains were not so bad as the spikes of the thorns.

Christ's sufferings are a rebuke to our softness and selfpleasing. It is not, indeed, wrong to enjoy the comforts and pleasures of life. God sends these; and, if we receive them with gratitude, they may lift us nearer to Himself. If the crown of thorns now becomes Christ so well as to be the pride and the song of men and angels, be assured that any twig from the crown which we may have to wear will one day turn out to be our most dazzling ornament.   —*James Stalker*

"Rest in the Lord, and wait patiently for Him." Yes, *for* Him. Seek not only the help, the gift, you need; seek Himself; wait for Him. Give God His glory by resting in Him, by trusting Him fully, by waiting patiently for Him.

*Just when I am disheartened, Just when by cares oppressed,*
*Just when my way is darkest, Just when I am distressed,*
*Then is my Savior near me, He knows my every care;*
*Jesus will never leave me, He helps my burdens bear.*

*And when they were come to the place, which is called Cal-*
*vary, there they crucified Him.*                    — Luke 23:33

This spot to which we have come is the center of all things. Here two eternities meet. The eyes of patriarchs and prophets strained forward to Calvary, and now the eyes of all generations and all races look back to it. This is the end of all roads. The weary heart of man, that has wandered the world over in search of perfect sympathy and love, at last arrives here and finds rest. Think how many souls every Lord's Day, assembled in church and chapel and meeting-house, are thinking of Golgotha! How many eyes are turned thither every day from beds of sickness and chambers of death! "Lord, to whom can we go? Thou hast the words of eternal life."

Though we cannot take in all the meaning of the scene before which we stand, yet we can fill mind and heart with it to the brim, and, as it sends through our being the pulsations of a life divine, rejoice that it has a breadth and length, a height and depth, which pass understanding. —*James Stalker*

*Who defeats my fiercest foes?*
*Who consoles my saddest woes?*
*Who revives my fainting heart,*
*Healing all its hidden smart?*
  *Jesus Christ, the Crucified.*

*Who is life in life to me?*
*Who the death of death will be?*
*Who will place me on His right,*
*With the countless hosts of light?*
  *Jesus Christ, the Crucified.*
      —Benjamin Hall Kennedy

# FEBRUARY 13

*He that believeth on me, as the Scripture hath said, out of his belly shall flow rivers of living water.* —John 7:37

The Bible calls the world a world of sorrow; but the same Bible tells us there is a way of making the vale of misery to laugh with springs and fountains. Remember, it is not just compensation, but *transformation* that you are to seek. Not Heaven yet. That looms before us always, tempting us on; but now the earth, with all its duties, sorrows, difficulties, doubts and dangers. We want a faith, a truth, a grace to help us now, right here, where we are stumbling about, dizzied and fainting with our thirst. And we can have it. One who was man, yet mightier than man, has walked the vale before us. When He walked it, He turned it all into a well of living water. To them who are willing to walk in His footsteps, to keep in His light, the well He opened shall be forever flowing. Nay, it shall pass into him and fulfill there Christ's own words: "Whosoever drinketh of the water that I shall give him shall never thirst; but the water that I shall give him shall be in him a well of water springing up into everlasting life." —*Phillips Brooks*

*My faith is strong when skies are bright,*
*But sunny days are all too brief;*
*When clouds arise, and sorrows come,*
*My lips are sealed, my heart is dumb,*
*And full of weary unbelief.*

*But this, dear Lord, my comfort is;*
*My troubled heart is known to Thee;*
*Thou knowest that I love Thee, Lord,*
*And, Savior mine, I have Thy Word*
*That this shall my salvation be.*
—Charles A. Dickinson

*Now thanks be unto God, which always causeth us to tri-umph in Christ.*
— 2 Corinthians 2:14

It is altogether like the Apostle Paul to give the glory for the key to triumphant living. It would be unlike Paul to take unto himself any glory.

A better translation of the verse reads, "But thanks be to God, who always leads us in triumphal procession in Christ . . ." (NIV). God in Christ has gone on before. It was Christ who was "tempted in all points like as we." It was Christ who suffered the pain and anguish of Calvary, who endured the death of the Cross that our sins might be cleansed and forgiven.

It is always Christ who leads His people — not only in triumph but in trouble as well, He goes on before, leading His child by the hand.

If anyone knew what it meant to be led of Christ, the Apostle Paul was that man. Paul had learned the lesson of complete and full surrender, and had put the lesson into practice in his own life, proving its utter workability. When Paul came to the end of his earthly journey he was able to rest in the realization that he as a runner in the race of life had "run a good race and fought a good fight." Paul would be the first one to acknowledge that his success in the Christian life was not the result of his own efforts, but the result of his complete consecration to Christ.

This lesson from Paul's life for you and me today, dear reader, opens to us the key to living a victorious life in Christ. The secret is surrender. The supplier is Christ!

> *Just Thee alone, my blessed Lord,*
> *For every time and place;*
> *Just Thee alone—until we all*
> *Shall see Thee face to face.*
> —Grace E. Troy

# FEBRUARY 15

*Your Father knows what things you need before ever you ask Him.* — Matthew 6:8

Why does God say "No"? Because of our shortsightedness and His omniscience. He sees "the distant scene" and He knows how the next step should be taken that the "distant scene" may be made clear to us.

What we mistake for God's denials are often God's wise and providential delays, which are not denials at all. He sees the peril lying ahead which we cannot see. It is only after long years have passed that we gain a true vision and say: "Well, if I had taken the road I had expected to take it would not have resulted as I had hoped it would."

Many an individual thanks God that he did not have his way, that things were taken from him, that difficulties were put in his way to block his advance in order that he might have the delight of overcoming, or the delight of awaiting God's time. How often that is true in the ordinary events of life, when we use our ability to the utmost and things do not seem to turn out as we had expected them. If we are children of God, they have turned out as He had expected them and it will be wonderfully beneficial and blessed to us just a little later on. He sees the perils that are in our path that we cannot see. He speaks to us in mercy and grace and He builds us up to meet the dangers and be prepared to receive the things we could not wisely use today. There are many things which we can employ tomorrow that we cannot wisely use today.

— A. Z. Conrad

*When I cannot understand my Father's leading,*
*And it seems to be but hard and cruel fate,*
*Still I hear that gentle whisper ever pleading,*
*God is working, God is faithful — Only wait.*
—A. B. Simpson

*Wait on the Lord: be of good courage, and he shall strength-en thine heart; wait, I say, on the Lord.* —Psalm 27:14

Give God time and, even when the knife is in the hand of Abraham for bloody execution, the ram will be caught in the thicket and the divine voice will speak and restrain (Gen. 22:10, 13).

Give God time and "stand still, and see the salvation of the Lord," even though hemmed in on every side and Pharaoh's hosts press hard upon your heels, for the Red Sea will open before you (Ex. 14:13-25).

Give God time and with Paul say, "Sirs, I believe God"; and then the strange and wonderful Presence will stand by (Acts 27:23-25).

Give God time even when the bed of the brook is dry and you seem forsaken, for Elijah's God still lives and He will guide you to Zarephath (1 Kings 17:8-16).

"Lean not upon thine own understanding." "In all thy ways acknowledge him, and he shall direct thy paths."

—*E. E. Wordsworth*

*I cannot, but God can;*
　*Oh, balm for all my care!*
*The burden that I drop*
　*His hand will lift and bear.*
*Though eagle pinions tire,*
　*I walk where once I ran,*
*This is my strength to know*
　*I cannot, but He can.*

*I see not, but God sees;*
　*Oh, all sufficient light!*
*My dark and hidden way*
　*To Him is always bright.*
*My strained and peering eyes*
　*May close in restful ease,*
*And I in peace may sleep;*
　*I see not, but He sees.*

—Annie Johnson Flint

*For we walk by faith, not by sight.* —2 Corinthians 5:7

It seems that God chooses the hour of human extremity to teach us most surely the greatest lesson of all the Scriptures— we walk by faith.

God would have us in time of storm, as well as when the seas are calm, trust Him implicitly. He would have us commit our way unto Him and lean not unto our own understanding. He would have us believe that "all things work together for good to them that love God." He would have us so rely on His wisdom and discretion that we can add a staunch "Amen" to Job's tribute, "Though he slay me, yet will I trust in him."

—*Jack Shuler*

There is no immunity pledged to us in the everlasting covenant of God from the burdens and bereavements of this passing scene. What is pledged to us, however, is something better. It is the miracle working presence of Him who can appear on our behalf at the darkest hour of our existence, and in a moment change our night to glorious day. Happy the sufferer who, in the crisis of his fate, knows how to bring his troubles to the Savior.

—*E. W. Moore*

*I will not doubt, though sorrows fall like rain*
*And troubles swarm like bees about a hive;*
*I will believe the heights for which I strive*
*Are only gained through anguish, and by pain.*
*And though I groan and tremble 'neath the crosses,*
*Yet shall I see, through my severest losses,*
*The greater gain!*

*Thus saith the Lord unto you, Be not afraid nor dismayed by reason of this great multitude; for the battle is not yours, but God's.*
                                                            —2 Chronicles 20:15

Who among us, dear reader, has not been "afraid" or "dismayed" when he has contemplated the magnitude of life? What comfort there is, then, in reflecting that ". . . the battle is not yours, but God's!"

There are times in life when all of us seem to reach "wits' end corner." Sad it is that we usually wait until this point in life before turning over the battle to the Lord. It seems that only when our own wisdom and strength fail are we willing to turn over the problem to Him. Yet, instead of giving way to despair and despondency, it is our privilege and right to go to God at the outset in the midst of our difficulties — as well as in all conditions, good or ill.

What a comfort it is to know that God is at our side not only in fair weather, but in the storm as well. It is a delight for God to fellowship with us no matter how difficult our path. In fact, it is our complete surrender to and reliance upon Him in the midst of our trial that He is seeking. It is when the crises of life are reached that our Lord shows Himself "a mighty present help." The experience of darkness, of prayers seemingly unanswered, of sin which seems to be triumphant, and affliction is the channel through which we ofttimes learn how truly great our God is.

It was Christ who prayed in Gethsemane, "Tarry ye here, and watch with me." That was His crisis hour. May we not in our own minor crises confidently ask Him to watch with us?

*Not she with traitorous kiss her Savior stung,*
*Not she denied him with unholy tongue;*
*She, while apostles shrank, could dangers brave,*
*Last at the cross and earliest at the grave.*
                                                            —E. S. Barret

> *And he spake a parable unto them to this end, that men*
> *ought always to pray, and not to faint.* —Luke 18:1

Why is it that God does not give to us the very first time we ask Him, the things that we ask of Him? The answer is plain: God would do more for us, and better for us, than to merely give us that thing. He would do us the far greater good of training us into persistent faith. The things that we get by our other forms of effort than prayer to God, do not always become ours the first time we make an effort to get them; for our own good God compels us to be persistent in our effort, and just so God does not always give us what we ask in prayer the first time we pray. Just as He would train us to be strong men and women along the other lines of effort, so also He would train us to be and make us to be strong men and women of prayer by compelling us to pray hard for the best things. He compels us to "Pray through." —*R. A. Torrey*

The spectacle of a nation praying is more awe-inspiring than the explosion of an atomic bomb. The force of prayer is greater than any possible combination of man-controlled powers, because prayer is man's greatest means of tapping the infinite resources of God. —*J. Edgar Hoover*

> *He doth not bid thee wait,*
> *Like driftwood on the wave,*
> *For fickle chance or fixed fate*
> *To ruin or to save.*
> *Thine eyes shall surely see,*
> *No distant hope or dim,*
> *The Lord thy God arise for thee,*
> *"Wait patiently for Him."*
> — Frances Ridley Havergal

*He brought me up also out of an horrible pit, out of the miry clay, and set my feet upon a rock, and established my goings.*
—Psalm 40:2

*God is the Lord, which hath shewed us light.*
—Psalm 118:27

The fact is that, when we turn our faces toward the light, the shadows fall behind us. Never allow yourself to believe that the grace of past days was but a delusion. Never allow the territory which you have won by God's grace and power to be wrested from you by the force of the evil one. When the heavens above you seem to be as brass, when there seems to be no response to the perpetual "Why?" of your heart, remember what God has been to you in the past, and sing with the psalmist: "He took me from the fearful pit, and from the miry clay, and on the rock He set my feet, establishing my way." And the light will surprise you as you sing, and the joy of the Lord will come into your heart and chase away the gloom.          —*J. Stuart Holden*

*He goes before you, O my heart!*
  *Fear not to follow where He leads;*
*He knows the strength each task demands,*
  *He knows the grace each trial needs.*
*He's just a little farther on*
  *Along the dark and lonely way,*
*His bleeding footprints you may trace,*
  *He goes before you all the day.*

*He goes before you, O my heart!*
  *Through deepest depth, o'er highest heights;*
*He knows where lurks the ambushed foe*
  *And what the battles you must fight;*
*He sees the pitfalls you will meet,*
  *The place where you will faint or fall;*
*The weariness, the pain, the tears,*
  *He goes before, He knows it all.*
                    —Annie Johnson Flint

# FEBRUARY 21

*The words of the Lord are pure words: as silver tried in a
furnace of earth, purified seven times.* — Psalm 12:6

One morning with a friend I walked out of the city of
Geneva to where the waters of the lake flow with swift rush
into the Rhone, and we were both greatly interested in the
strange sight which has impressed so many travelers. There
are two rivers whose waters come together here, the Rhone
and the Arve, the Arve flowing into the Rhone. The waters of
the Rhone are beautifully clear and sparkling. The waters of
the Arve come through a clayey soil and are muddy, gray, and
dull.

I went to the guidebook and maps to find out something
about this river that kept on its way undefiled by its neighbor
for so long. Its source is in a glacier that is between ten thousand and eleven thousand feet high, descending "from the
gates of eternal night, at the foot of the pillar of the sun." It is
fed continually by the melting glacier which, in turn, is being
kept up by the snows and cold. Rising at this great height,
ever being renewed steadily by the glacier, the river comes
rushing down the swift descent of the Swiss Alps through the
lake of Geneva, and on. There is the secret of purity, side by
side with its dirty neighbor.

Our lives must have their source high up in the mountains
of God, fed by a ceaseless supply. Only so can there be the
purity, and the momentum that will keep us pure, and keep
us moving down in contact with men of the earth. Constant
personal contact with Jesus is the ever new beginning of service.
—S. D. Gordon

*No service in itself is small,
    None great though earth it fill;
But that is small that seeks its own,
    And great that seeks God's will.*
—Anonymous

*And he said unto me, My grace is sufficient for thee; for my strength is made perfect in weakness. Most gladly therefore will I rather glory in my infirmities, that the power of Christ may rest upon me.* — 2 Corinthians 12:9

"Sufficient"—the grace of Christ is always and evermore sufficient. See that noble, rolling river; it has been flowing for thousands of years, watering the fields, and slaking the thirst of a hundred generations; yet it shows no sign of exhaustion. See the morning sun as he shoots his golden arrows high above the mountain crests, and as he gilds the curtains of the dawn with a glittering glory. He has been performing this daily miracle for millenniums; he has melted the snows of six thousand winters, and renewed the verdure of as many summers; yet he shines as gloriously as ever; his eye is not dimmed, and his natural strength is unabated. Do not these things try to speak to us of the grace of Christ? In Him are fountains that never run dry, and rivers that never cease their flowing. He is a sun that never languishes, and an ocean ever full. Certainly indeed is His grace "sufficient" for us. His "sufficiency" is simply the expression toward us of His infinite fullness.
— *J. Sidlow Baxter*

*His grace is sufficient, whatever the pathway,*
*His strength in thy weakness shall perfected be;*
*So great is His love it never can weary*
*Of meeting thy need and of caring for thee.*

*His grace is sufficient, thou ne'er canst exhaust it,*
*Be strong in that grace which floweth to thee,*
*Draw largely, continually, out from His fullness,*
*He still is sufficient, He careth for thee.*

# FEBRUARY 23

*For we have not an high priest which cannot be touched*
*with the feeling of our infirmities.* — Hebrews 4:15

The shadows of life have their purpose as well as the bright sunlight, and the dark hours of sorrow bring their own rich satisfaction. The one who has passed through trouble is equipped by his own experience to sympathize with others who pass that way. Our Great High Priest sympathizes with His brethren in their infirmities and is qualified to do so because of His own experience on earth. Similarly, those who know the trials and difficulties of life's road can enter into the feelings of others who are tried and can provide strength and encouragement for the weak and the weary.

No trial is ever too great to bear. The One who allows it provides the strength required in the time of testing (Heb. 4:16). Paul might be given a thorn in the flesh, but Divine grace was bestowed in the measure he needed (2 Cor. 12:7-9). And in every hour of trouble, there is the consciousness not only of His sufficiency and sympathy, but also of His companionship and sharing of the trouble. "In all their affliction He was afflicted" (Isa. 63:9). We do not walk alone in the shadows: the gracious Companion of the lonely pilgrim is nearer in the dark than in the light, and His fellowship is as real (if not more so) in days of adversity as in days of prosperity.

—*Frederick A. Tatford*

*The Savior can lift every burden,*
*The heavy as well as the light;*
*His strength is made perfect in weakness,*
*In Him there is power and might.*
—Oswald J. Smith

*He that putteth his trust in Me shall possess the land, and
shall inherit My holy mountain.* — Isaiah 57:13

Every act of trust increases your capacity for God. Every
time I trust Him I have more room for Him. He dwells
within me in ever richer fullness, occupying room after room
in my life. That is a glorious assurance, and one that is filled
with infinite comfort. Let me repeat it again, for it is the very
music of the soul; little acts of trust make larger room for
God. In my trifles I can prepare for emergencies. Along a
commonplace road I can get ready for the hill. In the green
pastures and by the still waters I can prepare myself for the
valley of the shadow. For when I reach the hill, the shadow,
the emergency, I shall be God-possessed: He will dwell in
me. And where He dwells He controls. If He lives in my life
He will direct my powers. It will not be I that speak, but my
Father that speaketh in me. He will govern my speech. He
will empower my will. He will enlighten my mind. He will
energize and vitalize my entire life. — *J. H. Jowett*

*I know not, but God knows;*
*Oh, blessed rest from fear!*
*All my unfolding days*
*To Him are plain and clear.*
*Each anxious puzzled "Why?"*
*From doubt or dread that grows,*
*Finds answer in this thought:*
*I know not, but He knows.*

*If I take the wings of the morning and dwell in the uttermost parts of the sea.* —Psalm 139:9

The higher way provides better vision. He who reaches the Alpine peaks of spiritual devotion is rewarded with a clear panoramic vision of the waiting fields in the valley of human need. His view will not be obstructed by the multitudinous mounds of self-interest which hinder the vision of one on a lower plane. Then, too, it is easier to descend to the ministry of work when once we have ascended to the mountain of worship. Lookout towers are ever on the heights, never in the valley. The reason is obvious. Nor is it less reasonable that elevation is of utmost importance in the spiritual realm.

The outlook of God's people is suffering irreparably in this day as a result of the course which is being followed. It reminds us of an aeroplane disaster in southern England during World War II. The plane had hit the tree tops and plunged into a burning heap of wreckage, killing all the occupants. The investigators returned this terse report of their findings: "flying too low." We would do well to covet that optional spiritual status of "mounting up with wings as eagles." We are flying too low. We haven't the vision which makes for an aggressive endeavor of the finer type. The higher way, near to the heart of God, gives one the proper outlook. —*S. Franklin Logsdon*

*I dare not choose my lot*
*I would not if I might,*
*Choose Thou for me, my God,*
*So shall I walk aright.*
—H. Bonar

*Let your light so shine before men, that they may see your good works, and glorify your Father which is in heaven.*
—Matthew 5:16

The secret of a holy life is God-possession. If you would be holy, God must be in the possession. There is only one Holy Life, there is none holy as the Lord. If you would be holy, you must let the Holy One indwell you.

Do you want to lead a holy life? Let Christ be absolute Master in your inmost being, let Him be the Fountain whence the streams of thought and word and action flow, let Him be the central Fire dwelling within the shrine and sending forth its light and heat even to the outer courts of your temple. "The light of Israel shall be for a fire, and his Holy One for a flame" (Isa. 10:17). Let our God, who is a consuming fire (Heb. 12:29), so take possession of us that He shall consume the dross out of us, and make our lives to glow with light and love to all men.

This is the life that men will turn aside to see. This is letting our light shine before them. We want to arrest their attention. It is no easy thing to do. Perhaps they will not listen to sermons preached for one half-hour a week; but will they not be struck by a sermon that is practiced all the week? Sure I am, at any rate, that the best sermon is a holy life. —*E. W. Moore*

*You never can tell when you do an act*
*Just what the result will be,*
*For with every deed, you are sowing a seed*
*Tho' its harvest you may never see.*

*I will lift up mine eyes unto the hills, from whence cometh
my help.*                                              —Psalm 121:1

Stars may be seen from the bottom of a deep well when
they cannot be discerned from the top of a mountain: so are
many things learned in adversity which the prosperous man
dreams not of. We need affliction as the trees need winter,
that we may collect sap and nourishment for future blossoms
and fruit. Sorrow is as necessary for the soul as medicine is to
the body:

> *The path of sorrow, and that path alone,*
> *Leads to the land where sorrow is unknown.*

The adversities of today are a preparatory school for the
higher learning.

Sunlight is never more grateful than after a long watch in
the midnight blackness; Christ's presence is never more
acceptable than after a time of weeping, on account of His
departure. It is a sad thing that we should need to lose our
mercies to teach us to be grateful for them; let us mourn over
this crookedness of our nature; and let us strive to express our
thankfulness for mercies, so that we may not have to lament
their removal. If thou desirest Christ for a perpetual guest,
give Him all the keys of thine heart; let not one cabinet be
locked up from Him; give Him the range of every room, and
the key of every chamber; thus you will constrain Him to
remain.                                        —C. H. Spurgeon

> *Seas of sorrow, seas of trial*
>> *Bitterest anguish, fiercest pain,*
> *Rolling surges of temptation,*
>> *Sweeping over heart and brain,*
> *They shall never overflow us,*
>> *For we know His word is true;*
> *All His waves and all His billows*
>> *He will lead us safely through.*
>>> —Annie Johnson Flint

*Serve the Lord with gladness; come before his presence with singing.*
—Psalm 100:2

It is of little importance what your service is or the place where God calls you to service: the important thing is to fill that particular place which the Lord has designated and delegated to you. If God's place for you is upon your sickbed, that is the place where you can serve Him just as truly, just as fully, just as fruitfully as the most brilliant silver-tongued orator who stands before the masses proclaiming the Word of the Living God.

The richest, the fullest, the most fruitful lives are those that have been in the crucible of testing, that have been broken upon the wheel of tribulation. We have no right to believe that God will do anything with our lives until He has broken us. There are in this world few entirely unbroken lives that are useful to God. There are few men and women who can fulfill their own hopes and plans without interruptions and disappointments all along the way. But man's disappointments are ever God's appointments, and what we believe are tragedies are only blessings in disguise, and the very opportunities through which God wishes to exhibit His love and grace.

—*M. R. DeHaan*

*Not now, but in the coming years,*
*It may be in the better land,*
*We'll read the meaning of our tears,*
*And there, some time, we'll understand.*

*Then trust in God thro' all the days;*
*Fear not, for He doth hold thy hand;*
*Though dark thy way, still sing and praise,*
*Some time, some time, we'll understand.*

# FEBRUARY 29

*If ye shall ask any thing in my name, I will do it.*
                                              —John 14:14

We need do but one thing: tell God about our condition, about our faith, our solicitude, and our worldly and prayer-weary heart; and then pray in the name of Jesus.

We can come before God and say to Him, "I do not have a right to pray because I do not have a truly prayerful heart. Much less do I have any right to receive what I ask for. Everything which Thou seest in my heart, O Lord, is of such a nature that it must close Thy heart to me and all my supplications. But hear me, not for my sake, not for the sake of my prayer, and not even because of my distress, for it is a result of my own sinfulness. But hear me for Jesus' sake."

We have learned that to pray in the name of Jesus is the real element of prayer in our prayers.

It is the helpless soul's helpless look unto a gracious Friend.
                                              —O. Hallesby


When the disciples locked the doors, Christ knew He was sure of a welcome. He could not get their ear because of the din and confusion that came through the open doors. Closing the door to the world meant opening the door to the Master. Don't be afraid of shutting the door. It is the best invitation for the Master to enter.                    —*Christian Herald*

> *Unanswered, does your prayer remain*
> *Though oft with tears you plead?*
> *And watch and wait and wonder if*
> *God does not care or heed?*
> *Unanswered? Well, perhaps, dear heart,*
> *You may have asked amiss;*
> *Is it God's glory that you seek,*
> *Or selfish avarice?*
>                     —Annie Woodsworth

*Ye also, as lively stones, are built up a spiritual house, an holy priesthood, to offer up spiritual sacrifices, acceptable to God by Jesus Christ.* —1 Peter 2:5

How can we build ourselves up? By the Gospel and that which is preached. The builders are the preachers; the Christians who hear the Gospel are they who are built, and the stones which are to be fitted on this cornerstone; so that we are to repose our confidence on Him, and let our hearts stand and rest upon Him. The house of stone or wood is not His house: He will have a spiritual house, that is, the Christian congregation. Those alone are the Holy and spiritual priesthood, who are true Christians and built upon this stone. Christ has been anointed the high and most exalted priest by God Himself; has also sacrificed His own body for us, which is the office of the high priest; besides, He prayed on the cross for us. He has also preached the Gospel and taught all men to know God and Himself. —*Martin Luther*

To the feeblest of God's children Christ says: *Ye are in Me.* "Abide in me. Ye shall bear much fruit." To the strongest of His messengers He still has the word, there can be nothing higher: "Abide in me, and ye shall bear much fruit." To one and all the message comes: Daily, continuous, unbroken abiding in Christ Jesus, is the one condition of a life of power and of blessing. Take time and let the Holy Spirit so renew in you the secret abiding in Him that you may understand His meaning: "These things have I spoken unto you that my joy might remain in you, and that your joy might be full." —*Andrew Murray*

*No vision, and you perish;*
  *No ideal, and you're lost;*
*Your heart must ever cherish*
  *Some faith at any cost.*

*Some hope, some dream to cling to,*
  *Some rainbow in the sky,*
*Some melody to sing to,*
  *Some service that is high.*

—Harriet Du Autremont

# MARCH 2

*Nevertheless God, that comforteth those that are cast down,*
*comforted us . . .*                                    —2 Corinthians 7:6

There are many results growing out of the infilling of the Holy Spirit, but not one is more glorious than the abiding presence of Jesus Christ. Jesus said to His disciples, "I will not leave you comfortless: I will come to you" (John 14:18). "For if I go not away, the Comforter will not come unto you: but if I depart, I will send him unto you" (John 16:7). Jesus Christ crucified, risen, glorified, can do more for us through the Holy Spirit in us, than He could have done in person on earth with us. And so, the meaning of the divine promise is that Jesus comes back to earth again in the Holy Spirit, and every believer who opens his heart and receives the infilling of the Holy Spirit has the everlasting Christ with him day by day. And, when He comes into your life, He will give that completeness which you need for life and for service.

—J. B. Lawrence

*Lean hard, sad heart, on Jesus, He knows thy secret grief,*
*And swift He is to succor, so swift to give relief;*
*Then let come cloud or sunshine, or skies be dull or clear,*
*Lean hard, sad heart, on Jesus, for thou hast nought to fear.*

*With Him 'tis ever sunshine, and clouds are far away,*
*With Him there is no darkness, but full meridian day;*
*Tho' winter's blast or summer's balm, or life or death should come,*
*Lean hard on Him, dear troubled heart, He's pledged to bring thee home.*

*Jesus . . . made a little lower than the angels for the suffering of death, crowned with glory and honor; that he by the grace of God should taste death for every man.* —Hebrews 2:9

The Cross. The true glory of God is revealed in the Atonement. To read the Word of God in Jesus you must read His life clear through to the end; there you come to the Cross. And only there do you see the heart of God laid bare. You have a small God if you have no Atonement in your creed.

Let me not view the Cross with idle sight. There I see the real nature of my God; for I read His name as Holy Love; Holy, because He could not overlook sin; Love, because He bore the weight of it Himself for me. And I see that for me, too, spiritual glory is far to be preferred to material; for there my King serves His enemies and my God saves by His shame.

A religion can lift you only as high as its core. At the heart of beautiful Bali, isle of the South Seas, is the dance; and unspeakable lusts grow out of its "lovely" religious rites. At the heart of Confucianism is the "superior man"; and ethics will make an upright but self-centered character. At the heart of Christianity is the Cross of holy love. How high should it lift me?
—*Bertha Munro*

*The cross was such an ugly thing!—*
*A shape to make the heart afraid;*
*A beam of death for lawless men,*
*A gibbett for the renegade.*

*The symbol of eternal hope;*
*The subject of a thousand songs;*
*The sign of truth and liberty.*

*The cross is such a lovely thing!—*
*The lamp in night where people grope;*
*The emblem of eternal life;*

*The cross was such an ugly thing*
*Until it went to Calvary.*

—Lon Woodrum

# MARCH 4

*Thou hast beset me behind and before, and lain thine hand upon me.*
— Psalm 139:5

How perfectly complete is the suggestion of an all encircling presence, round about me on every side. The ramparts are built up all about me, and the ring of defense is complete. Perhaps there is no experience in human life which more perfectly develops the thought of the Psalmist than the guardianship offered by a mother to her baby-child when the little one is just learning to walk. The mother literally encircles the child with protection, spreading out her arms into almost a complete ring, so that in whatever way the child may happen to stumble she falls into the waiting ministry of love. Such is the idea of "besetment."
—*J. H. Jowett*

*In the secret of His presence*
*All the darkness disappears;*
*For a sun that knows no setting,*
*Throws a rainbow on my tears.*
*So the day grows ever lighter,*
*Broadening to the perfect noon;*
*So the day grows ever brighter,*
*Heaven is coming, near and soon.*

*In the secret of His presence*
*Never more can foes alarm;*
*In the shadow of the Highest,*
*I can meet them with a psalm;*
*For the strong pavilion hides me,*
*Turns their fiery darts aside,*
*And I know, whate'er betides me,*
*I shall live because He died!*
—Henry Burton

*I can do all things through Christ which strengtheneth me.*
—Philippians 4:13

"But I do not feel strong," says Joshua, "and I am not at all courageous. The men who withstood Moses to the face and rewarded his patience with apostasy, will dispute my authority also; and what credentials can I carry that none shall dare to controvert?"

And the Unseen breaks in almost abruptly, and closes the conversation with this: "Have not I commanded thee? Be strong and of good courage; be not afraid, neither be thou dismayed: for the Lord thy God is with thee, whithersoever thou goest."

At that point the dialogue ceases, the disputation ends. Every doubt has been dissolved, the spirit of fear cast out. The man who had trembled upon his knees rises already a victor. He has conquered himself. Nay! shall I not rather say that God has conquered him? Yes! that is the better way of putting it, God has conquered him; and the man who has been subdued by the Holy Spirit will be subdued by none beside.
—*R. Moffat Gautrey*

*Stand up, my soul, shake off thy fears,*
*And gird the gospel armor on;*
*March to the gates of endless joy,*
*Where thy great Captain Savior's gone.*

*What though thine inward lust rebel;*
*'Til but a struggling gasp for life;*
*The weapons of victorious grace*
*Shall slay thy sins, and end the strife.*

*Then let my soul march boldly on,*
*Press forward to the heavenly gate;*
*There peace and joy eternal reign,*
*And glittering robes for conquerors wait.*
—Isaac Watts

# MARCH 6

*Yield yourselves unto God, as those that are alive from the dead, and your members as instruments of righteousness unto God.*
—Romans 6:13

We find that after yielding all to the Master, He comes so to possess us by His Spirit that our very frames-of-mind are governed by Him. Are we moved to pray? He gives that spirit of prayer, access into the presence of the living God. And our prayers have a force and a vitality that leads us to laugh at the impossible. Are we tried? He holds us in His bosom and the kisses of His mouth make our heart to sing. Are we tempted? He girds us with might— we are more than conquerors in Him.
—F. J. Huegel

*The world grows lonely, and, with many a tear,*
*I stretch out longing hands in vain, to clasp*
*The treasures of my life, and hold them here,*
*But "all dear things seem slipping from my grasp."*

*Oh, say not so, my heart! One stands beside*
*Whose love, in all its fullness, is thine own:*
*That love is changeless, and, whate'er betide,*
*He will not leave thee; thou art not alone!*

*God keeps my treasures, and some glad, bright day,*
*He'll give them to my longing sight again;*
*So Faith and Hope shall cheer me all the way,*
*And Love, their sweetest sister, soothe my pain.*

*Thus, taking God's full cup of comforting,*
*Let me give thanks! and, pouring out most free*
*My life in loyal service, let me bring*
*To other lives the joy God giveth me.*

*And Jesus answered him, saying, It is written, That man shall not live by bread alone, but by every word of God.*

—Luke 4:4

The Bible meets the crises of life with unquestioned success. The Bible, never to be outgrown, is never out-of-date. The most up-to-date book in any library, the Bible is forever inexhaustive in adequacy. Meaningless—comparatively—would be the world's libraries without its teaching. There are no problems it cannot solve, no burdens it does not lighten, no trouble it does not lessen, no doubt assailing Christian faith it does not vanquish. There is no weariness the Bible does not help remove, no grief it cannot console, no sin it does not condemn, no righteous deed it does not commend, no defilement it cannot cleanse. The softest pillow for the dying, the mightiest spur to the living, it furnishes to the weak power, to the strong greater strength, to the hopeless renewed assurance. Not one of its promises can ever fail, not one of its fires ever die out. The guarantees it gives of eternal life are unequivocal and entirely reliable.

Let us be able to say what the Psalmist said: "I turned my feet unto thy testimonies" (Psalm 119:59).    —*Robert G. Lee*

*Cling to the Bible, though all else be taken:*
*Lose not its promises precious and sure;*
*Souls that are sleeping, its echoes awaken,*
*Drink from the fountain, so peaceful, so pure.*

*Lamp for the feet that in byways have wandered.*
*Guide for the youth that would otherwise fall;*
*Hope for the sinner whose best days are squandered,*
*Staff for the aged, and best Book of all.*

—M. J. Smith

# MARCH 8

*Rejoice evermore.* — 1 Thessalonians 5:16

Some people seem to feel that an unhappy countenance or a mournful expression indicates spirituality and righteousness. God's Word indicates that the contrary is true. A Christian has every reason for rejoicing. God's way is a way of joy. Indeed, the only place that full and abundant happiness is found is in the proper relationship with God. The Psalmist wrote: "In thy presence is fullness of joy; at thy right hand there are pleasures for evermore" (Ps. 16:11). Christians are commanded to rejoice, and it is a command that it is no effort to obey. "Rejoice in the Lord alway; and again I say, Rejoice" (Phil. 4:4). This is God's injunction to His children. Christ declared: "I am come that they might have life, and that they might have it more abundantly" (John 10:10). Surely no abundance of life is possible unless there is peace and happiness in the heart.

After all, the Christian has every reason for rejoicing.

Even death itself holds no terrors, "For we know that if our earthly house of this tabernacle were dissolved, we have a building of God, an house not made with hands, eternal in the heavens" (2 Cor. 5:1). We are assured that because He lives, we shall live also (John 14:19). The grave may be dark, but beyond it is the glory of resurrection and the promise of an heavenly home where "God shall wipe away all tears . . ." (Rev. 21:4) from the eyes of men, where there is no sorrow or sighing, where nothing shall ever enter that mars and blights and destroys.     —*Bob Jones, Jr.*

*Joy is a fruit that will not grow*
*In nature's barren soil;*
*All we can boast, till Christ we know,*
*Is vanity and toil.*
*But where the Lord hath planted grace,*
*And made His glories known,*
*These fruits of heavenly joy and peace*
*Are found, and there alone.*
    —John Newton

> *Looking unto Jesus the author and finisher of our faith; who for the joy that was set before him endured the cross, despising the shame, and is set down at the right hand of the throne of God.*
> —Hebrews 12:2

Looking at Jesus changes the world for us. It is as though the light of His eyes fills our eyes and we see things all around as He sees them. Have you ever gone out, as a child, and looked intently at the sun, repressing the flinching its strength caused and insisting on looking? You could do it for a short time only. It made your eyes ache. But as you turned your eyes away from its brilliance you found everything changed. You remember a beautiful yellow glory-light was over everything, and every ugly jagged thing was softened and beautified by that glow in your eyes. Looking at the sun had changed the world for you for a little while.

It is something like that on this higher plane, in this finer sense. That must have been something of Paul's thought in explaining the glory of Jesus that he saw on the Damascus road. "When I could not see for the glory of that light." The old ideals were blurred. The old ambitions faded away. The jagged, sharp lines of sacrifice and suffering involved in his new life were not clearly seen. A halo had come over them.

— *S. D. Gordon*

> *But I look up—into the face of Jesus,*
> *For there my heart can rest, my fears are stilled;*
> *And there is joy, and love, and light for darkness,*
> *And perfect peace and every hope fulfilled.*
> —Annie Johnson Flint

# MARCH 10

*Watch and pray, that ye enter not into temptation.*
—*Matthew 26:41*

It is because of the fact, power and danger of temptation that Jesus urges us to watch and pray. Watching and praying are practically equivalent; for when we are watching against temptation, we are praying against it; and when we are praying against it, we are on guard against it. When we pray, we bring ourselves into vital contact with Christ, who knows all about the wiles and stratagems of the devil. He met the enemy and triumphed gloriously over him, and is therefore able to make us more than conquerors.

A British pilot had not flown very far before he noticed a peculiar noise. Looking down, he saw a rat gnawing away at a vital part of his plane. He could not stop to kill the rodent. What could he do? Up into the rarified air he zoomed, and the rat rolled over, dead. Does this not illustrate the power of prayer? When the rat of hell tempts us, prayer takes us up into the rare air of heaven, where everything not of God quickly dies.
— *Herbert Lockyer*

*I need Thee, precious Jesus!*
*For I am full of sin*
*My soul is dark and guilty,*
*My heart is dead within;*
*I need the cleansing fountain,*
*Where I can always flee,*
*The blood of Christ most precious,*
*The sinner's perfect plea.*
—Frederick Whitfield

*These things I have spoken unto you, that in me ye might have peace. In the world ye shall have tribulation; but be of good cheer; I have overcome the world.* —John 16:33

Trials are sometimes inflicted by God in order to teach His people their complete dependence upon Him. When days of prosperity are enjoyed, the felt need of Him diminishes, but when adversity breaks, the believer turns back to the Father with a cry for help. A small boy, busy building a toy boat, declined the proffered help of his father; but a few minutes later, he came running to his father plaintively with a bleeding finger. When trouble comes, the spirit of sturdy independence disappears and the comfort and strength of God are sought. Because He desires to teach the lesson of dependence upon Him and the uncertainty of everything else, He deliberately allows suffering and sorrow. At times, it is necessary for Him to deliver His people even from the enslavement of their tenderest and most sensitive affections, since, as another has said, "even legitimate affections, if tenaciously, selfishly and passionately nursed, may become the enemies of our souls." Therefore the sudden blow falls and we turn helplessly to Him and fall into the embrace of love. *—Frederick A. Tatford*

*When, in the hour of lonely woe,*
*I give my sorrow leave to flow,*
*And anxious fear and dark distrust*
*Weigh down my spirit to the dust.*

*When not e'en friendship's gentle aid*
*Can heal the wounds the world has made,*
*Oh, this shall check each rising sigh,*
*That Jesus is forever nigh.*

—Josiah Conder

# MARCH 12

*Blessed be the God and Father of our Lord Jesus Christ,
which according to his abundant mercy hath begotten us
again unto a lively hope by the resurrection of Jesus Christ
from the dead.* —1 Peter 1:3

In the words of Peter we have a living hope. Every Christian
has not only the blessed assurance of sins forgiven, but the
present bright hope of everlasting life.

Christians may suffer untold miseries in this life. We may
die of some torturing disease. We may drop in a moment
from a spasm of the heart. We may be burned, drowned or
crushed. We may die in youth or in advanced age. No matter
how, no matter when, the end of the corridor is lighted! The
collapsed heart may spell the end of the body, but it means
immediate life with Jesus Christ in heaven. Such is the living
hope of the Christian. —*Bernard Ramm*

*Naught shall e'er from Jesus sever:
Jesus lives, and I am sure
Satan's wiles and Satan's power,
Pain or pleasure, ye shall never!
Christian armor cannot rust:
Jesus is my Hope and Trust.*

*Jesus lives, and death is now
But my entrance into glory.
Courage! then, my soul, for thou
Hast a crown of life before thee;
Thou shalt find thy hopes were just:
Jesus is the Christian's Trust.*

(From the German by Chr. Furchtegott Gellert)

*When he heard that Jesus was come out of Judea into Galilee, he went unto him, and besought him that he would come down, and heal his son: for he was at the point of death.*
— John 4:47

The trouble in his home sent this man to Christ. Perhaps he never would have gone at all had it not been for his son's sickness. Many of those who went to Christ in the olden days were driven by their distress of heart. They tried everything else first, and then at the last moment they hurried to Jesus. The same is true in these days. Many persons who have never prayed before have gotten down upon their knees by the bedside of their sick and dying children and cried to God on their behalf. Many persons have first been sent to God by their own troubles. It was not until the prodigal was in sore want, and every other resource had been exhausted, that he said he would arise and go to his father. Many sinners never think of Christ until they are in despair under the scene of guilt. Not until they see the storm of wrath gathering do they seek the shelter of the Cross. But what a comfort it is that even going so late to the Savior He does not reject or cast away those who come!
— *J. R. Miller*

*The world and Satan I forsake;*
*    To Thee I all resign:*
*My longing heart, O Savior, take,*
*    And fill with love divine.*

*O may I never turn aside,*
*    Nor from Thy bosom flee;*
*Let nothing here my heart divide,*
*    I give it all to Thee.*

# MARCH 14

*I will say of the Lord, He is my refuge and my fortress: my God, in Him will I trust.*                    —Psalm 91:2

God is prepared to keep us in all our ways. Many of us believe that somehow God will bring us out at last, but we have no expectation that He can keep us in blamelessness of soul; we expect to be brought to heaven, but that we shall be battered, and beaten, and despoiled on the way. But surely our God can do better for us than that! He can keep us from yielding to passionate temper, jealousy, hatred, pride and envy, as well as to the grosser forms of sin.

The promise is clear: "He shall give His angels charge over thee, to keep thee in all thy ways" — the business ways, the social ways, the ways of service into which God may lead us forth, the ways of sacrifice or suffering. Let us simply and humbly ask for the fulfillment of the promises in this Psalm. He will answer your prayer. He will be with you in trouble. He will satisfy you with many years of life, or with living much in a short time, and He will show you the wonders of His salvation.                    —F. B. Meyer

*I know not, but God knows;*
*Oh, blessed rest from fear!*
*All my unfolding days*
*To Him are plain and clear.*
*Each anxious, puzzled "Why?"*
*From doubt or dread that grows,*
*Finds answer in this thought:*
*I know not, but He knows.*
                    —Annie Johnson Flint

*He that dwelleth in the secret place of the most High shall abide under the shadow of the Almighty.* —Psalm 91:1

To abide in the Will of God is to abide in absolute safety. David said to Abiathar, "Abide thou with me. Fear not; for he that seeketh my life seeketh thy life; but with me thou shalt be in safeguard" (1 Sam. 22:23). So speaks God to the humblest believer. Is not this the true interpretation of that Ninety-first Psalm, that to all commentators seems such a mystery? Is not that Secret Place of the Most High, where one abides under the very shadow of the Almighty, covered with His feathers and hiding trustfully under His wings simply the Will of God! There abiding, in vain does the Fowler spread his snares for our feet, or the adversary hurl at us his darts of death. Into that sacred chamber of the Divine Presence neither the pestilence that walketh in darkness nor the destruction that wasteth at noonday can find entrance. Here we tread upon the young lion and adder and trample under foot even the Dragon.

Fellowship with God is the all sufficient antidote to anxiety—the cure of care. Anxious thoughts are not only useless, but worse, for they burden us with the anticipation of troubles that never come, while they avert or avoid no real and inevitable troubles, and only double them by anticipation.

—A. T. Pierson

*Before He formed a star,*
  *Our God arranged our lot;*
*Our little lives were planned afar,*
  *When we as yet were not.*

# MARCH 16

*Forsake me not, O Lord.*   —*Psalm 38:21*

Do you wait until the time of trial and temptation to pray this prayer? Do you have the feeling that it is presumptuous on your part to pray this prayer—unless you are in dire circumstances? Stop and think. There is no moment in our lives when we can do without His constant upholding, His continual support. Whether we are riding the crest of a wave of prosperity and joy, or groping in the darkness of depression, we need to pray: "Forsake me not, O Lord."

The rudderless ship wanders aimlessly over the face of the sea. The child without a watchful adult is helpless. Just so the Christian who would get through any moment without the guiding hand of the Father is traveling aimlessly.

Our Father God will not forsake His own. God is pictured in His Word as a Shepherd who forsakes not His sheep, but stands ready to protect and care for His own in the face of any obstacle or danger. God is also pictured as a great Husbandman, who cares for His vineyard. You and I, as Christians, are part of the great Husbandman's vineyard, one of the Shepherd's sheep.

Should we not pray God that He forsake us not even in our joys, lest we become absorbed in them; in our sorrow, lest we murmur against Him; in our repentance, lest we lose the hope of pardon and fall into despair; in the day of our strongest faith, lest our faith degenerate into presumption? O Lord, forsake us not, for without Thee we are weak, but with Thee we are strong! Forsake us not, for our path is full of temptation and snares, and without Thy guidance we would fall by the wayside.

*Only, O Lord, in Thy dear love*
*Fit us for perfect rest above;*
*And help us this and every day,*
*To live more nearly as we pray.*           —John Keble

*But lay up for yourselves treasures in heaven.*

*—Matthew 6:20*

I read of a little child whose mother was sick, and the child was not old enough to understand about the sickness of the mother. She was taken away, and when the mother died, they thought they would rather have the child remember her mother as she was when she was well, and so they did not take her back till after the mother was buried.

They brought the child home and she ran into the drawing-room to meet her mother and her mother was not there. The little girl was disappointed, and ran into all the rooms, but could not find her mother. She began to cry and asked them to send her back; she did not want to stay; home had lost its attraction because mother was not there.

What is going to make heaven so delightful? It won't be the pearly gates; it won't be the jasper walls; but it will be that we shall see the King in His beauty, and shall behold Him, and not only Him, but those that have gone before us.

*—D. L. Moody*

Heaven is a place of complete victory and triumph. This is the battlefield; there is the triumphal procession. This is the land of the sword and spear; that is the land of the wreath and crown. Oh, what a thrill of joy shall shoot through the hearts of all the blessed when their conquests shall be complete in heaven, when death itself, the last of foes, shall be slain— when Satan shall be dragged captive at the chariot wheels of Christ—when He shall have overthrown sin—when the great shout of universal victory shall rise from the hearts of all the redeemed.

# MARCH 18

*He that spared not his own Son, but delivered him up for us*
*all, how shall he not with him also freely give us all things?*
—Romans 8:32

Mark the manner in which God gives: "How shall he not with him also freely give us all things?" God does not have to be coaxed; there is no reluctance in Him for us to overcome. He is ever more willing to give than we are to receive. Again; He is under no obligation to any; if He were, He would bestow of necessity, instead of giving "freely." Ever remember that He has a perfect right to do with His own as He pleases. He is free to give to whom He wills.

The word "freely" not only signifies that God is under no constraint, but also means that He makes no charge for His gifts, He places no price on His blessings. God is no retailer of mercies or barterer of good things; if He were, justice would require Him to charge exactly what each blessing was worth, and then who among the children of Adam could find the wherewithal? No, blessed be His name, God's gifts are "without money and without price," unmerited and unearned.

—*Arthur W. Pink*

*Rest, troubled heart, oppressed by care and sorrow,*
*Let every fear and vague foreboding cease;*
*Oh, rest in Him who giveth to the burdened,*
*After the day is over, blessed peace.*

*Rest, anxious heart, take no thought for the morrow,*
*Thou needest not wake, for He His watch doth keep;*
*Oh, rest in Him who giveth His beloved,*
*After the day is over, blessed sleep.*
—Annie Johnson Flint

*Who passing through the volley of Baca make it a well; the*
*rain also filleth the pools.* —Psalm 84:6

There is something very beautiful to me in the truth that
suffering, rightly used, is not a cramping, binding, restricting
of the human soul, but a setting of it free. It is not a violation
of the natural order, it is only a more or less violent breaking
open of some abnormal state that the natural order may be
resumed. It is the opening of a cage door. It is the breaking of
a prison wall. This is the thought of those fine old lines of an
early English poet:

> *The soul's dark cottage battered and decayed,*
> *Let's in new light through chinks that time has made.*
> *Stronger by weakness, wiser men become*
> *As they draw near to their eternal home.*

Oh, how many battered cottages have thus let in the light!
How many broken bodies have set their souls free, and how
many shattered homes have let the men and women who sat
in darkness in them see the great light of a present God!
"Stronger by weakness!" "Who passing through the vale of
misery use it for a well." —*Phillips Brooks*

> *His grace is sufficient,*
> *Then why need I fear,*
> *Though the testing be hard,*
> *And the trial severe?*
>
> *He tempers each wind*
> *That upon me doth blow,*
> *And tenderly whispers,*
> *"Thy Father doth know."*
> —Avis B. Christiansen

# MARCH 20

*Ye are my friends, if ye do whatsoever I command you.*
—John 15:14

There is a friendship infinitely higher than all human friendships. It is the friendship of which Jesus spoke to His faithful disciples in the night in which He was betrayed. Surely, no sweeter words ever fell upon mortal ears. They were given by one who was shortly to display in His death the great love which was involved in that friendship.

What is often overlooked, however, is the fact that Jesus himself conditions this friendship with obedience on our part. "If ye do whatsoever I command"; that is, willful and repeated disobedience on our part rules out the possibility of such a friendship. Notice further that this obedience is unlimited in its scope whatsoever I command you. And if then we would be inclined, almost rebelliously, to reply, "But Lord, is all that required?" He simply repeats, "If ye do whatsoever I command you, ye are my friends."
—S. G. Brondsema

*The path of Duty is the path of glory,*
*He that ever following her commands,*
*On with the toil of heart, on knees and hands,*
*Through the long gorge, to the far light, has won*
*His path upward, and prevailed,*
*Shall find the toppling crags of Duty, scaled;*
*Are close upon the shining table-lands*
*To which our God, Himself, is moon and sun!*
— Alfred Tennyson

*The joy of the Lord is your strength.*      —Nehemiah 8:10

God cannot be dissociated from joy. He is light and in Him is no darkness at all. Gloom has nothing to do with Deity, and those who serve Christ without joy are in that respect failing to represent Him truly. Moreover, as Nehemiah puts it in this superb sentence, strength comes from the joy of the Lord. There is nothing trivial about the Lord's joy. It is powerful, and it fortifies the heart in deepest distress.

Take your Bible, trace the theme joy throughout its pages, and you will see that there is no circumstance in which it is inappropriate to rejoice in the Lord. One of the unique elements of the Christian faith is its independence of earthly circumstances. In tribulation and in sorrow, in sickness and in peril, it is possible for you to rejoice. No matter, therefore, what faces you today, you may find strength in the joy of the Lord. "The joy of the Lord is your strength."

—*Frank E. Gaebelein*

*Where Jesus reigns there is no night,*
*For He is Wisdom, Love and Light;*
*No raging sea, nor tempest dread,*
*But quietness and calm, instead;*
*No anxious care, no blind unrest,*
*No heavy heart by guilt oppressed;*
*No discontent, nor gloomy days,*
*But brightest hope and sweetest praise;*
*No stumbling oft, nor galling chains,*
*No shame, no sin, where Jesus reigns.*
     — Melville Wynans Miler

# MARCH 22

*The meek shall eat and be satisfied: they shall praise the Lord that seek him: Your heart shall live for ever.* —Psalm 22:26

Sometimes if the road is rough, I steal away to the Psalms where the Sweet Singer of Israel fills all the palace with the tuneful melody of voice and harp. I call to David: "Can God satisfy?" He strums his harp and makes reply: "The Lord is my shepherd: I shall not want."

"David, one of these days your nimble fingers will stiffen on the strings and those lips will mumble their last phrase. Your strong body will bend and sag, and with dim eye you will face the valley's gloom. In that sad hour will our God suffice?" Hear the glorious strains! "Yea, though I walk through the valley of the shadow of death, I will fear no evil: for thou art with me; thy rod and thy staff they comfort me."

What better cure for the disheartened? "Surely goodness and mercy shall follow me all the days of my life." When the last streak of light is seen in the west and earth has donned the shroud of everlasting night, when we climb to the top of Jacob's ladder and look back on sorrows that shall nevermore return, when we exchange this frail body, for one immortal and perfect and awake in the image of Him whom we love and serve, we shall indeed be satisfied! Then shall we find rest from our toils in the shade of the tree of life and forget earthborne woes amid the murmurings of the crystal river that flows from the throne of God.

Discouragements will find an end, and like a day that is spent, be folded and laid away on the shelf of mortal history. But that happy day shall have no end. Eternal high noon! "I will dwell in the house of the Lord forever!"   —*Jack Shuler*

*Put on the whole armour of God, that ye may be able to stand against the wiles of the devil.* —Ephesians 6:11

It is only the Spirit-filled life which can victoriously defeat Satan, and armor us to quench his fiery darts, in a time like this. It is only the Spirit-filled Christian who will live not by human speculation or reasoning, but by supernatural revelation, so that his life can be lived on a triumphant plane, in spite of appearances. The Church is the "body of Christ," and as such is God's chosen instrument for the accomplishment of His plans and purpose. Therefore, if any member does his work outside the Spirit, that work is man's building, and is simply "wood, hay, and stubble" (1 Cor. 3:12). Only that which we accomplish in the Spirit can endure. Our prayer, therefore, must ever be that the Holy Spirit will keep us within the center of God's holy and righteous will.

If we pray to be filled with the Spirit, we must remember that persecution may begin with the filling, just as it did with Jesus after the Spirit came upon Him, at His baptism. But we should remember that true Christianity has always flourished in the soil of persecution— Christianity was made for heroes!

—*David M. Dawson*

*Prayer is the soul's sincere desire,*
*Uttered or unexpressed;*
*The motion of a hidden fire*
*That trembles in the breast.*

*Prayer is the burden of a sigh,*
*The falling of a tear,*
*The upward glancing of an eye,*
*When none but God is near.*

—Montgomery

# MARCH 24

*And lead us not into temptation but deliver us from evil: For thine is the kingdom, and the power, and the glory, forever, Amen.*  —Matthew 6:13

It is impossible to live in this world and escape temptation. In olden times men fled away from active life and from human companionships, hoping thus to evade enticement to evil. But they were not successful; for wherever they went they carried in their own hearts a fountain of corruption, and were thus perpetually exposed to temptation. The only door of escape from all temptation is the door that leads into heaven. We grieve over our friends whom the Lord calls away—the little child in its sweet innocence, the mother in her ripened saintliness, the young man in his pride of strength; but do we ever think that we have far more reason for anxiety, possibly for grief, over those who live and have to battle with sin in this world? Those who have passed inside, in the victorious release of Christian faith, are forever secure; but those yet in the sore battle are still in peril.

This petition is a prayer that we may never be called needlessly to meet temptation. Sometimes God wants us to be tried, because we can grow strong only through victory. We have a word of Scripture which says: "Blessed is the man that endureth temptation; for when he is tried, he shall receive the crown of life." Yet we ought never ourselves to seek any way of life in which we shall have to be exposed to the peril of conflict with sin. Temptation is too terrible an experience, fraught with too much danger, to be sought by us, or ever encountered save when God leads us in the path on which it lies. We must never rush unbidden or unsent into any spiritual danger. When God sends us into danger, we are under His protection; when we go where He does not send us, we go unsheltered.  —*J. R. Miller*

*And we know that all things work together for good to them
that love God, to them who are the called according to his
purpose.*
                                            —Romans 8:28

All other religions deny suffering or dodge it in some
manner. The religion of Jesus Christ uses it. The Holy Spirit
can and will take your suffering and transform it into good.
This is not idle philosophy. This is a fact. Radiant Christians
step from prison camps where they have seen their own
families murdered before their eyes! How is this possible?
Because our Lord accepted the fact of human suffering instead
of dodging it. He accepted it and made ready the one and
only way of using it redemptively. "He did not bring a
philosophy. He brought a fact." The fact of Himself. By the
very fact of allowing His own dear body to be broken on the
Cross. He took the world's greatest tragedy and turned it
triumphantly into the world's greatest testimony. He did not
just bear things; He used them.

This same Jesus Christ is alive today in all His resurrection
power with this practical way out of all our human sufferings.
And He does not expect us to do it alone. He explains little;
but if we are willing He will change anything.

He will take your suffering and your sin into His own heart
again right now, and there He will transform it into goodness
and joy for you. And best of all, out of your suffering will
come a new awareness and new nearness to Jesus, the Christ
of God.
                                            —*Eugenia Price*


*There's no trouble that can shake me,*
*  If my Savior's by my side;*
*There's no joy but is far sweeter,*
*  When with Jesus I abide.*
                          —Grace B. Renfrow

# MARCH 26

*And he said unto them, Why are ye so fearful? How is it that*
*ye have no faith?* — Mark 4:40

Is there no respite from this dread contagion of fear, no deliverance from the epidemic of uncertainty? For the believer there is, of course, release, full and complete, in God's gracious provision. But the world sunk in unbelief and sin can look for no relief. While the child of God must not expect to be immune from the temptations, dangers and commotions of this life, he can meet them victoriously, maintaining always the peace of God in his soul. He must not be under any illusion, however, that he will not run into dangers and storms in his journey.

Obeying Christ often involves suffering and persecution, as Christ suffered and was persecuted. "A servant is not greater than his lord. If they persecuted me, they will also persecute you . . ." (John 15:20). "Yea, and all that would live Godly in Christ Jesus shall suffer persecution" (2 Tim. 3:12). The true disciple of Christ is subject to hatred and scorn from the world — often tacit, unexpressed, but easily discoverable when the test is applied. "If the world hate you, we know that it hated me before it hated you. If ye were of the world, the world would love its own: but because ye are not of the world, but I have chosen you out of the world, therefore the world hateth you" (John 15:18,19). — *Merrill F. Unger*

*He knoweth the need of my soul—*
*The trial that calls for His grace,*
*The weakness that leans on His strength,*
*The fear that looks up to His face.*
*He knoweth what sifting is best*
*To scatter the chaff from the wheat*
*And lay all my self-righteous pride*
*Low down in the dust at His feet.*

*Now faith is the substance of things hoped for . . .*
—Hebrews 11:1

Faith always attaches itself to what God has said or promised. When an honorable man says anything, he also does it: on the back of the saying follows the doing. So also is it with God: when He would do anything, He says so first through His Word. When the man of God becomes possessed with this conviction and established in it, God always does for him what He has said. With God, speaking and doing always go together: the deed follows the word: "Shall He say it and not do it?" When I have a word of God in which He promises to do something I can always remain sure that He will do it. I have simply to take and hold fast the word, and therewith wait upon God: God will take care that He fulfills His word to me. Before I ever feel or experience anything, I hold fast the promise, and I know by faith that God will make it good to me.

Of Abraham it is reported that he was fully assured that that which had been promised, God was also able to fulfill. This is assurance of faith: to be assured that God will do what He has promised.                         — *Andrew Murray*

*Faith moves into the realm of God,*
  *And there in perfect peace,*
*We find the great reality—*
  *Our earthly strivings cease—*
*That which is unseen is greater*
  *Than that which we now behold,*
*The riches of eternity*
  *Outweigh all earthly gold.*
—Louis Paul Lehman, Jr.

# MARCH 28

*But ye are a chosen generation, a royal priesthood, an holy nation, a peculiar people.* — 1 Peter 2:9

Through our great High Priest we become believer-priests, restored to the position which God had planned for His children when sin kept them from direct communion with Him. Thus, as such believer-priests, we look to the inheritance of the Levitical priests, and surely we may also say, "The Lord is our inheritance" (Deut. 10:9).

Much anxiety and care are expended upon earthly inheritances and possessions, and God must look with loving pity upon His children who rush to and fro in such pursuits. Why do not God's true children remember that He is their inheritance? What does that mean to you and to me? Surely it does not make us careless or thoughtless in necessary earthly provisions and duties. But does it make us conscious of the priceless heritage we have in God? He is our portion; His grace is sufficient for the needs and desires of our souls, and He will fulfill our yearning for service to God and others.

*I have tasted heaven's manna,*
*And I want no other bread.*
*In green pastures I am dwelling,*
*And my hung'ring soul is fed.*

*At the living Fount of waters,*
*I have quenched my thirst for aye.*
*I am living in God's glory,*
*And my sins are washed away.*
                                    —Avis B. Christiansen

*Jesus wept. Then said the Jews, Behold how he loved him!*
—John 11:35, 36

"Jesus wept!" Then, with that tangible evidence of tears before their eyes, the onlookers never liked our Lord so much, and said one to another: "Behold how He loved him!"

Ah! *Here is a Revelation of our Lord's Sublime Sympathy.* He well knew how He was going to restore Lazarus to life again; and He could well picture how these poor grief-stricken friends would soon be glowing with gladness and rejoicing in rich reunion. He could fore-fancy the supper at Bethany, with the loved and living Lazarus in the midst. Yes, He could see it all. Yet, as perfect "Man of Sorrows," He suffered with these sufferers, wept with these weepers, and, in sublime sympathy, shared this bitter burden with the broken-hearted sisters.

Such is Love Divine! "Behold how He loved him!" Yes, but behold also, how He loved Martha and Mary! He knew their sorrows, He groaned beneath their burden. He saw their tears and was touched with the feelings of their infirmities (Heb. 4:15).

Thus it is with all His own to this day. "There is a loving One who sticketh closer than a brother" (Prov. 18:24, *Rotherham*). Oh, precious comfort for all in Christ who are cast down by sorrow and grief! —*John G. Ridley*

*How broad is His love? Oh, as broad as man's trespass,*
*As wide as the need of the world can be;*
*And yet to the need of one soul it can narrow—*
*He came to the world and He came to me.*

*How great is His love? Oh, it passeth all knowledge,*
*No man's comprehension its measures can be;*
*It filleth the world, yet each heart may contain it—*
*He so loves the world and He so loves me.*
— Annie Johnson Flint

# March 30

*And call upon me in the day of trouble: I will deliver thee,*
*and thou shalt glorify me.* — Psalm 50:15

We make a most serious mistake when, in any time of need or pressure, we turn to the creature for help or sympathy. We are sure to be disappointed. Creature-streams are dry. Creature-props give way. Our God will make us prove the vanity and folly of all creature-confidences, human hopes and earthly expectations. And on the other hand, He will prove to us, in the most touching and forcible manner, the truth and blessedness of His own Word, "They shall not be ashamed that wait for Me."

No, never! He, blessed be His name, never fails a trusting heart. He cannot deny Himself. He delights to take occasion from our wants, our woes and weaknesses, to express and illustrate His tender care and loving-kindness, in a thousand ways. But He will teach us the utter barrenness of all human resources.

Thus it must ever be. Disappointment, barrenness and desolation are the sure and certain results of trusting in man. But, on the other hand — and mark the contrast — "Blessed is the man that trusteth in the Lord, and whose hope the Lord is: for he shall be as a tree planted by the waters, and that spreadeth out her roots by the river, and shall not see when heat cometh, but her leaf shall be green; and shall not be careful in the year of drought, neither shall cease from yielding fruit." —*Charles E. Fuller*

*Jesus, who knows full well*
*The heart of every saint,*
*Invites us all our griefs to tell*
*To pray, and never faint.*
—John Newton

*So Jesus had compassion on them, and touched their eyes:
and immediately their eyes received sight, and they followed
him.*
—Matthew 20:34

Our blessed Lord left the ivory palaces for a world of sin, sorrow and shame because He cared for us. He who was rich became poor because He cared for us. He turned from heavenly praise of the seraphim to hear the jeers and taunts of blasphemous men because He cared for us. He voluntarily endured not one but a thousand deaths on the old rugged Cross with its unspeakable shame and reproach because He cared for us. He graciously and freely supplies us with celestial resources for every daily need because He cares for us. He tenderly invites us to come unto His throne, there to place our supplications for dispensing grace to help in the nick of time, because He cares for us. He is now, through love, interceding unceasingly at the throne of heaven in our behalf because He cares. In due course He will come with triumphant glory to evacuate His bride from this place of sin, sorrow, death and impending wrath, all because He loves us with an everlasting love.
— *S. Franklin Logsdon*

*Does Jesus care when my heart is pained
    Too deeply for mirth and song;
As the burdens press, and the cares distress,
    And the way grows weary and long?*

*Oh, yes, He cares, I know He cares,
    His heart is touched with my grief.
When the days are weary, the long nights dreary,
    I know my Savior cares.*

# APRIL 1

*Behold the half was not told me.*                    —1 Kings 10:7

Such was the testimony given by the Queen of Sheba when she visited King Solomon in Jerusalem. She had heard a great deal about the city itself and of the wisdom and riches of its king. It was so wonderful that she could not believe it until she went and saw for herself, and then she declared first that she had never been told half enough, and next that Solomon's servants who stood continually before him were an exceedingly happy set of men. From which we may learn that it is not sufficient to hear about Jesus and of His wondrous love, but we must go to Him and prove His wisdom, love and power for ourselves.

We may learn also that those who do go to Him and experience His work in their hearts have to confess that, although they had heard much, the half had never been told. His power and willingness to pardon, purify, fill and use is beyond man's power fully to describe. Solomon's servants were happy, but oh, the indescribable joy possessed by those who stand continually before the Lord Jesus! His service is indeed real liberty and everlasting joy.

Think also of the presents the Queen of Sheba gave to King Solomon. The gold amounted to 120 talents, and one talent is worth more than $30,000.00 and, in addition to all the gold, she gave a number of precious stones. We cannot do this, but we can do something else, which to our King will be most valuable, and that is yield to Him our entire beings. Let us do this, and then our experience with regard to Christ and His "great salvation" will be "the half has never been told."

—*John Roberts*

> *O may I never turn aside,*
> *Nor from Thy bosom flee;*
> *Let nothing here my heart divide,*
> *I give it all to Thee.*

*I am crucified with Christ: Nevertheless I live; yet not I, but Christ liveth in me: and the life which I now live in the flesh I live by the faith of the Son of God who loved me, and gave himself for me.*
—Galatians 2:20

Sing, my soul, sing about Redemption, and forget not to revel daily in its rich refrain:—"The Son of God who loved me and gave Himself for me." Here is love's ultimate goal — "Me." The poor, wretched, guilty, vile sinner is looked upon, longed for, and loved. Jesus, the tender, sympathizing Savior, has set His holy heart upon the sinner. He must seek him; He must save him; He must succor him; He must have him. Oh, blessed be God that I am that sinner and Jesus is my Savior.

Here is Love's uttermost gesture:—"gave Himself for me." To gain the sinner, to gather the guilty, to rescue the rebel, to lure the lost, Love will go to the uttermost gesture of grace and give Himself a ransom for all, including me. It is indeed an uttermost gesture. He cannot do more. He will not do less. It is Love's uttermost limit of love.
—*John Ridley*

*He ever lives above*
*For me to intercede,*
*His all-redeeming love,*
*His precious blood to plead;*
*His blood atoned for all our race,*
*And sprinkles now the Throne of Grace.*

*Five bleeding wounds He bare,*
*Received on Calvary;*
*They pour effectual prayers,*
*They strongly plead for me.*
*"Forgive him, O forgive," they cry,*
*"Nor let that ransomed sinner die."*
—Charles Wesley

# APRIL 3

*Even as the Son of man came not to be ministered unto, but to minister, and to give his life a ransom for many.*
—*Matthew 20:28*

There are two well-known pictures each with the same title, "The Shadow of the Cross." One by Holman Hunt represents the interior of a carpenter's shop, with Joseph and the Boy Jesus at work. Mary also is present. The Boy Jesus pauses in His work, and as He stretches Himself the shadow of the Cross is formed on the wall. The other picture is a popular engraving which depicts the Infant Jesus running with outstretched arms to His mother, the shadow of the Cross being cast by His form as He runs. Both pictures are fanciful in form, but their underlying idea is assuredly true. If we read the Gospels just as they stand, it is clear that the death of Jesus Christ was really in view from the outset of His earthly appearance. —*W. H. Griffith-Thomas*

Till He hung on it, the Cross was the symbol of slavery and vulgar wickedness; but He converted it into the symbol of heroism, self-sacrifice and salvation. It was only a wretched framework of coarse and blood-clotted beams, which it was a shame to touch; but since then the world has gloried in it; it has been carved in every form of beauty and every substance of price; it has been emblazoned on the flags of nations and engraved on the scepters and diadems of Kings. The Cross was planted on Golgotha a dry, dead tree; but lo! it has blossomed like Aaron's rod; it has struck its roots deep down to the heart of the world, and sent its branches upwards, till today it fills the earth, and the nations rest beneath its shadow and eat of its pleasant fruits. —*James Stalker*

*Greater love hath no man than this, that a man lay down his life for his friends.*
                                                                    —John 15:13

The character of our Lord Jesus Christ is nowhere more perfectly demonstrated than on the Cross. He who died for sinners did not even in suffering on Calvary forget His own. He made provision for His mother and His friend, and what a tender provision it was. He had nothing on earth to give them. He died without property or possession. Though He made all things, He had no lands to leave. Though He, in creation, had hidden the gold in the hills, He died without money. Even His robe had been taken from Him and the soldiers were casting lots for it in the shadow of the Cross. He had nothing of material value to leave to His mother and not even a keepsake to bequeath to His friend, so He gave them to each other —to the heartbroken mother, a son, upon whom the affection of a mother's heart could be lavished; to John, a mother, whose heart was capable of all the devotion a mother possesses.

His divine compassion showed itself in His prayer for those who crucified Him. "Father, forgive them; for they know not what they do." His enemies, His tormentors, His persecutors came within the embrace of His divine compassion in the prayer.

It was not until He had made provision for His loved ones and prayed for His enemies that He thought of Himself.

                                                        — *Bob Jones, Jr.*

*O love divine, that stoop'd to share*
*Our sharpest pang, our bitt'rest tear,*
*On Thee we cast each earth-born care,*
*We smile at pain while Thou art near.*
                                        —Oliver W. Holmes

*Comfort ye, comfort ye my people, saith your God.*
—Isaiah 40:1

Believer, you are one of those whom God calls "my people"! What a multitude of meaning is bound up in those two words. God, who created the heavens and the earth, who reigns supreme, who made man in His own image, purchased you for His own, through the shed blood of His Son, and says that you are one of His children.

All the nations of the world are His; the whole world is subject to His power; yet you are one of His people, for He has done more for you than for anyone else — He has made it possible for you to be one of His own children.

Not only are you one of His children, but He is your God! What a world of blessing and meaning is wrapped up in those four words. The God who rules the universe, the God who sees even the sparrow's fall, is your God. Can you doubt His tender love? Can you ignore His precious promises?

You are the personal care of your Father; you are His child. Revel in the depth of meaning in God's words, "My people."

*He knoweth the way that I take;*
  *Each step of that way He hath planned;*
*And, walking through sunshine or storm,*
  *I walk in the shade of His hand.*
*In deserts untrodden and drear,*
  *Where foes in the darkness may hide,*
*He leaveth me never alone;*
  *He sendeth me light and a guide.*
    —Annie Johnson Flint

*And Simon Peter answered and said, Thou art the Christ,*
*the Son of the living God.* —Matthew 16:16

My dear friend, one thing is certainly true about Christ. All that He has ever been He must forever be. All that He was to those first disciples, He must be ready to be to any one, even the least of His disciples. His power is nothing at any one point if it is not powerful at all points; nothing, if not eternal. How is it possible, then, that Christ should do for you and me what He did for Peter and John, and Matthew and Nathanael? It is not hard to see, and to many people living just such lives as we live it has become the most real of experiences. Jesus, the Jesus of the Gospels, fastens His life to our life. By His life and death, bearing witness of His love, He twines Himself into our being. To love Him becomes a real thing. He is close by our side. He is right in our lot every day. Then as we go on living thus with Him some crisis of our life occurs, some need of action. We are put to some test, and as we stand doubting, or as we go and do the act in our low way, Christ, right by our side, does it in His higher way. Not that His hands visibly touch our tools and do the work we have to do. But it becomes evident to us what He would do under our circumstances, what one only thing it would be possible for Him to do as we are situated.

The gates of that nobler life which He has opened shine before us, and His love draws us on to be with Him.

—*Phillips Brooks*

*Always with us, always with us —*
*Words of cheer and words of love;*
*Thus the risen Savior whispers*
*From His dwelling place above.*
—Nevin

# April 7

*Blessed are they which do hunger and thirst after righteousness: for they shall be filled.* —Matthew 5:6

The writers of the great devotional books were people who were not satisfied. They were satisfied that the Christ who dwelt in their hearts was all-sufficient, but they were never satisfied with what they had received of God's grace. They were always pushing forward. They were always seeking to know Him better. They were always creating the conditions whereby they could receive new fillings with His Spirit. This hunger on their part and the way God continually met it make their writings blessed to us today.

Every spiritual blessing we have prepares us for a greater blessing. Every filling with the Holy Ghost creates a capacity for an additional filling with the Holy Ghost. Every experience of the presence of God we enjoy leads the way to a richer experience of the presence of God. As long as we live in this life we can go on from blessing to blessing, from filling to filling with the Holy Spirit, from experience to experience of God's presence until, finally, we see Him face to face when He returns to receive us into His glory. Then we will be satisfied. Then we will need nothing more.

—*Raymond H. Davis*

*How could I walk faint-heartedly*
*With Thee, O Christ, when Thou hast prayed,*
*"Keep them which Thou hast given me"?*
*Lord, I walk unafraid!*

*How could I let a single care*
*O'ershadow heaven's mercy seat,*
*When Thou art interceding there?*
*Lord, I am at Thy feet!*

*Thou art my hiding place; Thou shalt preserve me from trouble; Thou shalt compass me about with songs of deliverance.*
                                                    —Psalm 32:7

How blessed the thought that God Himself becomes our bomb-proof shelter. Our lives are hidden with Christ in God. Nothing can touch us to do us harm until all the defensive power of His omnipotence is exhausted. Is there any possible excuse for you to carry around that load of worry under these circumstances? When great cities prepare to withstand a siege it is usual for their armies to provide a multiple ring of defenses. Even so every Christian is provided with numerous encirclements, each one of them invincible before the fiery assaults of Satan. It is interesting and significant that one of these lines of defense is "songs of deliverance" with which, according to our verse, God encompasses us.

The power of trustful rejoicing in times of testing is greatly underestimated. God wants you to have a singing heart. Let it be one of your lines of defense.                 —*J. Elwin Wright*

I know not, but God knows;
    Oh, blessed rest from fear!
All my unfolding days
    To Him are plain and clear.
Each anxious, puzzled "why?"
    From doubt or dread that grows,
Finds answer in this thought:
    I know not, but He knows.
                        —Annie Johnson Flint

> Oh that men would praise the Lord for his goodness, and for his wonderful works to the children of men!
>
> —Psalm 107:8

The Upturned Face. A bird looks up, a pig looks down, when it drinks. I will look up. I will remember the source of all the good things I have. I will cultivate the attitude of the remembering, thankful heart.

You recall the two boys looking at half a glass of water. One said, "It's half-empty"; the other, "It's half-full." You can choose your point of view. The first may be human nature; the second is certainly Christian nature.

The thankfulness that really counts is the thankfulness that is a perpetual soul-bent "In everything give thanks."

The most important stipulation about our thanksgiving is that it be wholehearted. "All that is within me" must bless the Lord, for it is the heart that He sees.

We can be thankful always because, in reality, our reason for thankfulness is God Himself and not things. If only things, then when things go our reason for thanks has gone and our gratitude with it. To be thankful whatever your situation, think about God.

He is the one original Blesser; yet He tells us that He can be blessed by us, that is, by our thanks. If I can make Him happy or add to His well-being, let me not be tongue-tied or slow. Even if it is hard for me to express my feelings, let me "offer the sacrifice of praise . . . giving thanks" — and marvel that He cares.

> Awake, my soul, to joyful lays,
> And sing thy great Redeemer's praise.

—Bertha Munro

*Then saith he to the disciple, Behold thy mother! And from
that hour that disciple took her unto his own home.*

—*John 19:27*

Home is the holy of holies of a man's life. There he
withdraws from all the world, and, shutting his door, is alone
with those who are his own. It is the reservoir of his strength,
the restorer of his energies, the resting place from his toil, the
brooding place for his spirit, the inspiration for all his activities
and battles.

Home is where love lives. Not where it boards, nor pays
occasional visits, even long visits, nor even where it may be a
sort of permanent guest, with familiar access to certain rooms
and cozy corners. But where it owns the front-door key, sits
by the glow of a hearthfire of its own kindling, and pervades
the whole house with its presence. It may be a king's spacious,
luxurious palace. It may be the poor man's narrow-walled
cottage, or anywhere in between these two extremes.

There may be present the evidences of wealth and culture
and of the sort of refinement that these give, and even the
higher refinement they can't give, and yet the place not be a
home. And there may be the absence of all this, except the
real refinement that love always breeds, and yet there may be
a home in the sweet, strong meaning of that word.

—*S. D. Gordon*

*O happy house! where Thou art loved the best,*
  *Dear Friend and Savior of our race,*
*Where never comes such welcome, honored Guest,*
  *Where none can ever fill Thy place;*
*Where every heart goes forth to meet Thee,*
  *Where every ear attends Thy word,*
*Where every lip with blessing greets Thee,*
  *Where all are waiting on their Lord.*

—C. J. Ph. Spitta

*The Lord gave, and the Lord hath taken away; blessed be the name of the Lord.* —Job 1:21

God uses the experience of His children to silence the enemy of the Word of God and the Lord Jesus Christ. Probably the best example of this is the story of the patriarch Job. Remember that Job was a wealthy man, but he was also a spiritual and godly man, and when the Lord called Satan's attention to the fact that Job was a godly man who feared the Lord perfectly with all his heart, the devil accused Job of doing it only for the gain and for the profit which came to him materially and personally as a result of his fearing the Lord. You will recall that God gave Satan the privilege, the right, to lay his hand upon Job and to take away his possessions and his family, and the result was that Satan was silenced, for Job, instead of murmuring and complaining and turning in bitterness against Almighty God, praised the Lord and was able to say, "The Lord gave, and the Lord hath taken away; blessed be the name of the Lord."

Is it not wonderful to think that God is willing to use us to silence the adversary, the devil, by the testing and the trial and the tribulations which come upon us? Many a time I have stood at the bedsides of God's patient sufferers and have seen the enemy silenced — he who would say that we serve God only in sunshine. I can take you to the bedside of many who for years and years have been racked with pain, and, I can show you smiles never seen on other faces, smiles which indicate the gratefulness, the gratitude and the praise to God which belong only to those who have been trained in the school of affliction. If you are one of God's "Satan-silencers," praise Him for it. —*M. R. DeHaan*

*He led them on safely.* —Psalm 78:53

"Safely." That is always the accompaniment of God's leading. He may take you along a perilous Path, but when He goes before and points out the way, you are absolutely safe. It is said that the expert Alpine guide can now take even the inexperienced climber safely up the precipitous slopes of the Matterhorn, where several lives were lost on Whymper's first ascent. So the Lord guides you and me safely, always safely, over the steep and dangerous places in our lives. It may be that you are standing today in a hard place and that, as you look ahead, the path appears of impossible difficulty. Never fear. Just trust yourself to your divine Guide, and He will lead you safely.
—*Frank E. Gaebelein*

What a world of meaning is wrapped up in the one word "safely." Just to say the word seems to wrap one in the loving arms of the Savior. Safety is the result of being saved. One reaches safety only after receiving salvation. It is Christ who saves, who keeps and satisfies. It is Christ with His overshadowing Presence who keeps the child of God day by day in blessed safety. With such a One to keep us safe, why should we be troubled? Simply lean on the everlasting arms, dear reader, secure in the safety that Christ the Peace-giver affords.

> *"Be still and know that I am God,"*
> *That I who made and gave thee life*
> *Will lead thy faltering steps aright;*
> *That I who see each sparrow's fall*
> *Will hear and heed thy earnest call.*
> *I am God.*
>
> —Doran

> *And go quickly, and tell his disciples that he is risen from the*
> *dead; and, behold, he goeth before you into Galilee; there*
> *shall ye see him: lo, I have told you.* —Matthew 28:7

We, too, must meet the Lord in Galilee on the other side of Calvary, on the other side of an Easter morning, in the light of an eternal glory that belongs to all that are in Jesus Christ. May we constantly appear in the presence of the Father, in the Holy of Holies, obtaining mercy and finding grace to help in time of need, because, in all these things, He who wants to meet us in our Galilee has gone before us. He has gone before us; He will lead the way. We need not fear the judgment, for He was judged on our behalf; we need not fear death, for He died that we might live; we need not fear to stand in the presence of the Living God because we are clothed in the righteousness of our Savior, Jesus Christ; we need not seek to accumulate for ourselves the treasures of earth which do not satisfy, for ours is an eternal weight of glory in Him. So, in the light of all that He is to us and all that He has done for us, may we meet Him in Galilee that from henceforth He may lead us in paths of righteousness, in ways of blessing, and of peace. —*Larry Love*

> *Thy way, not mine, O Lord,*
> *However dark it be;*
> *Lead me by Thine own hand,*
> *And choose the path for me.*
> *I dare not choose my lot;*
> *I would not if I might;*
> *Choose Thou for me, my God,*
> *So shall I walk aright.*
> —A. Bonar

*If ye abide in me, and my words abide in you, ye shall ask what ye will, and it shall be done unto you.* —John 15:7

Someone has well said, "To abide in Christ is more than to be in Him since it represents a condition maintained by communion with God and by the habitual doing of His will." Abiding in Christ does not suggest mountaintop experiences interspersed by valley disappointments, but rather a life of constancy, of steadfastness, and of full blessing as a continuing experience.

It is the abiding life that is the believer's safeguard against being engulfed with the world, by the fear of the things that are coming on the earth.

It is the abiding life that is the secret of a prayer ministry that reaches the throne of God, the most distant parts of the earth, as well as the people and the needs that are closest to home. —*S. P. Anderson*

Rejoice, O trembling heart! The Holy Spirit has come to indwell thee, and He will not leave His residence. He has chosen thee as His temple, and He will not be driven forth. He has given thee glimpses, yearnings, first fruits, which are the earnest of an inheritance that He cannot do otherwise than grant. He has begun a good work, and will carry it on to the day of Jesus Christ. There are no unfinished pictures in His gallery, no imperfected blocks in His studio. "The work which His grace has begun, the arm of His strength will complete." —*F. B. Meyer*

*Abide with me: fast falls the eventide;*
*The darkness deepens; Lord with me abide:*
*When other helpers fail, and comforts flee,*
*Help of the helpless, O abide with me.*
—H. F. Lyte

*Now the God of hope fill you with all joy and peace in believing, that ye may abound in hope, through the power of the Holy Ghost.* —Romans 15:13

The fullness of the Spirit is something for which most Christians long. They see the spiritual power evidenced in the lives of other men, and they yearn for a similar enduement. Many spend hours in confession of sin and agonizing in prayer for the gift of the Holy Spirit, but confession and agony seem fruitless and ineffective.

There may be someone reading these lines who longs intensely to be "out and out" for God. You have seen the vision of life's possibilities and you yearn to live wholeheartedly for Christ, to be gloriously victorious over sin, and to be a spiritual power for God. But you cannot find the way! You resolutely determine never to sin again, but scarcely has the resolution been registered than you find yourself committing the same sins as before. With all your heart, you intend to follow the Lord, but you are always losing the way. Defeated, disappointed and despairing, you feel it impossible ever to achieve your desire. Penitence and regret, new resolutions and decisions seem of no avail. What is the secret of real life and power?

If the enjoyment of the Spirit's fullness is God's norm for the Christian, how is it possible to appropriate this blessing? What is the secret for which so many search so ceaselessly and unavailingly? The answer is that it is necessary merely to yield to the sovereignty and sway of the Holy Ghost. Just as the sinner yields to Christ for salvation, so must the Christian yield to the Spirit for life and power. —*Frederick A. Tatford*

*All to Jesus now I give,*
*From this hour for Him to live;*
*While before His cross I bow,*
*He doth hear my humble vow.*

*Be careful for nothing; but in every thing by prayer and supplication with thanksgiving let your requests be made known unto God.* —Philippians 4:6

I am not sure that deliverance from care is not a greater proof of God's power even than deliverance from sin. Cares surround us at every step of our heavenward journey. Travel the journey of life as pleasantly as you may, you cannot expect to escape the encounter with care.

There are *temporal cares*. There are the cares for daily bread, against which the Lord so graciously warns us when He says, "Take no thought for your life, what ye shall eat, nor yet for your body what ye shall put on" (Matt. 6:25).

Then there are *spiritual cares*—cares for the souls of others—cares from which, in a true sense, we can have no desire to be exempt. And yet, even in this respect, we are to be without carefulness, for we are to cast all our care on Him who careth for us. There are cares for the work of God, cares for its success and progress all over the world, cares for our own work and how best to advance it in the Master's name. In all these ways we are exposed to care. Yet care, in the hurtful and prejudicial meaning of the term, we have a right to be free from, for care is a most serious evil. —*E. W. Moore*

Words cannot set forth the preciousness of the Lord Jesus to His people. Dear reader, what would you do in the world without Him, in the midst of its temptations and its cares? What would you do in the morning without Him, when you wake up and look forward to the day's battle? What would you do at night, when you come home jaded and weary, if there were no door of fellowship between you and Christ? Blessed be His name, He will not allow us to go through life without Him.

*On mine arm shall they trust.* —Isaiah 51:5

In seasons of severe trial, the Christian has nothing on earth that he can trust to, and is therefore compelled to cast himself on his God alone. When his vessel is on its beam-ends, and no human deliverance can avail, he must simply and entirely trust himself to the providence and care of God. Happy storm that wrecks a man on such a rock as this! O blessed hurricane that drives the soul to God and God alone!

There is no getting to our God sometimes because of the multitude of our friends; but when a man is so poor, so friendless, so helpless that he has nowhere else to turn, he flies into his Father's arms, and is blessedly clasped therein. When he is burdened with troubles so pressing and so peculiar, that he cannot tell them to any but his God, he may be thankful for them; for he will learn more of his Lord then than at any other time. Oh, tempest-tossed believer, it is a happy trouble that drives you to the Father.

—*C. H. Spurgeon*

*The way I may not*
*Always see,*
*But this I know:*
*God cares for me.*

*It matters not*
*What seems to be,*
*Since this is true;*
*God cares for me.*

*Though tempests rage*
*On land and sea,*
*I'm safe because*
*God cares for me.*

—Glenville Kleiser

*And God shall wipe away all tears from their eyes.*
—Revelation 7:17

*Some glorious morning sorrow will cease,*
*Some glorious morning all will be peace;*
*Heartaches all ended, school-days all done,*
*Heaven will open, Jesus will come;*

*Oh, what a meeting, there in the skies,*
*No tears nor crying shall dim our eyes;*
*Loved ones united eternally,*
*Oh, what a daybreak that morn will be.*

Human hands are poor at drying tears. If they succeed in removing one set, others come that they cannot wipe away. Only the hand that made the spirit can reach the deep sources of its sorrows or dry up the streams that issue from them.

What joy comes to the physician who sees the tears of pain and fear vanish away! Have you ever thought about God's great handkerchief? All manner of tears have been wiped away by that handkerchief. It is embroidered with love and tender sympathy, and it is the pierced Hand that put it to the eyes of the weeping ones. Christ is the wiper away of every tear: tears of misfortune and poverty, tears of bereaved affection, tears of sympathy and mercy, tears of doubt and discouragement, tears of pain, tears of fear, tears of disappointments, tears of neglect, tears of yearning for what cannot now be ours; tears—each tear and every tear—wholly wiped away by the Great Physician.     —*Howard W. Ferrin*

*God knows the way, He holds the key,*
*He guides us with une'rring hand;*
*Some time with tearless eyes we'll see:*
*Yes, there, up there, we'll understand.*
—Maxwell N. Cornelius

# APRIL 19

*According as his divine power hath given unto us all things
that pertain unto life and godliness, through the knowledge
of him that hath called us to glory and virtue.* —2 Peter 1:3

God's standard for life is higher than the world can conceive or appreciate, and holier than the Church is wont to believe and accept. It is one of absolute justice and purity. Perhaps it is too high for Christians to reach? But then, a standard of godliness is not to be reached; it is to keep one reaching. It is the incentive which keeps one pressing on. It is that vision of higher and greater things which makes us dissatisfied with our strongest effort for Christ. It is that impelling challenge which elicits prayerful devotion to the Lord. It is a constraint which the trusting heart cannot avoid. God's standard for life is a towline which gracefully directs the barge of human energies into the channel of spiritual productiveness. It is the indispensable inducement which brings the desires of true disciples into sweet concurrence with the divine will.

—*S. Franklin Logsdon*

We often make a great mistake, thinking that God is not guiding us at all, because we cannot see far in front. But this is not His method. He only undertakes that the steps of a good man should be ordered by the Lord. Not next year, but tomorrow. Not the next mile, but the next yard. Not the whole pattern, but the next stitch in the canvas.

—*F. B. Meyer*

*Oh, mighty power that holds me,*
  *A helper forever near!*
*Oh, perfect peace that folds me*
  *In danger and storm and fear!*
                —Annie Johnson Flint

*And he arose, and rebuked the wind, and said unto the sea,
Peace, be still. And the wind ceased, and there was a great
calm.* —Mark 4:39

Believing God is the panacea for every inward disturbance.
We would be in a happy condition indeed if we never doubted
God or never questioned His care or concern for us. How
much worry and anxiety we would spare ourselves! What
quietness and confidence would be ours even though the sea
about us might be lashed into fury and the snarling waves
break into our frail craft. But the Master of the sea and the
Lord of creation knows our human frailty. Though He may
seem to be asleep in the hinder part of the boat and oblivious
to our peril, yet when the furious tempest is upon us and the
swirling waves threaten to engulf us, when we call upon Him
He will arise for our help and we may say with the Psalmist:

> *My help cometh from Jehovah
> Who made heaven and earth.
> He will not suffer thy foot to be moved:
> He that keepeth thee will not slumber.
> Behold, He that keepeth Israel
> Will neither slumber nor sleep*
>
> (Ps. 121:2-4).

"He that keepeth thee will not slumber!" Can we, dare we,
believe that this is true always — under all trials and
tribulations, in every circumstance and condition of life?
Sometimes, when we cannot, and the situation appears
hopeless, and we struggle vainly in the fury of the tempest,
He, the infinitely gracious One, nevertheless will still the storm,
which no one else but He can calm. Those who look to Him
in times of trouble and commotion and unfalteringly trust
Him experience the "great calm." —*Merrill F. Unger*

# APRIL 21

*. . . praying always for you.* —Colossians 1:3

Prayerfulness is evidence of grace, the art of dependence, the soul of expression, the harbinger of joy, the bringer of blessing, the hand of power, the killer of sin, the road to victory, the remover of rust, the breath of summer, the secret of fruitfulness, the soil of love, the developer of faith, the helper of others, and brightener of hope. Prayer brings us into touch with God, and keeps God in touch with us.

Prayer is the delight of the saint, the armor of the soldier, and the supplier of the servant. God works when men pray. No spiritual power is existent apart from prayer. Prayer changes things within and without. —*Robert G. Lee*

The prayer of faith swings open the windows of heaven through which God's answers can come down to us. Faith holds God to His word, and this is always pleasing to Him. "What things soever ye desire, when ye pray, believe that ye receive them, and ye shall have them" (Mark 11:24). Just put out your hand in simple faith and accept! Many of us know how to ask, but all too few of us know how to receive! We should be large in our expectation of answered prayer. Was it Carey who said: "Attempt great things for God, and expect great things from God"? —*David M. Dawson*

*O the pure delight of a single hour*
*That before Thy throne I spend,*
*When I kneel in prayer, and with Thee, my God*
*I commune as friend with friend!*
—Fanny Crosby

*And therefore will the Lord wait, that he may be gracious unto you, and therefore will he be exalted, that he may have mercy upon you: for the Lord is a God of judgment: blessed are all they that wait for him.* —Isaiah 30:18

Someone has said that God is never in a hurry, but that He is always on time. In orderly procession of day and night, summer and winter, we can see the purpose and plan of God in the operation of this universe. Nothing is ever ahead of schedule but everything is always on time.

God has a purpose and plan for every life, and that purpose is planned according to His knowledge and His schedule. The time for everything in the Christian's life is in His hands. How much happier and how much more fruitful our lives would be if we could just remember and believe that. It is when we are unwilling to believe that or unwilling to wait for His plan and His time that we get into difficulties and trouble.

There was a Christian wife who had prayed for her husband through the years, but he was not saved. He said, "If I have to go down to an altar to be saved, I'll never be saved." This wife still continued to pray and finally the Lord called her home without answering her prayer. The day after the funeral a revival began in a nearby church. That husband attended the meeting, and he was the first to go down to the altar and seek salvation. God answered, but in His own time.

Are you impatient to see the result of some labor or to see some loved one saved? Remember that God sees the end from the beginning and the result or reward will come in due time—His time. —*Sallie Lee Bell*

*Dismiss your doubts and feelings,*
*"Stand still" and see it through:*
*And the God who fed Elijah*
*Will do the same for you.*
—Author Unknown

*Behold, we count them happy which endure. Ye have heard of the patience of Job, and have seen the end of the Lord; that the Lord is very pitiful, and of tender mercy.*
—James 5:11

The Christian attitude in physical suffering is the one most likely to speed recovery regardless of all the medical help. This attitude is one of trust in God, committal to His will and way, rest upon His promises, and faith in His purposes. The Christian thanks God for all His blessings, for every ministry given him by others, for every step on the way to recovery, and for every evidence of mercy and grace. God responds to Christian attitudes and is able to do His best for the sufferer.

Physical sufferers, rightly oriented with God, learn some things that others miss. They come to a more correct evaluation of what is really worthwhile in life, their spirits are chastened, their motives are purified, their sympathies are deepened, and their characters are sweetened. —*Faris D. Whitesell*

*My Jesus, as Thou wilt!*
*O may Thy will be mine;*
*Into Thy hand of love*
*I would my all resign.*
*Thro' sorrow or thro' joy,*
*Conduct me as Thine own,*
*And help me still to say,*
*"My Lord, Thy will be done."*

*My Jesus, as Thou wilt!*
*All shall be well with me;*
*Each changing future scene*
*I gladly trust with Thee.*
*Straight to my home above*
*I travel calmly on,*
*And sing in life or death,*
*"My Lord, Thy will be done."* —*Benjamin Schmolck*
(Trans. by Jane Borthwick)

*Whatsoever He saith unto you, do it.* — John 2:5

That is the word for all Christ's servants. That is the motto of true consecration at all times and in all places. Every word in this sentence is emphatic and intense in its meaning. "Whatsoever He saith." There is no other one who has a right to command us. We belong to Christ because He has redeemed us. He is our only Lord and Master. "Whatsoever He saith." We may not choose some of His commands for obedience and some for neglect, inattention, or rejection. We are not to do the pleasant things He bids us to do, and leave undone the things that are not according to our taste and feeling. We are to do even the things that cost pain and personal sacrifice. It was thus that Jesus did the will of His Father.

"Whatsoever He saith." But how can we know what He saith? We cannot hear His voice as the servants at the wedding heard it. He speaks now in His Word, and the reverent heart may always hear what He says, as the sacred pages are prayerfully pondered. He speaks in the conscience that is kept tender by loyal obeying; He speaks in the providence that brings duty to our hand. There never is any real uncertainty as to what He says, if we are truly intent on knowing His will. "Whatsoever He saith unto you, do it!" It is the doing that is important. We should never ask questions nor make suggestions when Jesus has spoken; the one thing for us is obedience. We should never ask what the consequences may be, what it may cost us; we are simply to obey. Christ knows why He wants us to do the thing, and that should be reason enough for us.
— *J. R. Miller*

# APRIL 25

*Be still, and know that I am God: I will be exalted among the heathen, I will be exalted in the earth.* —Psalm 46:10

One of the seeming paradoxes of the Christian life is that when one spends enough time with God, in prayer and Bible study, he will have a strange sense of leisure and quietness in doing his regular tasks, and apparently more time. It is something like tithing. Those who give a tenth of their income to God can testify that what is left seems to go further than if they kept the whole sum for themselves. When we are careful to be alone with God for a certain time every day preferably the first thing in the morning— we shall find that other things fall into their rightful place, and the work of the day goes more smoothly. —*Philip E. Howard, Jr.*

Beyond measure it is desirable that we as believers should have the person of Jesus Christ constantly before us, to enliven our love toward Him, and to increase our knowledge of Him. But to have Jesus ever near, the heart must be full of Him, welling up with His love, even to running over; thus the apostle prays "that Christ may dwell in your hearts." See how near he would have Jesus to be! "That He may dwell": not that He may call upon you sometimes, as a casual visitor enters into a house and tarries for a night, but that He may *dwell*, that Jesus may become the Lord and Tenant of your heart.

*Take time to be holy, Speak oft with thy Lord;*
*Abide in Him always, and feed on His Word;*

*Take time to be holy, The world rushes on;*
*Spend much time in secret, With Jesus alone;*

*Take time to be holy, Be calm in thy soul;*
*Each tho't and each motive beneath His control.*
—W. D. Longstaff

*For I know that my Redeemer liveth.*  —Job 19:25

It is good to know that Job could speak in such terms of certainty regarding God. The buffeted patriarch had all manner of doubt-suggesting circumstances with which to contend. Wave after wave of trouble broke over his head. Heart-breaking domestic calamities suddenly robbed him of life's tenderest joys. Loathsome physical disorders made him an object of revulsion, and a burden to himself. Added to all this, he was harassed by the exasperating verbosity and controversiality of would-be comforters who were as undiscerning as they were dogmatic. Yet from this tempestuous sea of adversity there rises up in solemn grandeur this solid rock of unshakable conviction—"I know that my Redeemer liveth, and that He shall stand at the latter day upon the earth: and though after my skin worms destroy this body, yet in my flesh I shall see God." Yea, and what glorious certainty this is which Job possessed! Here is (1) the supreme reality of the present— "My Redeemer liveth." Here is (2) the supreme prospect of the future—"He shall stand at the latter day upon the earth." Here is (3) the supreme miracle of all history—"And though after my skin worms destroy this body, yet in my flesh shall 1 see God."

—*J. Sidlow Baxter*

*He that believeth shall not make haste*
*In useless hurry his strength to waste;*
*Who walks with God can afford to wait,*
*For he can never arrive too late.*

*He that believeth shall walk serene,*
*With ordered steppings and leisured mien;*
*He dwells in the midst of eternities,*
*And the timeless ages of God are his.*

—Annie Johnson Flint

# APRIL 27

*For the law of the Spirit of life in Christ Jesus hath made me
free from the law of sin and death.*　　　—Romans 8:2

The seventh chapter of Romans shows us the futility of trying to lead a Christian life through our own effort. Paul acknowledged that he was carnal, sold under sin. Notice how many times in this chapter he used the word "I."

In contrast, when we get over into the eighth chapter, we find him talking about the Spirit instead of himself. The word "Spirit" occurs twenty-eight times in just a few verses. Here is the secret: "The law of the Spirit of life in Christ Jesus hath made me free from the law of sin and death" (Rom. 8:2).

In our physical world the law of gravitation is always at work with its downward pull. But the power of the sun, sweeping over the ocean, pulls the water upward and overcomes the law of gravitation. There are two laws at work, the upward pull of the sun and the downward pull of gravitation.

And so, in the spiritual realm, the moment I fully yield myself and reckon that I am dead unto sin I find that I am instantly made free from the law of sin and death. The lack of this knowledge is the reason why so many well-meaning Christians go on, year in and year out, defeated and discouraged. Notice in the twenty-sixth verse of the eighth chapter how the Spirit helps us in our infirmities and weaknesses, making intercession for us. "He that searcheth the hearts knoweth what is the mind of the spirit, because He maketh intercession for the saints according to the will of God" (Rom. 8:27).　　　—*Charles E. Fuller*

*Jesus bore all your burdens and care,
All your suff'rings and sin when He died;
They were nailed to His cross: leave them there;
You are free through the Christ crucified.*
　　　—George B. Wetherbee

*Grace be to you and peace from God the Father, and from our Lord Jesus Christ.* —Galatians 1:3

This greeting of the Apostle is strange to the world and was never heard of before the preaching of the Gospel. These two words, grace and peace, comprehend in them whatever belongs to Christianity. Grace releases sin, and peace makes the conscience quiet. But Christ has vanquished these two monsters, sin and conscience. This the world does not know, therefore it can teach no certainty of the overcoming of sin, conscience and death. Only Christians have this kind of doctrine, and are exercised and armed with it to overcome sin, despair and everlasting death. Peace of conscience, however, can never be had unless sin be first forgiven. And sin is not forgiven by the fulfilling of the Law; for no man is able to satisfy the Law. Much less is sin taken away by the works and inventions of men; there is no work that can take away sin. There is no means to take away sin, but grace alone. By grace alone we have remission of sins and peace with God. And the Apostle fitly distinguishes this grace and peace from all other kinds of grace and peace. He wishes to the Galatians grace and peace, not from the emperor, or kings and princes, not from the world, but from God the Father, and from our Lord Jesus Christ, which is as much as to say, he wishes them a heavenly peace. In affliction and in the hour of death, the grace and favor of the world cannot help us. But when the grace and peace of God are in the heart, then is man strong, so that he can neither be cast down with adversity, nor puffed up with prosperity, but walks on bravely and keeps the highway. This peace of God Paul wishes to Galatians. —*Martin Luther*

Peace is not the absence of conflict from life, but the ability to cope with it. —*Author Unknown*

# APRIL 29

*And he said unto me, My grace is sufficient for thee.*
*—2 Corinthians 12:9*

"My strength is made perfect in weakness!"

This inspiriting truth, like a high, silvery battle trumpet, has aroused myriads of Christians in the hour of trial. The sentence is very simple in word, short in length, but the Holy Spirit has filled it with a rich diversity of meanings. Here are three:

1. It means that the believer himself, never accepts the all-sufficiency of the grace of God until a great task come upon him for which he is unequal. Then as the work comes to glorious completion, his confidence strikes root in his Savior. He knows that the grace of God upon him is the sufficient enablement, however pitiful may be his own weakness.

2. It means, also, that men of obviously simple endowments working in the power of the Holy Spirit, are the unanswerable proof of God to an unbelieving world—"they took note of them that they had been with Jesus."

3. And, it means that the power of God is never able to operate to its highest excellency until it has an unmistakably humble instrument at its disposal. Christian servants, highly gifted and highly conscious of it, do not help the All-Powerful; they hinder Him.      *—Richard Ellsworth Day*

> *There are riches of grace in the ages to come*
> *That God to His own will unfold:*
> *There are vast and exceeding great riches of grace*
> *Far better than silver or gold.*
>
> *Unsearchable riches God gives unto all*
> *Who let Him come into their heart;*
> *And riches of glory through ages untold,*
> *God willingly still will impart.*

*But it is good for me to draw near to God: I have put my trust in the Lord God, that I may declare all thy works.*
—Psalm 73:28

The Devil can discourage most of us when we begin to take notice of the prosperity of the wicked. This is true on all levels of life, from the personal to the international.

The Psalmist found the answer to these problems. In the sixteenth and seventeenth verses he writes: "When I thought to know this (the prosperity of the wicked), it was too painful for me; until I went into the sanctuary of God; then understood I their end." An entire change in his attitude is shown from the seventeenth verse to the end of the Psalm.

The difference came when the discouraged man entered the sanctuary where his eyes were lifted from the world to God. God is omnipotent. He loves us and will make a practical application of His love if we keep our eyes upon Him.

The sanctuary of God may not be in the church. God's sanctuary for you may be the place of prayer by your bedside. It may be in the fields, or in an automobile. But regardless of place, God's sanctuary for you is the place where your vision is lifted from the hard-to-understand things of this world to His eternal purposes.
—*Leslie Parrott*

*Oh, for the peace of perfect trust,*
*Unwavering faith, that never doubts,*
*Thou chooseth best for me.*

*That hears Thy voice—a Father's voice—*
*Directing for the best.*
*Oh, for the peace of a perfect trust,*
*A heart for Thee at rest.*

*Thanks be unto God for his unspeakable gift.*
—2 Corinthians 9:15

The one great work of God's love for us is, He gives us His Son. In Him we have all. Hence the one great work of our heart must be to receive this Jesus who has been given to us, to consider Him and use Him as ours. I must begin every day anew with the thought, I have Jesus to do all for me. In all weakness or danger or darkness, in the case of every desire or need, let your first thought always be, I have Jesus to make everything right for me, for God has given Him to me. Whether your need forgiveness or consolation or confirmation, whether you have fallen, or are tempted to fall, in danger, whether you know not what the will of God is in one or another matter, or know that you have not the courage and the strength to do His will, let this always be your first thought, the Father has given me Jesus to care for me.             —*Andrew Murray*

*At what great cost God gave the world,*
  *His Son, His wonderful Son!*
*But how many walk in darkness today,*
  *As though He had never come;*
*As though He had never been born at all,*
  *And never had left the throne*
*To walk in humility here on earth,*
  *And die on the Cross alone.*

*Oh, let us accept Him, God's wonderful Son,*
  *As our personal Savior today;*
*He seems to be calling as never before*
  *To us and to those far away.*
*Let us claim for ourselves His undying love,*
  *And thank Him for what He has done,*
*That the light in our lives may sing to the world,*
  *"He's come! The Savior has come!"*
                    —Alice Mortenson

*I have chosen you . . . that ye should go and bring forth fruit.*
— John 15:16

If we do the little duties of life faithfully, punctually, thoughtfully, reverently—not for the praise of man, but for the "Well done" of Christ—not for the payment we may receive, but because God has given us a little piece of work to do in His great world—not because we must, but because we choose—not as the slaves of circumstances, but as Christ's freed ones—then far down beneath the surge of common life the foundations of a character are laid, more beautiful and enduring than coral, which shall presently rear itself before the eyes of men and angels, and become an emerald islet, green with perennial beauty, and vocal with the songs of Paradise.

We ought, therefore, to be very careful how we fulfill the common tasks of daily life. We are making the character in which we have to spend eternity. We are either building into ourselves wood, hay and stubble which will have to be burnt out at great cost; or the gold, silver and precious stones, that shall be things of beauty and joy forever.     — *F. B. Meyer*

*Since Thou hast chosen us, O Lord,*
    *Fruitful we, too, would be;*
*We would not come with empty hand*
    *At close of day to Thee.*

*Oh, give us fruit that shall remain,*
    *Nor let us toil in vain.*
*Use us to bring the lost ones in*
    *Till Thou shalt come again!*
                — Cora Mae Turnbull

# MAY 3

This wisdom is obtained by hearkening to God's voice, for "we apply our heart to understanding" when we "incline our heart unto wisdom." The wisdom of God can only come from God, and He gives it to those who feel their need of it and plead with Him to have that need supplied. When God said to Solomon, "Ask what I shall give thee," he replied: "Give Thy servant an understanding heart . . . that I may discern between good and bad." God not only granted him his request, but said, "I have also given thee that which thou hast not asked—both riches and honor"; and in 1 Kings 4:29 we are told that "God gave Solomon wisdom and understanding exceeding much, and largeness of heart."

God is just the same today. He is still able and willing to do all for those who yield themselves fully to Him—"exceeding abundantly above all that we ask or think according to the power that worketh in us." Yea, if we accept the Lord Jesus in all the offices to which He has been made of God unto us, He will be in us as our wisdom," as well as "righteousness, and sanctification, and redemption" (1 Cor. 1:30). Therefore, when Christ's warriors lack wisdom, let them "ask of God" as Solomon did, and it shall be said of them as it was of him: "The wisdom of God" is in them "to do judgment" and to do God's work wisely and well.

> *I've found my "Pearl of Greatest Price,"*
> *My heart doth sing for joy;*
> *And sing I must, for Christ I have—*
> *Oh, what a Christ have I!*
> *My Christ, He is the Lord of lords,*
> *He is the King of kings,*
> *He is the Sun of Righteousness,*
> *With healing in His wings.*

—*John Roberts*

*He delivereth the poor in his affliction, and openeth their ears in oppression.*
— Job 36:15

It is good for us that we sometimes have some wearinesses and crosses; for they often call a man back to his own heart; that he may know that he is here in banishment, and may not set his trust in any worldly thing.

It is good that we sometimes endure contradictions; and that men think ill or meanly of us; and this, although we do and intend well. These things help often to humility, and defend us from vain glory: for then we the more seek God for our inward witness, when outwardly we are condemned by men, and when no good is believed of us.

And therefore a man should settle himself so fully in God, that he need not seek many consolations of men.

When a man of good will is afflicted, tempted, or troubled with evil thoughts; then he understands better the great need he has of God, without whom he perceives he can do nothing that is good.
—*Thomas à Kempis*

*O Holy Savior! Friend unseen!*
*The faint, the weak, on Thee may lean:*
*Help me, throughout life's varying scene,*
*By faith to cling to Thee.*

*Though hope and faith awhile be tried,*
*I ask not, need not aught beside:*
*How safe, how calm, how satisfied,*
*The souls that cling to Thee.*

*Blest is my lot, whate'er befall:*
*What can disturb me, who appall,*
*While, as my strength, my rock, my all,*
*Savior, I cling to Thee?*

# MAY 5

*For we wrestle not against flesh and blood, but against principalities, against powers, against the rulers of the darkness of this world, against spiritual wickedness in high places.*
—Ephesians 6:12

At no time in the Christian's pilgrimage is he free from peril. Temptations of every hue beset his path. The farther along the road, and the greater the grace, the more subtle the snares, and the more intense the opposition. It was at the end of the road in the hour of greatest achievement, in the moment of loftiest spiritual attainment, that the Savior experienced the sharpest and grimmest conflict; and so it is with the Christian. He will never know how determined and how mighty the foe is, how cruel the enemy, how potent the opposition, until he forges his way to the highest spiritual attainment. It is when he asserts his claim to a place with Christ in the Heavenlies, that the great Adversary, the Prince of Darkness, begins to employ his subtlest tactics, and brings into action his most telling weapons.
—F. J. Huegel

*Faithful is He who has promised,*
*He will never let you fall,*
*Daily will the strength be given*
*Strength for each and strength for all.*

*So till then just keep on trusting,*
*Through the sunshine and the rain,*
*Through the tears and through the heartaches,*
*Through the smiles and through the pain;*

*Knowing that our Father watches,*
*Knowing daily strength He'll give,*
*Victory for each passing hour;*
*This is life, so let us live!*
—John E. Zoller

*He maketh me to lie down in green pastures; he leadeth me
beside the still waters.*                                    —Psalm 23:2

These words are a gracious reminder that even in the midst
of life's pilgrimage God gives us sweet foretastes of heaven.
For the sheep, green pastures were a sweet foretaste of the
sheep's paradise.

David is seeking to remind us that God as the great and
good Shepherd gives to him as His sheep, here and now,
sweet foretastes of the glory that is yet to be for all of God's
redeemed children in that land where the body will never
grow old, that land of eternal Springtime.

The Bible is strewn with promises of green pastures. "When
the poor and needy seek water, and there is none, and their
tongue faileth for thirst, I the Lord will hear them, I the God
of Israel will not forsake them. I will open rivers in high
places, and fountains in the midst of the valleys: I will make
the wilderness a pool of water, and the dry land springs of
water" (Isa. 41:17,18). "Come ye yourselves apart into a desert
place, and rest awhile," He said to His disciples (Mark 5:31).
The prayer meeting on the Mount of Transfiguration was a
sweet foretaste of heaven. The Emmaus Road experience was
another.

The same Good Shepherd has green pastures for you in
the treasures of His Word, in the place of quiet prayer, in the
fellowship of His people, and in all the many means of grace.
"My meditation of him shall be sweet," wrote David in Psalm
104. No life is so poor but it has such experiences. If you
would experience the green pastures, if you would know these
exquisite moments that "Sweeten toil and banish care," then
you must become one of His sheep, one of those who have
been redeemed by His precious blood.          —*Robert Barr*

# May 7

> *But they that wait upon the Lord shall renew their strength;*
> *they shall mount up with wings as eagles; they shall run, and*
> *not be weary; and they shall walk, and not faint.*
> —Isaiah 40:31

The gradation is a remarkable one. At first sight it would appear that it should pass from walking to running, and from this to flying; but the order is reversed, as though it were easier to mount with wings than walk without fainting. And so, indeed it is. Any racehorse will start at full speed; but how few have staying power! To pursue the common track of daily duty—not faltering, not growing weary—to do so when novelty has worn off, when the elasticity of youth has vanished, when the applause of the crowd has become dim and faint, this is the greatest achievement of the Christian life. For this earthly and human strength will not avail. But God is all-sufficient. Never faint or weary Himself, He is able to infuse resistless energy into the soul that waits on Him.          —*F. B. Meyer*

> *Oh, wonderful promises given*
> > *To those who wait on the Lord;*
> *Strength for the faint who have fallen,*
> > *Power for weakness outpoured.*
>
> *Blessed the threefold assurance*
> > *Thrilling the soul like a song:*
> *They shall mount up as the eagles*
> > *On wide wings and swift wings and strong.*
>
> *Run with the stride of the racer,*
> > *Leaping unwearied and free,*
> *Till he comes to the end of his journey*
> > *And the crown of his effort shall see.*
>
> *Oh, promise for those who are walking,*
> > *Who falter and stumble and fall,*
> *The courage, the strength and the patience,*
> > *This is the sweetest of all.*
> > > —Annie Johnson Flint

*Lord, teach us to pray, as John also taught his disciples.*
—Luke 11:1

Without doubt these disciples were praying men. He had already talked to them a great deal about prayer. But as they noticed how large a place prayer had in His life, and what some of the marvelous results were, the fact came home to them with great force that there must be some fascination, some power, some secret in prayer, of which they were ignorant. This Man was a master in the fine art of prayer. They really did not know how to pray, they thought.

How their request must have delighted Him! At last they were being aroused concerning the great secret of power. May it be that this simple recital of His habit of prayer may move everyone of us to get alone with Him and make the same earnest request. For the first step in learning to pray is to pray, "Lord, teach me to pray." And who can teach like Him?

Prayer brings power. Prayer is power. The time of prayer is the time of power. The place of prayer is the place of power. Prayer is tightening the connections with the divine dynamo so that the power may flow freely without loss or interuption.

—S. D. Gordon

Prayer is the key that unlocks all the storehouses of God's infinite grace and power. All that God is, and all that God has, is at the disposal of prayer. But we must use the key.

—R. A. Torrey

*I know not by what methods rare,*
*But this I know, God answers prayer;*
*I know that He has given His word,*
*Which tells me prayer is always heard,*
*And will be answered, soon or late;*
*And so I pray, and calmly wait.*

# MAY 9

*Come unto me, all ye that labor and are heavy laden and I will give you rest.* —Matthew 11:28

Our Lord was not speaking of physical rest alone. Many who are quite restless in their souls can obtain that of themselves. Soul-rest is the only true and abiding rest, nor is there one among us who does not sigh for it. But there is no soul-rest except through Jesus Christ. He is the only fully restful One who has ever walked on the earth, and the restful alone can give rest; the peaceful alone are the ones who can bequeath peace to others. But what a bequest He has left us: rest and peace such as the world cannot give nor take away. Nor will the tribulations of the world disturb us.

But there is another rest—a rest that comes to us only when we take His yoke upon us and learn of Him. It seems strange that after telling us to cast all our cares and burdens upon Him that we might obtain rest, He should at once proceed to inform us that we must now take another yoke upon us. Observe, however, that it is His yoke, and His yoke is easy, and the burden which He lays upon us is not like the burden which we formerly carried and found to be so heavy, for His burden is light. —*Howard W. Ferrin*

*Once my life was full of effort,*
  *Now 'tis full of joy and zest;*
*Since I took His yoke upon me*
  *Jesus gives to me His rest.*
  —A. B. Simpson

*As many as I love, I rebuke and chasten: be zealous there-fore, and repent.*
—Revelation 3:19

It is mental and spiritual deception to use the glorious Bible statement, "God is love," as an argument for soft, sentimental conclusions. Such lying conclusions as these: "Since God is love, He can never have wrath; since God is love, He has no intention to punish or execute judgment." Avoid such folly! that kind of a god, were he to become a mother, couldn't raise a decent family of children. Such attitudes in a mother's heart wouldn't be *love* at all, but *sentiment*, so cheap and shallow, that only a miracle could keep her brood from becoming social problems. God's love is not a flimsy amorphous texture; but a love that squares up with the highest ideals of justice. That is what John said; Herein is love, the real article, that God loved us and sent His Son to be "a sacrificial adjustment" for our sins. This new phrase, "sacrificial adjustment" is a high explosive, but our hearts are warmed by it, just the same. The death of Jesus is "a sacrificial adjustment" enabling God's love to redeem man without violence to God's holy character. The death of Jesus is "a sacrificial adjustment" enabling God's love to purge us of the taint of sin.

Behold, love, the highest love, *God's love*, has as its supreme goal not our *immediate comfort* but our *ultimate Christ-likeness*. Therefore God's love is love at the utmost. He rebukes and chastens, because he *does* love us. Be faithful, dear reader, under your manifold trials! Look well to yourself; be zealous and repent of every weakness, which only *the light of pain* has power to expose!
—*Richard Ellsworth Day*

"Love seeketh not her own," and so
He did not stay as God above,
But chose a manger and a cross
To show that He was Love.

—Marion Wilmshurst

# MAY 11

*And being found in fashion as a man, he humbled himself,*
*and became obedient unto death, even the death of the cross.*
—Philippians 2:8

Our physical nature revolts at the thought of suffering. A normal man will, when he can, turn aside from pain, but to do God's will costs some men physical suffering. Christians have been fed to wild beasts, burned at the stake, beheaded. To do God's will may not mean physical anguish for us, but there is a pain which can be even greater, that is pain of the heart and of the mind. To do the will of God may mean turning our back on all we love and going alone to the place of God's appointment for us. To follow Christ may mean separation from that which we cherish most, a turning away from that which is dearest to our own heart. It means turning aside from that which we would choose, to that which God chooses for us. No man can truly claim to be obedient to God until he, like the Savior, is willing to be obedient even unto death. Anything which stops short of that sort of obedience is not obedience. What would you think of a soldier who refused to obey a command because his obedience might result in his death? If obedience "even unto death" is naturally expected of a good soldier, is such obedience not necessary if one would be perfect in his obedience to God?     —*Bob Jones, Jr.*

*"Take up thy Cross," the Savior said,*
*"If thou wouldst My disciple be;*
*Deny thyself, the world forsake,*
*And humbly follow after Me."*

*Take up thy cross, and follow Christ;*
*Nor think till death to lay it down;*
*For only he who bears the Cross*
*May hope to wear the glorious crown.*
—Charles W. Everest

*To the praise of the glory of his grace, wherein he hath made us accepted in the beloved.* —Ephesians 1:6

Every believer in the Lord Jesus Christ has the seal of God's approval and favor. We are "accepted in the beloved." In our Lord's high priestly prayer, He prayed that the love wherewith the Father loved Him might be in us as we abide in Him. The same love that the Father has for Jesus Christ is poured out upon all who are in Jesus Christ, because Christ is in them and they are in Him. He prayed, "As Thou, Father, art in Me and I in them, that they may also be one in us." The Father loves us because we are in the beloved. As we who believe in Christ contemplate this precious phrase, our hearts can say with the Apostle Paul, "Blessed be the Father of our Lord Jesus Christ who hath blessed us with all spiritual blessings in heavenly places in Christ according as He hath chosen us in Him before the foundation of the world."

—*Larry Love*

*No distant Lord have I,*
*Loving afar to be;*
*Made flesh for me, He cannot rest*
*Until He rests in me.*

*I need not journey far*
*This dearest Friend to see,*
*Companionship is always mine;*
*He makes His home in me.*

*Oh, glorious Son of God,*
*Incarnate Deity,*
*I shall forever be with Thee*
*Because Thou art with me!*

*But he knoweth the way that I take: when he hath tried me,*
*I shall come forth as gold.* — Job 23:10

The omniscience of God is one of the wondrous attributes of Deity. "For his eyes are upon the ways of man, and he seeth all his goings" (Job 34:21). "The eyes of the Lord are in every place, beholding the evil and the good" (Prov. 15:3). Spurgeon said, "One of the greatest tests of experimental religion is, What is my relationship to God's omniscience?" What is your relationship to it, dear reader? How does it affect you? Does it distress or comfort you? Do you shrink from the thought of God knowing all about your way? To the sinner this is a terrible thought. He denies it, or if not, he seeks to forget it. But to the Christian, here is real comfort. How cheering to remember that my Father knows all about my trials, my difficulties, my sorrows, my efforts to glorify Him. Precious truth for those in Christ, harrowing thought for all out of Christ, that the way I am taking is fully known to and observed by God. — *Arthur W. Pink*

*Christ leads me through no darker rooms*
*Than He went through before;*
*He that unto God's kingdom comes*
*Must enter by this door.*

*Come, Lord, when grace has made me meet*
*Thy blessed face to see;*
*For if Thy work on earth be sweet,*
*What will Thy glory be!*
—Richard Baxter

*Though I walk in the midst of trouble, thou wilt revive me.*
—Psalm 138:7

God has promised to be with us and keep us in all places, to walk with us to the last foot of the last mile of Life's journey. Treasure these words: "The Lord God is a sun and shield . . . no good thing will he withhold from them that walk uprightly." "Though I walk through the valley of the shadow of death, I will fear no evil." "Teach me, O God, I will walk in thy truth." "He is a buckler to them that walk uprightly." "They that wait upon the Lord shall . . . walk and not faint." "He that followeth me shall not walk in darkness, but shall have the light of life." "He that walketh uprightly walketh surely."

And looking beyond this world with its sickness to the world where sickness is never known, beyond this world with its darkness to the world where there is no night, beyond this world with its sin and shame to the world where nothing that defileth ever entereth, beyond this world with its death to the world where no death enters, let us yield our feet unto Him as instruments of righteousness so that when we shall see Jesus we shall know all He means when He says: "They shall walk with me in white."
—*Robert G. Lee*

*I do not know, I cannot see,*
*What God's kind hand prepares for me,*
*Nor can my glance pierce through the haze*
*Which covers all my future ways;*
*But yet I know that o'er it all*
*Rules He who notes the sparrow's fall.*

*I will not leave you comfortless.* —John 14:18

What a blessed word of assurance from the Lord Jesus Himself! It is our guarantee that whatever happens, it is absolutely certain that we shall never be forsaken by our Lord. Some things are spiritually impossible, and one of them is for a single Christian soul ever to be deserted. The Lord has given to every believer His pledged word according to that precious Scripture, in Hebrews 13:5, "I will never leave thee, nor forsake thee."

And why could Christ, so soon to depart out of this world through the way of the Cross—why could Christ so definitely promise that His disciples, though bereft of His bodily presence, would not be left comfortless? Every saved soul should know the answer, for every saved soul has the witness of the Holy Spirit, the Comforter who abides with us forever, even the eternal Spirit of the Lord Jesus Christ. Yes, Christians may be called upon to suffer much for their Lord; they may lose possessions and even their dearest relatives. But God will never put them in a place of separation from the Lord Jesus, for He has promised not to leave them orphans, and His own Spirit dwells forever in the believing heart.

—*Frank E. Gaebelein*

*Here let my faith unshaken dwell;*
*Immovable the promise stands;*
*Not all the powers of earth or hell*
*Can e'er dissolve the sacred bands.*

*Here, O my soul, thy trust repose!*
*If Jesus is forever mine,*
*Not death itself, that last of foes,*
*Shall break a union so divine.*

—Anne Steele

*And, behold, there arose a great tempest in the sea, insomuch that the ship was covered with the waves: but he was asleep.*
—Matthew 8:24

Storms may arise even when we are in the plain line of duty. We should not be discouraged by the difficulty or trouble that comes, and conclude that we are in the wrong path. Christ's presence with His disciples does not keep the storms away. There are no Promises in the Bible that Christian people shall not meet trials. Religion builds no high walls about us to break the force of the winds. Troubles come to the Christian just as surely as to the worldly man. There are the storms of temptation; these sweep down with sudden and terrific power from the cold mountains of this world. Then there are storms of sickness, of disappointment and adversity, of sorrow, that make the waves and billows to roll over the soul.

On the Sea of Galilee travelers say that a boat will be gliding along smoothly over a glassy surface, unbroken by a ripple, when suddenly, without a moment's warning, a tempest will sweep down, and almost instantly the boat will be tossed in the angry waves. Thus many of life's storms come. Temptations come when we are not looking for them. So disasters come. We are at peace in a happy home. At an hour when we think not, without warning, the darling child we love so much lies dead in our arms. The friend we trusted, and who we thought could never fail us, proves false. The hopes cherished for years wither in our hands in a night, like flowers when the frost comes. The storms of life are nearly all sudden surprises. They do not hang out danger-signals days before to warn us. The only way to be ready for them is to be always ready.
—J. R. Miller

# MAY 17

*The Lord hath done great things for us; whereof we are glad.*
—Psalm 126:3

One cannot adequately praise his God with a heart so bowed down with care that it will not lift because of the weight of woe hanging heavily upon it. What then are we to do? Are we not to cast our burdens upon the Lord, who has promised to sustain us? Are we not to lay hold upon His vital promises and look through and beyond the overhanging storm clouds, into the sunlight, clear and shining, which is God's eternal hope let down by His own hand for us?

Should we not rejoice in a heavenly Father who has our welfare ever at heart and who is working constantly for our good?

We should be rejoicing Christians, looking "not at the things which are seen, but at the things which are not seen: for the things which are seen are temporal; but the things which are not seen are eternal."

We have a great God. "In his hand are the deep places of the earth: the strength of the hills is his also"; and wonder of wonders, we are His, and nothing can pluck us out of His hands! Is not this a cause for the greatest rejoicing?
—*Grace Noll Crowell*

*Shall I tell you what it is that keeps me singing,*
*Never minding whether it be shade or shine?*
*'Tis because His own glad song is singing in me,*
*'Tis because the Savior's joy is always mine.*

*Shall I tell you why my foes no longer vex me,*
*And my cares and fears and doubtings all are o'er?*
*'Tis because I've given my burdens all to Jesus,*
*And He leads me forth in triumph evermore.*
—A. B. Simpson

*For whom the Lord loveth he chasteneth, and scourgeth
every son whom he receiveth.* —Hebrews 12:6

There are those who sometimes wonder if God has forsaken them; the chains of circumstances bind them down in undesirable places and their prayer seems shut out from God. No great faith is required to trust God when the skies are bright and you feel full of natural vitality and can come and go as you please. Saints are not made in the easy places; they are refined in the white-hot furnace of affliction. Do not "despise" the chastening of the Lord. Hear the words of Jeremiah. Broken because of the sins of others and chained in a dungeon, he cried out: "He hath led me, and brought me into darkness . . . my flesh and my skin hath he made old; He hath hedged me about, that I cannot get out; he hath made my chain heavy" (Lam. 3:2, 4, 7). And yet out of that crushed and broken life came the prophecies which gave hope and assurance to Israel in the dark days of her captivity. Our God has not changed. His specifications are still the same, calling for finished products, refined and molded under divine pressure.

To follow Christ means a life given over to the complete lordship of the Son of God, a life willingly surrendered to the breaking process that will inevitably come (in one way or another) to "every son whom he receiveth."

—*Marcus L. Haskell*

> *He kindles for my profit purely*
> *Affliction's glowing, fiery brand,*
> *And all His heaviest blows are surely*
> *Inflicted by a master's hand;*
> *So I say, praying, "As God will!"*
> *And hope in Him, and suffer still.*
> —Julius Sturm

*Doth God take care for oxen?* —1 Corinthians 9:9

The Lord cares for all things, and the meanest creatures share in His universal providence, but His particular providence is over His saints. "The angel of the Lord encampeth round about them that fear Him." "Precious shall their blood be in His sight." "Precious in the sight of the Lord is the death of His saints." "We know that all things work together for good to them that love God, to them that are the called according to His purpose." Let the fact that, while He is the Savior of all men, He is specially the Savior of them that believe, cheer and comfort you. You are His peculiar care; His regal treasure which He guards as the apple of His eye; His vineyard over which He watches day and night. "The very hairs of your head are all numbered." Let the thought of His special love to you be a spiritual pain-killer, a dear quietus to your woe: "I will never leave thee, nor forsake thee." God says that as much to you as to any saint of old. Think you see Him walking on the waters of your trouble, for He is there, and He is saying, "Fear not, it is I; be not afraid." Oh, those sweet words of Christ! May the Holy Ghost make you feel them as spoken to you; forget others for awhile—accept the voice of Jesus as addressed to you, and say, "Jesus whispers consolation; I cannot refuse it; I will sit under His shadow with great delight."     —*Charles H. Spurgeon*

*Father! whate'er of earthly bliss*
*Thy sov'reign will denies;*
*Accepted at Thy throne of grace,*
*Let this petition rise.*
        —Anne Steele

*God is our refuge and strength, a very present help in trouble.*
—*Psalm 46:1*

Don't run away from your troubles. Don't magnify them. Don't dwell on them, taking them to bed with you, spoiling your digestion by feeding upon them all day, and making everybody unhappy by throwing their shadow upon them. But with a resolute, courageous and trustful spirit take them to God in prayer and then go forth to meet and vanquish them, and you will find they are much less formidable than you feared.

An old farmer plowed around a rock in one of his fields for many years. He had grown actually morbid over it, for he had broken a cultivator and two plows besides losing a lot of valuable land in its vicinity. One day he made up his mind that he would dig it out and have done with it. Lo, when he put his crowbar under it he found it was less than a foot thick and that he could loosen it with a trifling effort and carry it away in his wagon. He smiled to think how all through the years it had haunted him.

One day we shall look back on our trials and our anxious cares and find how needless many of them were, so unreal and yet so distressing, that we can say like the old lady when she was reviewing her past life: "I've had so many trials, especially those that never came." —*A. B. Simpson*

*Who trusts in God, a strong abode*
  *In heaven and earth possesses;*
*Who looks in love to Christ above,*
  *No fear his heart oppresses.*
*In Thee alone, dear Lord, we own*
  *Sweet hope and consolation:*
*Our shield from foes, our balm for woes*
  *Our great and sure salvation.*
    —Joachim Madeburg

# MAY 21

*Peace I leave with you, my peace I give unto you: not as the world giveth, give I unto you. Let not your heart be troubled, neither let it be afraid.* —John 14:27

There is no blessing that brings more positive benefits to the life than the enjoyment of God's peace. While all Christians have experienced peace with God by virtue of exercising saving faith in Christ (Rom. 5:1), many of God's children know little of the "peace of God which passeth all understanding" because their lives are not dominated by believing, prevailing prayer, which God's Word so closely connects with the enjoyment of His peace.

It is impossible to enjoy God's peace, however, and not face war. Still the anxiety that paralyzes the world need not affect the child of God. God desires to guard our hearts and minds against it. It is His gracious will that we walk undisturbed and undismayed through our earthly pilgrimage. However severe the storm without may be, the Christian must not allow it to get within. He must avail himself of the garrison God has set to guard his heart and mind against anxiety and fear. That garrison, which has never lost a battle nor suffered one fortress to be invaded or taken, is the peace of God. "And the peace of God, which passeth all understanding, shall guard your hearts and minds through Christ Jesus."

—*Merrill F. Unger*

*Jesus, Deliverer!*
*Come Thou to me!*
*Soothe Thou my voyaging*
*Over life's sea!*

*Thou, when the storm of death*
*Roars, sweeping by,*
*Whisper, O Truth of Truth!*
*"Peace! it is I!"*
—Anatolius

*And if I go and prepare a place for you, I will come again, and receive you unto myself; that where I am, there ye may be also.*
—John 14:3

It is this fact that Christ will someday return to earth that supplies Christianity with practical vitality. Here is the basis for fulfillment of every grand promise of salvation, the weight in every warning of wrath to come; the motive behind the divine commission to disciple the earth; the incentive to purify ourselves as He is pure. It is the one excuse for the existence of the Church, and the greatest inducement to perform faithfully the task Christ placed it in the world to do. We retain or lose our power to persuade men in proportion as we regard or disregard this blessed hope.

In these days of darkness when men grope for that which gives peace to the living and hope to the dying, may we, like the early disciples, catch the significance of His pledge, "I will come again." May it be to us a guiding ray. May it comfort our hearts as we look toward that dawning when our sainted dead shall rise to meet Him in the skies. May it add to our trophies the crown of righteousness, promised to all those who love His appearing. For Jesus shall come, and in that day every knee shall bow and every tongue confess that Jesus Christ is Lord.
—*Jack Shuler*

*We long to hear Thy voice,*
*To see Thee face to face,*
*To share Thy crown and glory then,*
*As now we share Thy grace.*
*Should not the loving bride*
*Her absent Bridegroom mourn?*
*Should she not wear the signs of grief*
*Until her Lord return?*
*Come, then, Lord Jesus, come!*

*This then is the message which we have heard of him, and declare unto you, that God is light, and in him is no darkness at all.*
—1 John 1:5

Always do we need the guidance of the light of God. Unless we have it we stray far from the path of righteousness.

After we have learned God's will comes the most critical step of all, the following faithfully and persistently of the directions given us. Often we must go forward in the face of severe criticism and real difficulties. Perhaps it seems overwhelmingly discouraging, even almost impossible. That is the great test; unless we want to court inevitable failure, we must lift our eyes to the "kindly Light" and follow blindly, if need be for a time, but with the blessed assurance that in God's own good time the way will become clear and bright before us. This sudden clearing and lighting of the way after darkness and discouragement is one of the most precious and inspiring experiences that can come to a child of God.

Let us therefore put our trust in God and pray earnestly from the heart, "Lead Thou me on." —Bernice D. Richtmyer

*Lead, kindly Light, amid the encircling gloom,*
*Lead Thou me on!*
*The night is dark, and I am far from home;*
*Lead Thou me on!*
*Keep Thou my feet; I do not ask to see*
*The distant scene; one step enough for me.*

*So long Thy pow'r hath blest me, sure it still*
*Will lead me on*
*O'er moor and fen, o'er crag and torrent, till*
*The night is gone,*
*And with the morn those angel faces smile,*
*Which I have loved long since, and lost awhile!*
—John H. Newman

*They that trust in the Lord shall be as mount Zion, which cannot be removed, but abideth for ever.* —Psalm 125:1

Joseph R. Sizoo, one-time pastor of the New York Avenue Presbyterian Church in Washington which Abraham Lincoln often attended, says he will never forget the day he held in his hands for the first time the Bible from which Lincoln's mother had read to him as a child. She had taught him to commit to memory many of its passages. It was the only possession Lincoln carried from Pigeon Creek to the Sangamon River. And book in my hand, I wondered where it would fall open. It opened to a page which was thumb-marked and which he must have read many times. It was the thrity-seventh Psalm. "Fret not thyself because of evildoers. . . . Rest in the Lord, and wait patiently for him" (Ps. 37:17). —*James Hastings*

"Abide in Me," says our Lord. Just rest peacefully in Him so far as your life of victory is concerned. At every alarm, at every approach of temptation, just "hide in Him," the Rock of Ages, just as the rabbit takes cover in his rock of defense. "Consider the lilies of the field, how they grow"—not by self-effort, toiling or striving. They just abide in the sunshine and drink in its life. "Which of you being anxious can add one cubit to his stature?" asks our Lord in the Sermon on the Mount. And in His mind was something more than physical stature.

It is not our faith but His faithfulness that maintains the Victorious Life. "Trust in the Lord," and then "do good; so shalt thou dwell in the land and verily thou shalt be fed" (Ps. 37:3).

*Lord, I cannot hope to triumph*
  *Over every form of sin,*
*And to live but for Thy glory,*
  *While my own will reigns within;*

*So I bring my will to Thee, Lord;*
  *Rule Thou me in all my ways,*
*And the glory shall be Thine, Lord,*
  *And the honor and the praise—*
    *That is victory!*

—Eva L. Webster

---

*Be careful for nothing.* —Philippians 4:6

The word careful means "full of care or anxiety." God has promised to throw an impenetrable wall of fire around your heart so that no enemy can ever successfully reach you. You have a garrison on guard which can never be overcome. Therefore, you have nothing to worry about. You are not kept by your own power but by the power of God.

Certainly, your faith will be tried, but "the trial of your faith (is) much more precious than of gold that perisheth, though it be tried with fire" (1 Pet. 1:7). Take your pen and mark the occurrences of the word "suffer" or "suffering" in 1 Peter. You will find it fourteen times. The suffering, the trials, are necessary but not an occasion for the least anxiety. It is found "unto praise, and honor and glory at the appearing of Jesus Christ: whom having not seen, ye love; in whom, though now ye see Him not, yet believing, ye rejoice with joy unspeakable and full of glory." —*Charles E. Fuller*

*Nor does He merely sit as a refiner*
*Of gold beside the crucible He views;*
*But walks the furnace with us, our Shekinah,*
*With His own might our souls to interfuse.*

*Ah, yes! I know! Have I not sensed His nearness,*
*His soothing touch upon my quivering nerve,*
*Heard the soft whisper, realized the dearness*
*Of that High Presence which still stoops to serve!*

*We know in part: but then swift understanding*
*Will flash upon each earthly sign and groan,*
*As face to face, unveiled at His commanding,*
*We each shall know, as we ourselves are known.*
—Henry Howard

---

*Take my yoke upon you, and learn of me; for I am meek and lowly in heart: and ye shall find rest unto your souls.*
—Matthew 11:29

Surely we can come to know Jesus Christ personally in no better way than being quiet before Him. Time spent in feeding our inward lives with His lovely presence will ultimately make it possible for us to carry this inner life out into the market place. Time spent in silence before God teaches us what it really means to "pray without ceasing." We come to live on two levels at once. The calm of the deep, quiet, unchanging inner level where we are Christ's and Christ is God's, where the pool of His peace is never disturbed by any tornadoes blowing from without, will begin to be felt in the bustle and turmoil of our exterior lives. Those who spend time with us will not only know that we "have been with Jesus," but that we are with Jesus. Our very lives will speak for Him, because Jesus Christ the living Lord will speak through our lives to an anguished, frightened world: "Come unto me . . . Look unto me, and be ye saved . . . I and my Father are one . . . be still, and know that I am God."
—*Eugenia Price*

*I would go deeper with Jesus, seeking the utmost He'd give,*
*Striving to please Him forever, e'er in abundance to live.*
*I would go deeper with Jesus, forsaking the glitter of earth,*
*Knowing the beauty of service, knowing its blessing and worth.*

*I would go deeper with Jesus, trusting, though oft through the vale,*
*Close in His keeping, untroubled, finding Him never to fail!*
*I would go deeper with Jesus, Jesus Redeemer above,*
*Deeper, yea deeper forever, into His wonderful love.*
—Connie Calenberg

# MAY 27

*Behold, God is mine helper.* — Psalm 54:4

The word "helper" has an appeal all its own. It comes from a Greek word which is a compound of two verbs, the one meaning to cry (for help), and the other meaning to run: so that the compound word gives the picture of one ready to run at the cry of another. Such is our tenderhearted Lord toward His loved ones. Says Puritan Thomas Brooks: "You know the tender father, the indulgent mother, the careful nurse, they presently run when any of them hears the child cry, or sees the child in any danger or distress; so when God sees His poor children in any danger or distress, when He hears them complain and cry out of their suffering, their bonds, their burdens, their oppressions, their dangers, He presently runs to their relief and succor."

Consider, then, the solid comfort of this great fact, troubled believer, that the Lord Himself is your helper, and you can say this boldly, for it is grounded in His own sure word. Wipe the mist of uncertainty from your eye. Let limping doubt become leaping faith. Let this *Magna Charta* of your eternal security turn sighing into singing and repining into rejoicing. Think over some of your Lord's attributes in His condescending role as your Helper, and it will be as the very joy of heaven to make the heart glad.           —*J. Sidlow Baxter*

*Our God, our help in ages past,*
*Our hope for years to come,*
*Be Thou our guide while life shall last,*
*And our eternal home.*
(From Psalm 90)
—Isaac Watts

*He restoreth my soul: he leadeth me in the paths of righteousness for his name's sake.* — Psalm 23:3

Who of us who has planted his feet in that way of the blessed would tread any other path? Can we not sing as we go through the dark valleys that lie between us and the Celestial City: "He leadeth me in the paths of righteousness for His name's sake." Think of it! For His great Name's sake He must lead me aright. To no other would He entrust this great task. No other is competent. No one amongst the sons of men, no one among the radiant celestial beings who daily hymn His praise around the eternal throne could qualify to lead His beloved in the way of the blessed. Amazing grace, unspeakable condescension, that He Himself, the Lord of Glory, should come to pilot me safely on this strait and narrow way to our eternal home!

*—James H. Hunter*

*Hast thou wondered why He led thee*
*By such strange and lonesome ways,*
*Why thy future lay enshrouded*
*In a dark, mysterious haze?*

*Wondered why thy feet are guided,*
*Where the shadows thickly lie,*
*Why the storms and why the darkness,*
*Why that cold and cloudy sky?*

*Hush! He speaks, He whispers to thee:*
*"By a way thou hast not known,*
*I have led thee by a pathway*
*Marked out solely for Mine own."*

*Faithless child, He fain would teach thee,*
*What a God of love thou hast,*
*Guiding all thy steps with wisdom*
*Leading safely home at last!*

*—M. E. Rae*

*For thou art an holy people unto the Lord thy God: the Lord thy God hath chosen thee to be a special people unto himself, above all people that are upon the face of the earth.*
—Deuteronomy 7:6

The people of God are a special people. "The Lord thy God hath chosen thee to be a special people." The word "special" is as choice as it is rare. It means to shut up securely as jewels and precious treasures are protected, or to embrace as the breast encloses the heart. "They shall be mine, said the Lord of Hosts, in that day when I make up my jewels." Yes, the people of God are His jewels. But more impressive still is the intimation in the above definition that the people of God are in the bosom of the Father, gathered unto His heart and contained in His affections as the heart is held within the breast of man. This is how our life is "hid with Christ *in* God."
—S. Franklin Logsdon

When I go down to the grave I can say, like so many others, I have finished my work; but I cannot say that I have finished my life. My day's work will begin the next morning. My tomb is not a blind alley. It is a thoroughfare. It closes with the twilight to open with the dawn.     —*Victor Hugo*

*Bow down Thine ear, O Lord, to hear*
*For I, Thy loving child, come near*
*To rest in Thee, my only dwelling place;*
*For joy in service, strength through prayer,*
*Relief from every shade of care,*
*For bliss of sins forgiven through Thy grace,*
*I sing my praises to Thy name,*
*Yesterday, today, the same,*
*And also evermore!*
—Grace W. Haight

*Behold I give unto you power . . . over all the power of the enemy.*
—*Luke 10:19*

Once the believer gets the fact of this power fixed in his mind and heart and begins to act on it, then, indeed, he becomes more than conqueror. He no longer quails before the enemy. Like David before the giant Philistine who had defied Israel's hosts and, blaspheming her Lord, had made her army tremble, he says: "I come to thee in the name of the Lord of hosts, the God of the armies of Israel, whom thou hast defied . . . This day will the Lord deliver thee into mine hand; and I will smite thee."

Once a little cat that was being madly chased by a big dog, suddenly stopped and, turning on the dog, bristled defiance and arched as if to strike. The result was that the dog fell back, cowed, and slunk away defeated. The believer, who would be victorious in all the circumstances of life, must no longer cower before Satan. He must realize that the enemy is a defeated foe. He must once and for all settle it that according to God's Holy Word, the Devil's rights have all been annulled.

Taking his stand firmly on such a text as, for example, Hebrews 2:14, where we read that through death the Redeemer destroyed him that had the power of death, that is the Devil, he exercises authority in the Name of his all-triumphant Lord. If, in the hour of conflict with the powers of darkness, he does this, he will find that he is able to move mountains—mountains of Satanic oppression. He finds that as he withstands in the evil day according to Ephesians 6:13, and having done all stands, he comes off the field of battle more than conqueror.
—*F. J. Huegel*

# MAY 31

*By Me if any man enter in, he shall . . . find pasture.*
—John 10:9

The shepherd takes care that his sheep are well fed. Christ also feeds His people, and leads them out to find pasture. The Bible is His pastureland, and the pasturage there is always good. Every chapter is a field of rich grass. Some of these fields seem at first to be bare and sterile; but even in the barest there is enough pasture to feed a hungry soul.

Then there are the pasture-fields of prayer. These lie very close to the border of heaven. They are always up in the quiet valleys among the mountains. The good Shepherd leads us to them through the gates of prayer. We bow down in lowly humility, and enter with Him into the green pastures, and feed our souls until their hunger is satisfied.

In our common life in this world, if we are faithfully following Christ, we are continually in fields of rich pasture. Christ never leads us into any places in which there is nothing to feed us.

Even in the hot plains of trial and sorrow there is food. We sometimes think there is only barrenness in our toilsome life, filled with temptations, cares and sacrifices; but the Good Shepherd is ever with us, and there is always pasture.

Thus the whole world is a rich field when Jesus leads His flock. If any Christians are not well fed, it is because they will not feed. The trouble must be that they do not hunger for spiritual food. The saddest thing in this world is not a passionate cry for bread, but a soul that has no hunger. Many souls die in the midst of the provision made by the Good Shepherd, not for want of food, but for want of appetite.    —*J. R. Miller*

*If any man serve me, let him follow me.* —John 12:26a.

Service is not a substitute for devotion; service expresses devotion in practical living. If any man serve me, let him follow me . . . (John 12:26a). Here Jesus indicates that devotion is the true price of service. We cannot serve God our own way; it must be His Way.

There are rigors to this call which we must face unhesitatingly if we would be obedient. The world hated our Lord and Master; it will hate us if we follow Him truly. "If the world hate you, ye know that it hated me" (John 15:18). Do not be surprised or confounded; the moral issues of right and wrong are timeless—forever the same. True holiness, likeness to God, our Father, is incompatible with the prevailing spirit of our age. Men still talk about the "foolishness" of God and the "reproach" of the Cross.

Self-denial is inevitable if we would follow our redemptive mission. Our path we cannot choose, nor would we if we could, when we follow the meek and lowly Nazarene. His ways are still higher than our ways and His thoughts than our thoughts. If we would lay claim to God's resourceful strength, then we must follow the Master in complete commitment.

Our view of success now is in terms of His will. Our reward is the Divine Presence. ". . . if any man serve me, him will my Father honor" (John 12:26b). That is enough for me.

—*Samuel Young*

Go, labor on; spend and be spent—
   *Thy joy to do the Father's will;*
*It is the way the Master went;*
   *Should not the servant tread it still?*

—Horatius Bonar

# JUNE 2

*Behold, I am with thee, and will keep thee in all places
whither thou goest.* —Genesis 28:15

*Be quiet, soul:
Why shouldst thou care and sadness borrow,
Why sit in nameless fear and sorrow,
   The livelong day?
God will mark out thy path tomorrow
   In His best way.*

The best place is wherever He puts us, and any other
would be undesirable, all the worse because it would please
our fancy, and would be our own choice. Do not think about
distant events. This uneasiness about the future is
unwholesome for you. We must leave to God all that depends
on Him, and think only of being faithful in all that depends
upon ourselves. When God takes away that which He has
given you, He knows well how to replace it, either through
other means or by Himself. —*François de la Mothe Fenelon*

Be not afraid of those trials which God may see fit to send
upon you. It is with the wind and storm of tribulation that
God separates the true wheat from the chaff. Always
remember, therefore, that God comes to you in your sorrows,
as surely as in your joys. He lays low, and He builds up. You
will find yourself far from perfection, if you do not find God
in everything. —*M. de Molinos*

God has provided a sweet and quiet life for His children,
could they improve and use it; a calm and firm conviction in
all the storms and troubles that are about them however things
go, to find content, and be careful for nothing.
—*R. Leighton*

*. . . when he hath tried me, I shall come forth as gold.*
*—Job 23:10*

It is said that a bar of steel worth five dollars when made into ordinary horseshoes will be worth only ten dollars. If this same five-dollar bar is manufactured into needles, the value rises to $350, but if it is made into delicate springs for expensive watches, it will be worth $250,000. This original bar of steel is made more valuable by being cut to its proper size, passed through the heat again and again, hammered and manipulated, beaten and pounded and finished and polished, until it is finally ready for its delicate task.

This truly is a parable which sets forth a vital truth concerning the child of God. Let us realize that God expends His effort only on that which gives promise of having value. The farmer does not spend time tilling the sand hill that has no value for crops; he puts most of his work and time into the heavy field which has the greatest promise of an abundant harvest. When God leaves us utterly alone, and does not visit us with difficulties and testings and trials, we may be sure that our lives are barren.

Someone has said, "Sunshine all the time only makes a desert." We need the clouds, the dark days, the storms, the rain, just as much as we need the sunshine, and God who is molding our lives, seeking to make us like the Lord Jesus Christ, is the One who knows what is best for us.

*—M. R. DeHaan*

*Hold Thou my cup of life;*
*With joy or sorrow fill*
*As best to Thee may seem:*
*Choose Thou my good and ill.*
—Horatius Bonar

*For as he thinketh in his heart, so is he: Eat and drink, saith he to thee; but his heart is not with thee.* —Proverbs 23:7

The real test of a man's life is his home life. It is not in what his lips say, nor in what his church profession may be, but in what he is, and in what he is in the one place where his life comes out most plainly, the home. If there be a seamy side, it will surely stick out here. If there be a sweet masterful keeping of the seams out of existence, so far as the eyes can see, it will be felt here. Character is not revealed best by public service or by church activities, nor by righting public evils, invaluable as all of this is. The real man may be found only at home. You don't know a man's character until you know his home life.

A Scottish missionary, home on furlough from her work in India, told this story. She had been teaching a group of children one day, telling them the story of Jesus, bringing out, bit by bit, incidents showing His character. As she was talking, one child, listening intently, grew excited, and then more excited. At last she was unable to restrain herself, and blurted out eagerly: "I know him; He lives near us."

Was there ever such praise of a human? Have any of us ever been taken or mistaken for Jesus? When the home folks begin to wonder in their secret hearts if it can possibly be that Jesus is back, living in you, in disguise, the sweetest victory of His grace will be told.          —*S. D. Gordon*

Prayer covers the whole of a man's life. There is no thought, feeling, yearning, or desire, however low, trifling, or vulgar we may deem it, which, if it affects our real interest or happiness, we may not lay before God and be sure of sympathy. His nature is such that our often coming does not tire him. The whole burden of the whole life of every man may be rolled on to God and not weary him, though it has wearied the man.

          —*Henry Ward Beecher*

When Father prays he doesn't use
    The words the preacher does;
There's different things for different days,
    But mostly it's for us.

When Father prays the house is still,
    His voice is slow and deep,
We shut our eyes, the clock ticks loud,
    So quiet we must keep.

He prays that we may be good boys,
    And later on good men;
And then we squirm, and think we won't
    Have any quarrels again.

You'd never think, to look at Dad,
    He once had tempers, too.
I guess if Father needs to pray,
    We youngsters surely do.

Sometimes the prayer gets very long
    And hard to understand,
And then I wiggle up quite close,
    And let him hold my hand.

I can't remember all of it,
    I'm little yet, you see;
But one thing I cannot forget,
    My father prays for me.

                                    —Author Unknown

# JUNE 5

*. . . I will be their God, and they shall be my people.*
*—2 Corinthians 6:16*

What a wealth of meaning is combined in our Lord's words to His people, "My people"! What depth of truth and blessed assurance in the words, "Their God."

In the words "my people" is *specialty* — though the whole world is God's, the heavens and the firmament, and though He reigns over all, supreme in glory, yet He has chosen a select group and called them "My people."

In these words there is also the thought of ownership on God's part. All the nations of the earth are His and the whole world is in His power, yet with particular meaning are His chosen His possession, for He has done more for them than for the others; He has loved them with everlasting love; He has purchased them with His precious Blood.

In the words, *"their* God" is the sweet assurance of a close relationship with the One who not only saves but keeps and satisfies. What a multitude of meaning is wrapped up in these brief words from our God of love. How refreshing it is to dwell upon the deep spiritual truths and blessings contained in these phrases!

*He knoweth the way that I take;*
*Each step of that way He hath planned;*
*And, walking through sunshine or storm,*
*I walk in the shade of His hand.*
*In deserts untrodden and drear,*
*Where foes in the darkness may hide,*
*He leaveth me never alone;*
*He sendeth me light and a guide.*
*—Annie Johnson Flint*

*A little while, and ye shall not see me: and again, a little while, and ye shall see me, because I go to the Father.*
*—John 16:16*

There will not be many more earthly sunsets until there will be an eternal and a heavenly sunrise. Only a little while until the shadows will flee away. Only a little while until we shall lay our burdens down at the end of the journey. Only a little while until aching hearts will ache no more, until our sorrows shall be no more. Only a little while until all of God's redeemed of all the ages will be gathered in that glorious resurrection morning. Only a little while until, as God has promised, we shall see Jesus' face and, with His, the faces of redeemed loved ones.

As victors who cannot be vanquished, we have in Christ a resurrection that can never be thwarted, a destiny that can never be changed, a hope that can never be disappointed, a glory that can never be dimmed or denied.    *—Robert G. Lee*

*Thou art our Master! Thou of God the Son,*
*Of man the friend;*
*By Thee alone the victory is won:*
*Our souls defend!*

*Thou art the Master! Let us love Thy word:*
*Thou Crucified!*
*Now from Thy starry throne look gently down,*
*With us abide!*

*Thou art our Master! At Thy feet we cast*
*Our burdens now.*
*The yoke of Love we take; O, bind us fast!*
*To Thee we bow.*

# JUNE 7

*Evening, and morning, and at noon, will I pray, and cry aloud: and he shall hear my voice.* —Psalm 55:17

Prayer takes practice. It is not a mere rushing into the presence of God and rushing out again without waiting for a reply. It is a conversation, speaking and listening. It is not something we can treat as a medicine bottle, to be used in times of sickness and despair. David once said, "In my distress I called upon the Lord"; but David also speaks of praying morning, noon and night, and his prayers were made up of praise and thanksgiving as well as petition. Nor is prayer a mere duty, nor is it a charm to ward off dangers. The prayer that brings to our souls a divine stillness, that calms our fears, that makes us strong to face a world full of sin and difficulties and discouragements is that prayer in which we wait in the presence of the Lord, look up into His face, and see His smile, and hear His voice speaking to our hearts — the prayer in which we are content just to know that He is there.

You have heard the story of the son of a preacher who came to his father's study one Saturday morning. The father said, "Son, I'm very sorry, but I'm too busy this morning to have you around." The little boy answered, "But, Daddy, I just want to come in and sit with you. I won't say a single word." And for two hours the youngster sat there, quiet, content just to be in the presence of his father. There was no need for words. Have you ever felt like that in the presence of your Heavenly Father?        —*Esther Sabel*

*Lord, the newness of this day*
*Calls me to an untried way:*
*Let me gladly take the road,*
*Give me strength to bear my load,*
*Thou my guide and helper be—*
*I will travel through with Thee.*
                —Henry van Dyke

*For sin shall not have dominion over you*     —Romans 6:14

How many a child of God spends weary hours, fruitlessly striving and struggling to overcome the old Adamic nature and to conquer its lusts and desires, only to experience frustration and constant defeat. Victory seems impossible and the battle seems permanently lost. Yet the New Testament emphatically declares that "sin shall not have dominion over you." Is radiant, joyful Christianity merely a myth or is it a glorious possibility still? Thank God, the victorious life is possible, but it is possible only by giving up struggling and striving and just yielding to the Holy Spirit.

The Holy Spirit stands waiting to assume complete control. He waits to receive the keys to the Christian's life. He waits to take complete possession and to fill every room with the spiritual fragrance and freshness of the Breath of God.

—F. A. Tatford

A sergeant of the British forces over in Egypt, manifesting a fine Christian spirit in his dealings with the men, was called before his chaplain who said, "Sergeant, tell me how you were converted." "It's very simple," replied the sergeant, "we were back at camp where we were having great sport with a Christian soldier, the only Christian in the regiment. He was the butt of jokes, jeered and mocked. One night I took my boots and cracked him on the head as he knelt beside me in prayer. He said nothing. In the morning, Chaplain, I found my boots beside my bed, all shined up and ready for me to get into. In this way I was paid by the one I had so cruelly wronged. Chaplain, it was too much. It broke my heart. I couldn't resist such a testimony. I surrendered to Christ."

# JUNE 9

*The eternal God is thy refuge, and underneath are the ever-lasting arms: and he shall thrust out the enemy from before thee; and shall say, Destroy them.* —Deuteronomy 33:27

Underneath are the everlasting arms! These words came from the lips of an old man who according to this world's way of thinking would soon be going under. But he had no fears about it. Let it be described as "a going under," what matter when underneath were the everlasting arms?

His assurance of this fact had behind it a whole lifetime of experience. Many a time Moses had cause to feel like going under. The burdens he had to bear had been so heavy, the people he had to meet were so trying, and the enemies so powerful. But always he had found that no matter how far down people or circumstances might crush him, always underneath were the everlasting arms. And this was the thought he sought to pass on to his people. They would have their difficulties in days to come, periods of depression when they would feel like going under. But let them never be downcast or fearful. God's arms would always get deeper than the deepest depression. Underneath were the everlasting arms.

*Standing on the promises of Christ my king*
*Thro' eternal ages let His praises ring;*
*Glory in the highest I will shout and sing,*
*    Standing on the promises of God.*

*Standing on the promises that cannot fail.*
*When the howling storms of doubt and fear assail,*
*By the living word of God I shall prevail,*
*    Standing on the promises of God.*
                                    —B. Kelso Carter

*In my Father's house are many mansions: if it were not so,*
*I would have told you. I go to prepare a place for you.*
—John 14:2

Nothing brings heaven closer or makes it more real to our human sensibilities than the passing of a loved one to those happy shores of the land of rest. Let no one mistake it . . . there are strong ties between the Church militant and the Church triumphant! Home on earth is dear to each of us mostly because our loved ones are there; for the same reason heaven is precious to the believer. There the longing heart of the world-weary pilgrim sets its affections. To that home his whole being aspires for there is the throne of the God he worships, there is the blessed physical presence of the Christ he adores and there are the kindred spirits of his loved ones gone before. How he longs to see those faces which, though now long absent from this earthly scene, still remain cherished and sacredly enshrined in the temple of his memory!

—*Henry Bosch*

*We shall meet beyond the river,*
  *Where the surges cease to roll!*
*Where in all the bright forever,*
  *Sorrow ne'er shall press the soul!*

*We shall meet there many a loved one*
  *That was torn from our embrace!*
*We shall listen to their voices*
  *And behold them face to face!*

*We shall meet with Christ our Savior,*
  *When He comes to claim His own!*
*We shall know His blessed favor,*
  *And sit down upon His throne!*

*Abide in me, and I in you. As the branch cannot bear fruit of itself, except it abide in the vine; no more can ye, except ye abide in me.*                    —John 15:4

Our Lord is with us all the days; but often our eyes are holden, that we do not know Him; and if for a radiant moment we discern Him, He vanishes from our sight. There is an experience in which we do not only believe that He is near, but we perceive His presence by the instinct of the heart. He becomes a living, bright reality; sitting by our hearth, walking beside us through the crowded streets, sailing with us across the stormy lake, standing beside the graves that hold our dead, sharing our crosses and our burdens, turning common joy into heavenly bliss.

Then the believer leans hard on the ever-present Lord, drawing on His fullness, appropriating His unsearchable riches, claiming from Him grace to turn every temptation into the means of increasing likeness to Himself. And if the branch abide constantly in the Vine, it cannot help bearing fruit; nay, the difficulty would be to keep fruit back.        —*F. B. Meyer*

*Dear Lord, from Thy hand have come blessings untold,*
*Joys that have proved far more precious than gold.*
*And, oh, if the future should sorrow unfold,*
*Let not faith in Thee depart or grow cold.*

*And as from Thy hand I rich blessings receive,*
*Beyond what my heart and my mind can conceive,*
*Use me burdened hearts to cheer and relieve,*
*And help sin-sick souls in Christ to believe.*
                    —Dorothy C. Wagner

*And Jacob was left alone; and there wrestled a man with him until the breaking of the day.* —Genesis 32:24

What were the results of this wrestling?—First, *trust*. Jacob was a broken man, and what could a broken man do? How could a man with a limb disjoined wrestle? No, he must give up wrestling. There was but one thing he could do—cling to his adversary. It is to this that God must bring us. This is the end of all His wrestling with us. It is that you may cling round Him; it is that you may "cease to doubt" and "cease to resist" Him; it is that you may be content to live, what as yet you have perhaps little understood—a life of faith, a life of dependence on the Son of God. We are not only made alive by faith; we live by it, and the life of faith is a deeper life than many think.

And what beside trust? Why, *triumph*. "As a prince hast thou power with God" (v. 28). His strength was gone, and yet in that hour he conquered. He conquered in a power which was not his own.

And then one thing more. *Transformation*. Jacob now triumphant must be transformed, and so the angel asks him, "What is thy name?" And he said, "Jacob." Crafty, cunning, defeated Jacob — is that your name? Thanks be to God, your name shall be no more called Jacob, you shall have another name. You shall rise above your old self, you shall be called Israel, a prince with God.

Reader, would you be transfigured too? Then you must be willing to be broken, for then in that very inward death you shall find the life of God. —*E. W. Moore*

*It isn't that I cling to Him*
 *Or struggle to be blest;*
*He simply takes my hand in His*
 *And there I let it rest.*

*So I dread not any pathway,*
 *Dare to sail on any sea,*
*Since the handclasp of Another*
 *Makes the journey safe for me.*
—Author Unknown

# JUNE 13

*Fear none of those things which thou shalt suffer. . . .*
—Revelation 2:10

John wrote these words to the suffering saints at Smyrna. Their being cast into prison was simply God "trying" them.

How much we lose by forgetting this! What a stay for the trouble-tossed heart to know that no matter what form the testing may take, no matter what the agent which annoys, it is God who is "trying" His children. What a perfect example the Savior sets us. When He was approached in the garden and Peter drew his sword and cut off the ear of Malchus, the Savior said, "The cup which My Father hath given Me, shall I not drink it?" (John 18:11). Men were about to vent their awful rage upon Him, the Serpent would bruise His heel, but He looks above and beyond them. Dear reader, no matter how bitter its contents (infinitely less than that which the Savior drained), let us accept the cup as from the Father's hand.

Dear Christian reader, there are no exceptions. God had only one Son without sin, but never one without sorrow. Sooner or later, in one form or another, trial—sore and heavy—will be our lot. "And sent Timotheus our brother . . . to establish you, and comfort you concerning your faith: That no man should be moved by these afflictions; for yourselves know that we are appointed thereunto" (1 Thess. 3:2, 3). And again it is written, "We must through much tribulation enter into the kingdom of God" (Acts 14:22). *—Arthur W. Pink*

*The stars shine over the mountains, the stars shine over the sea,*
*The stars look up to the mighty God, the stars look down on me;*
*The stars shall last for a million years, a million years and a day,*
*But God and I will live and love when the stars have passed away.*
—Robert Louis Stevenson

*The Lord knoweth them that are His.*     —2 Timothy 2:19

This verse brings great comfort to God's people in times of trial. When war strikes, families are separated, sons go off to battle, homes are broken by the invader and parents lose contact with children, but in the midst of all the turmoil and chaos and confusion, the Lord still knows His own. To whatever spot they may have been removed His eye has followed them. In a world that has been cursed with war upon war, amid the destruction of armies, God's eye has seen as His own have fallen on the field of battle. Amid the carnage on the seas He has watched as His children have gone down to death in the deep waters. He has watched planes speeding through the flaming air and has seen the fall of His own to the earth.

Just as the Lord called His friend Lazarus by name, bidding him come forth from the grave, so on some glorious day the dead in Christ shall rise at the sound of His voice speaking to His own, "Come forth!" God's family will some day be united; but now scattered over the earth He knows them that are His, and He keeps watch also even above the scattered dust of His sleeping children. The Lord knows them that are His and in all the darkness of bloody days "standeth God within the shadows keeping watch above His own." *—Bob Jones, Jr.*

> *Lord, it belongs not to my care*
>    *Whether I die or live;*
> *To love and serve Thee is my share,*
>    *And this Thy grace must give.*
>         —Richard Baxter

**5**

*...make ye this ado, and weep?* —Mark 5:39

"Perpetual Motion" has penetrated our lives. We can be so busy working for the kingdom that we miss God Himself. Who had more to do and less time to do it than Christ? Yet, "seeing the multitude, he went into a mountain." We need bread but we cannot live by it alone. For the best Christian service, we must create time for meditation. Great spiritual leaders such as Paul and Moses have set us the example. "Freely ye have received, freely give." But the receiving comes first.

Meditation shows us the primacy of God. "Be still and know that I am God." Isaiah began his life of service with a vision of God. "I saw the Lord high and lifted up." Our deepest needs are not met with material things but with God. Chemistry can melt the hardest stone, but it cannot dissolve hate. Surgery can actually operate on the human heart, but it cannot mend a broken one. Jet planes can fly faster than sound, but with all their power they cannot usher us into the presence of God. In material things there is no limit to the inventive genius of science, but all the research in the world cannot create God's love. Meditation brings us to God. "Be still and know that I am God." —*Lora Lee Parrott*

We Christians know far too little about meditation upon the person of the Lord. Were more of our prayer time to be spent in quietly thinking of Him instead of in petition alone, were we to search the Word daily to learn of Him instead of looking only for things we think might immediately help us in our own concerns, we should have a higher appreciation of the loveliness of Christ. —*Frank E. Gaebelein*

*Thou hast put gladness in my heart . . .*  —Psalm 4:7

David was still a fugitive through the cruel treatment of his son Absalom, but instead of being filled with sadness his heart was running over with gladness. And what was the secret of it all? The Lord his God was the fountain-head of this river of joy. "Thou hast put gladness in my heart." There are many with smiles upon their faces while experiencing feelings of wretchedness and loneliness within their hearts. Divine joy, on the other hand, is the result of inward peace. Those who let the "peace of God rule in their hearts" know the experience of "the peace that passeth all understanding" keeping their "hearts and minds through Christ Jesus."

See also in our meditation for today David's condition compared with that of his foes. His worst experiences were superior to their greatest blessings. When exclaiming, "Thou hast put gladness in my heart," he was cut off from home and the sanctuary of his God. He was literally in a desert land where no water could be found, while they were in their home and in their city, amidst their harvest of plenty and apparent prosperity, for "their corn and their wine increase." But God's blessing was not with it, so that they felt sharp thorns within their feather pillows. David, it is true, was driven from his home, but he could not be driven from his God, and so he had "gladness" put within his "heart," causing him afterwards to exclaim: "Happy is the people whose God is the Lord."

—*John Roberts*

It is wonderful how glorious that life of faith becomes for him who is content to have nothing, or feel nothing, in himself, and always to live on the power of his Lord. He learns to understand what a joyful thing it is to know God as his strength.

—*Andrew Murray*

*Thou rulest the raging of the sea: when the waves thereof arise, thou stillest them.* —Psalm 89:9

An elderly Christian man of our acquaintance was rushed to the hospital for an emergency operation. The son, arriving just as the father was being wheeled to the operating room, inquired, "How are you, Dad?" The father replied with quiet confidence, "Even though the storm is raging without, son, there is always calmness when the Prince of Peace is in the vessel." This is what we, too, must learn. "Peace I leave with you, my peace I give unto you; not as the world giveth, give I unto you. Let not your heart be troubled, neither let it be afraid," Jesus said on one occasion (John 14:27).

The peace which our Savior gives is exclusive in its origin, for it is a peace which the world cannot give. It is exceptional in its character for it is not what the world speaks about, fights and dies for — an uncertain, unstable, unsatisfying something to grasp at but never to be sure the grip is firm and lasting. No, it is something real, something restful, something refreshing. It is excellent in its exhilarating force, for it is the assurance of forgiven sins, the confidence of a present salvation and the certainty of future glory. It is the joy of a bestowed victory, the knowledge of a new relationship and the satisfaction of a new life. It is second only to love in sweetness, in sound and in significance. —*S. Franklin Logsdon*

*Could fear remain when His voice spoke?*
*Could waves His will defy?*
*Twelve fearful men regained their peace,*
*When once He said, "Tis I."*

*The stormy winds blow hard today,*
*Our boat is tossed about;*
*But Jesus comes, and still He bids*
*His trustful child step out.*
—Dorothy Langlord

> *Commit thy way unto the Lord; trust also in Him; and He shall bring it to pass.*
>
> —Psalm 37:5

Yes, this is a familiar promise. You may have read it a thousand times, but today it stands before you as new and encouraging as the day you first saw it.

Let us look at it today with some little care. "Commit," it begins. Now the Hebrew word thus translated is *galal*, meaning "roll." So we are reminded that there are times when our way through life becomes a heavy burden. Then it is that we are "to roll" the whole thing—i.e. our entire course through life, including every single care and problem and burden, upon Him who cares for us.

And what is our Lord's part? Simply this: "And He shall bring it to pass." But take your Bible, beloved, and look carefully at those words. As you do so, you will see that the word "it" is italicized, which means that it is not in the original text. So there is actually in this place a blank. "And He shall bring . . . to pass." O believer, realize that you may fill in that blank with your dearest and most hallowed wish, your deepest need, your hardest problem. —*Frank E. Gaebelein*

> *Not half the storms that threaten me*
> *E'er broke upon my head.*
> *Not half the pains I've waited for*
> *E'er reached me or my bed.*
>
> *Not half the clouds that drifted by*
> *Have overshadowed me —*
> *Not half the dangers ever came*
> *I fancied I could see.*
>
> *Dear Heavenly Father, hold my hand*
> *Each moment lest I fall.*
> *Thine is the power to keep—my part*
> *To let Thee, that is all.*

*Wherefore be ye not unwise, but understanding what the will of the Lord is.* —Ephesians 5:17

There is a fourfold test by which I believe Christians may fully determine the will of God for the events of everyday living. First, the Bible cannot be ignored. It lays down broad and unmistakable principles by which life may be governed. God never wills anything for us which is contrary to revealed truth.

Secondly, the illumination and leadership of the Holy Spirit cannot be ignored. The Spirit of God and the Word of God must be combined.

Another test is the providential circumstances we meet in our daily walk wherein we find doors closed or opened. These, joined with the preceding spiritual exercises, will enable us to determine what is the will of God for a given situation.

Another factor that must be taken into account is the power of a sound mind. We read, "For God hath not given us the spirit of fear; but of power, and of love, and of a sound mind" (2 Tim. 1:7). A sound mind is one which is instructed in the truth and quickened by the Spirit, thus giving the Christian discernment.

It is said that a man had to descend into a deep well for some purpose. He misjudged the distance to the bottom and clung for his life to the end of the rope. It was too dark to see the bottom and he was too weak to climb up. Finally through sheer exhaustion he let go and dropped only a few inches to the bottom. Many of us have failed to trust ourselves to the whole will of God. We have gone part way until a "drop" of sheer faith was necessary, and we discovered that when we could do nothing else than fall into His plan for us, we were safe and secure. —*R. S. Beal*

*Be thou there until I bring thee word.*        —Matthew 2:13

All our movements should be under the direction of God. In very olden times God guided His people by a pillar of fire and cloud, which lifted and moved when they were to move, showing them the way, and which rested and settled down when they were to halt. In these days of so much fuller revelation there is no need for any such visible token of guidance, yet the guidance is no less real and no less unmistakable.

It was an angel that brought to Joseph the bidding to flee into Egypt. Angels do not usually appear to our eyes; but who will say that they do not whisper in our ears many a suggestion which we suppose to come from our own hearts? At least we know that in some way God will always tell us what to do; and if only we have ears to hear we shall never fail of guidance. We should always wait for God's bidding before taking any step. Especially in times of danger, when we are moving under His guidance, should we wait and not move until He brings us word.

It ought to give us great comfort and a wonderful sense of safety to know that God is caring for us so faithfully. Our whole duty is to be ready always to obey. Whenever the voice comes bidding us arise and depart, there is some reason for it, and we should not hesitate to obey. Wherever we are sent we should quietly stay till again God sends to call us away. The place of duty is always the place of safety, and we should never move until God brings us word.        —*J. R. Miller*

> *Back of the loaf is the snowy flour,*
> *And back of the flour the mill;*
> *And back of the mill is the wheat, and the shower,*
> *And the sun, and the Father's will.*
> —Maltbie D. Babcock

# JUNE 21

> *And the light of Israel shall be for a fire, and his Holy One for a flame: and it shall burn and devour his thorns and his briars in one day.* —Isaiah 10:17

Isaiah informs us of certain effects of the glory of God which are not at all pleasant; these are chastenings which seem for the present to be grievous, very grievous. "The Light of Israel will be for a Fire and His Holy One for a Flame."

Every bush that has ever glowed with the fire of God, can tell a story of *purging*; it was not all romance and splendor. The Glory of Israel is also *painful*! His initial ministry must consume "thorns and briars." The Light of the world cleanses Pilgrim by fire in order to make him ready for radiance; for *the price of shining, is purging*. A man must pass through lowly valleys to enter the Gates of Light; yea lower and lower must he sink in self-estimation as he comes near the Ancient of Days.

But rejoice, look up! Our God may bring us to His flame, but His purpose is never to destroy!

—*Richard Ellsworth Day*

If there is ever a time when God is near, it is when we are ill. Some of our greatest spiritual blessings come when we are laid aside from the daily round. While it may not always be His will to strengthen the body, He ever works to strengthen the soul of the afflicted believer. It is impossible for a child of God to suffer illness with a submissive will and not be spiritually blessed. Let us remember that when God makes our bed in our sickness, as the psalmist beautifully phrases it, He may be sending us to His school of advanced instruction in the life of the soul.

—*Frank E. Gaebelein*

*Because he believed in his God.*　　　　—Daniel 6:23

Oh, the conquests of real, vital faith in the Living God! The Lord Jesus has told us that if we have faith, as a grain of mustard-seed, we shall be able, in the power of the Spirit, to accomplish wonders for our God. Our faith, however, must be of the mustard-seed kind. That is to say, the proper kind. The importance is not in the size, but in the quality. A mustard-seed has life, and though it is small and may be buried in the earth out of sight, give it time and something will happen.

So it is with real living faith in the True and Living God. Daniel is a beautiful illustration of this. For his faithfulness both to God and man he was thrown into a lions' den, but without doubt it was one of the best all-nights of prayer and praise he had ever experienced. And in the morning, when the king called upon him to say, "Is thy God, whom thou servest continually, able to deliver thee from the lions?" he was able to reply: "My God has sent His angel, and hath shut the lions' mouths, that they have not hurt me."

Daniel was then "taken up out of the den, and no manner of hurt was found upon him." But why? The answer should be stamped upon our heart and memory and life: "Because he believed in his God." Well might our Master say, "All things are possible to him that believeth," because "all things are possible to God." O Lord, "Increase our faith," our faith in Thee, in Thy love, Thy power, Thy grace, and Thy providence!

—*John Roberts*

> *God knows, not I, the reason why*
> *His winds of storm drive through*
> *my door;*
> *I am content to live or die*
> *Just knowing this, nor knowing*
> *more.*
> *My Father's hand appointing me*
> *My days and ways, so I am free.*　　—Margaret E. Sangster

# JUNE 23

*There is no fear in love; but perfect love casteth out fear:
because fear hath torment. . . .* —1 John 4:18

Fear is the first-born of sin. "And the Lord God called unto Adam, and said unto him, Where art thou? And he said, I heard thy voice in the garden, and I was afraid, because I was naked; and I hid myself" (Genesis 3:9,10). "I was afraid." Ever since that sad evening, fear has sung its frightful shadow over the sons of men. The dragon of fear waits before every expectant mother to devour her child with its deadly fangs. How early does a child begin to fear! Love came in Bethlehem, with the Savior, and then followed the cry: "Fear not; it is I."

Ever since Bethlehem love has been the foe of fear. John would have us "fearless on the day of judgment," and so points us in a profound passage to "perfect love" as the foe of fear.

On what ground is our confidence based? "Because as he is, so are we in this world" (v. 17). He is righteous. So are we righteous in Him. The sum of righteousness is love. Christ is all love. We, in this world, indwelt by Christ and dwelling in God, are as He is.

We are in this world, but not of it. We belong to that world where Love rules and reigns. When that Love has gained the throne of our hearts it drives out fear; it hurls fear from the throne; it wrenches the scepter from the foul and filthy hand of fear. Fear has torment. It dreads the judgment. It trembles, and tries to hide from the face of Him who sitteth on the Throne (Revelation 6:15-17).

Perfect love gives faith in place of fear; trust in place of torment; peace in place of trembling; boldness in place of dread. —*John G. Ridley*

*Though He slay me, yet will I trust in Him.* —Job 13:15

To stand with the good things of life all stripped away, to stand beaten and buffeted by storms of disaster and disappointment, to stand with all our brethren saying, "Behold, how God hates him," and yet to know assuredly in our own hearts that God loves us, to know it so assuredly, with the communion that lies between our heart and His, that we can freely let go the outward tokens of His love, as the most true and trusty friends do not need to take gifts from one another for assurance of their affection — this surely is the perfection of a faithful life. It is the gathering up of all happiness into one happiness which is so rich that it can live without them all, and yet regally receives them into itself as the ocean receives the rivers. —*Phillips Brooks*

When the trials and tests of life come, let us remember Abraham's experiences of faith. Even though everything be dark and there seems to be no way out, and our prayers go unanswered, and the burdens become heavier, we can believe that God is dealing with us and permitting, yes, even sending, trials and tribulation in order to train, discipline and prepare us for even greater blessings and victories, and to make us more like the Lord Jesus, who Himself had to endure sufferings. God grant us faith and grace to trust Him always, in every trial of life. —*M. R. DeHaan*

> *Thou, Lord, alone, art all Thy children need,*
>   *And there is none beside;*
> *From Thee the streams of blessedness proceed,*
>   *In Thee the blest abide—*
> *Fountain of life, and all-abounding grace,*
> *Our source, our center, and our dwelling-place.*
> —Madame Guyon

# JUNE 25

*Casting all your care upon Him; for he careth for you.*
—1 Peter 5:7

Again and again throughout His Word, our Lord exhorts us to avoid anxious care. Clearly, care, even though occasioned by real problems, is, if carried to excess, a sin in the sight of God. Again and again throughout Scripture God tells His children to cast all their cares upon Him.

The very essence of anxious care is a presumption on the creature's part that he is wiser than his Creator. Anxious care is in reality trusting ourselves to do what we cannot trust our Lord to do.

In reality, we try to think of those things which we fancy God has forgotten. We stagger about beneath a load which we have been unwilling to turn over to our Heavenly Load-bearer. This presumption on our part is plain disobedience to His commands and lack of belief in His Word.

More than this, however, anxious care often leads into acts of sin — forsaking God as Counselor and relying instead upon human wisdom. It is as if one were to go to a broken pump for water instead of going directly to the spring which provided the water for the pump.

On the other hand, if we cast our burden upon Him, cast each burden as it comes along upon Him, in simple faith, and if we are "careful for nothing" because He takes care of us, it will keep us in close communion with Him and strengthen us to meet every temptation. It was truly a wise man who said, "Thou wilt keep him in perfect peace whose mind is stayed (resting) on thee, because he trusteth in thee" (Isaiah 26:3).

*It's never easy, but take God's hand*
*And pray till night has passed;*
*Just trust nor ask to understand—*
*And peace will come—at last.*
—Phyllis C. Michael

*And whatsoever ye shall ask in my name, that will I do, that the Father may be glorified in the Son.* —John 14:13

Prayer puts God in the matter with commanding force: "Ask of Me things to come concerning My sons," says God, "and concerning the work of My hands command ye Me." We are charged in God's Word "always to pray," in everything by prayer, continuing instant in prayer," to "pray everywhere," "praying always." The promise is as illimitable as the command is comprehensive. "All things whatsoever ye ask in prayer, believing, ye shall receive," "whatever ye shall ask," "if ye shall ask anything." "Ye shall ask what ye will and it shall be done unto you." If there is anything not involved in "All things whatsoever," or not found in the phrase "Ask anything," then these things may be left out of prayer. Language could not cover a wider range, nor involve more fully all things. These statements are but samples of the all-comprehending possibilities of prayer under the promises of God to those who meet the conditions of right praying. —*E. M. Bounds*

We will never know the glory of the impossible until we have learned to pray in His name. If the blessed Name of Jesus is stamped on our prayers, they will always reach their destination. But no prayer ever reaches God the Father except through the precious Name of God the Son. Hear Him: "I am the way, the truth, and the life; no man cometh unto the Father, but by me" (John 14:6).

We have nothing to commend us at our heavenly Father's throne, but when we present ourselves in the matchless Name of the Father's Son, a throne of judgment is changed into a throne of Grace, and we are accepted in the Beloved!

— *David M. Dawson*

# JUNE 27

*Behold, I stand at the door, and knock: if any man hear my voice, and open the door, I will come in to him, and will sup with him, and he with Me.* —Revelation 3:20

I doubt that I know of a passage in the whole Bible which throws greater light upon prayer than this one does. It is, it seems to me, the key which opens the door into the holy and blessed realm of prayer.

This teaches us, in the first place, that it is not our prayer which moves the Lord Jesus. It is Jesus who moves us to pray. He knocks. Thereby He makes known His desire to come in to us. Our prayers are always a result of Jesus' knocking at our hearts' doors.

From time immemorial prayer has been spoken of as the breath of the soul. And the figure is an excellent one indeed.

The air which our body requires envelops us on every hand. The air of itself seeks to enter our bodies and, for this reason, exerts pressure upon us. It is well known that it is more difficult to hold one's breath than it is to breathe. We need but exercise our organs of respiration, and air will enter forthwith into our lungs and perform its life-giving function to the entire body.

The air which our souls need also envelops all of us at all times and on all sides. God is round about us in Christ on every hand, with His many-sided and all-sufficient grace. All we need to do is to open our hearts.

Prayer is the breath of the soul, the organ by which we receive Christ into our parched and withered hearts.

He says, "If any man open the door, I will come in to him." Notice carefully every word here. It is not our prayer which draws Jesus into our hearts. Nor is it our prayer which moves Jesus to come in to us. All He needs is access. He enters in wherever He is not denied admittance. —*O. Hallesby*

Only through prayer is God's purpose wrought in this age. Therefore, as "workers together with Him," we must pray "with all prayer and supplication in the Spirit, and watching thereunto in all perseverance and supplication for all the saints" (Eph. 6:18). True prayer is the Holy Spirit's voice echoing in our souls. We must, therefore, be completely dominated by the Spirit, or we may be found praying for that which is diametrically opposed to God's eternal purposes for our lives and His work. Praise God, "The Spirit also helpeth our infirmities: for we know not what we should pray for as we ought" (Rom. 8:26). God, by His Spirit, prays in us, and through us! Effectual prayer would be impossible for us if we were left to ourselves. —*David M. Dawson*

*Prayer is the breath of God in man,*
*Returning whence it came;*
*Love is the sacred fire within,*
*And prayer the rising flame.*

*It gives the burdened spirit ease,*
*And soothes the troubled breast;*
*Yields comfort to the mourners here,*
*And to the weary rest.*

*When God inclines the heart to pray,*
*He hath an ear to hear;*
*To Him there's music in a groan,*
*And beauty in a tear.*

*The humble suppliant cannot fail*
*To have His wants supplied,*
*Since He for sinners intercedes*
*Who once for sinners died.*
—Benjamin Beddome

# JUNE 28

*The Lord also will be a refuge for the oppressed, a refuge in*
*times of trouble.*                                    —Psalm 9:9

It will always give a Christian the greatest calm, quiet, ease
and peace, to think of the perfect righteousness of Christ.
How often are the saints of God downcast and sad! I do not
think they ought to be. I do not think they would if they could
always see their perfection in Christ. When the believer says,
"I live on Christ alone; I rest on Him solely for salvation; and I
believe that, however unworthy, I am still saved in Jesus";
then there rises up as a motive of gratitude this thought —
"Shall I not live to Christ? Shall I not love Him and serve
Him, seeing that I am saved by His merits?" "The love of
Christ constraineth us," "that they which live should not
henceforth live unto themselves, but unto Him which died
for them." If saved by imputed righteousness, we shall greatly
value imparted righteousness.

It certainly is not possible for us to be in a position where
Omnipotence cannot assist us. God has servants everywhere.
There are "treasures hid in the sand," and the Lord's chosen
shall eat thereof. When the clouds hide the mountains they
are as real as in the sunshine; so the promise and the
Providence of God are unchanged by the obscurity of our
faith, or the difficulties of our position.

When we are at our worst let us trust with unshaking faith.
Recollect that then is the time when we can most glorify God
by faith.                                    —*Charles H. Spurgeon*

*There is a Rock the earthquake cannot shake.*
*There is a Light the shadows cannot hide.*
*There is a heart that sorrow cannot break.*
*There is a friendship that is true and tried.*
*And though I walk the valley dark and grim,*
*God's word is sure; I shall have peace in Him.*
                                    —Myra Brooks Welch

*I press toward the mark for the prize of the high calling of God in Christ Jesus.* —Philippians 3:14

Always stand at the bow! Leave the stern with its backward look and make for the bow. To spend time in sad review of past sins and failures is not to put them to the best account. Confess them, and believe that for Christ's dear sake they are absolutely forgiven! Failure often provides the material for success, and our dead selves may become the stepping-stones to better things. Did not our Lord say to His disciples: "Sleep on now and take your rest"—the past is irreparable—but immediately He added: "Arise, let us be going!"—the future is available. Therefore, leave the stern with its backward look, and make for the bow.

True, the sky before us may be dark with storm-clouds. The weather-prophets say that the world is shedding its old sanctions without replacing them with better ones; that seven civilizations have already passed, and we are to see the death of the eighth. Be it so, but they forget that when the earth was without form and void, the Spirit of God brooded in the chaos and darkness, creating the heavens and earth.

Look out to the vast circle of the horizon, and prepare for the new lands to be explored, the wonderful discoveries that await us, the great missions hidden in the future which are waiting to be fulfilled. Never doubt that the clouds will break. Never dream that wrong will triumph. Never count yourself God-forsaken or forgotten. The Master may seem to be asleep on His pillow, oblivious and uncaring, but His hand is on the helm. He guides our course. He rules the waves and they obey Him.

In all His dispensations God is at work for our good. In prosperity He tries our gratitude; in mediocrity, our contentment; in misfortune, our submission; in darkness, our faith; under temptation, our steadfastness; and at all times, our obedience and trust in Him. —*Anonymous*

# JUNE 30

*He said unto them, When ye pray, say, Our Father . . .*
—Luke 11:2

We must pray—probably the most important of all Bible directions for living the Christian life, and the most difficult. Jesus prayed—probably the strongest argument for our need of prayer.

Inspired directly by His perfect prayer habits and prayer technique, the disciples requested a lesson on prayer, and He responded immediately. He prayed Himself, and He expected us to pray. He prayed effectively and acceptably to God; He expects His followers to learn to do the same.

*How pray?* Person to person, directly. As man to God, reverently, but as child to Father, simply, trustfully; for we have been adopted into the family of heaven. Sincerely, for in secret, with no eye to show or parade; however many may be listening, we are closeted in spirit, shut in alone with God.

How pray? In orderly fashion. We are not to rush in to that Presence uttering the first words that come into our minds, or that come to our lips without ever reaching our minds. Of course we are free to do so if we wish, but we may waste our words. God will pay attention when we pay attention.

Jesus suggests an order which takes time to realize first to whom we are speaking—first and last. If we would follow that suggestion faithfully, our prayers would have a grip of faith and power. Time can be wasted in saying prayers, but not in talking with God.

*There's a blessing in prayers, in believing prayer,*
*When our Savior's name to the throne we bear;*
*Then a Father's love will receive us there —*
*There is always a blessing, a blessing in prayer.*
—Bertha Munro

*But if we hope for that we see not, then do we with patience wait for it.*
—Romans 8:25

God wants to strengthen our faith. Only exercise can give strength. We know how true this is in the physical realm; we must use our bodies and our muscles as well as our minds if our bodies are to grow. The same is true of our faith. The faith which is not exercised is a faith which will not grow; a faith which is not tried will never be strong. Faith is believing what we cannot see and understand.

According to Scripture, faith is the substance of things hoped for, the evidence of things not seen. The very fact that you cannot understand why God deals with you in the way in which He does is for the purpose of making you exercise your faith. If we could understand all of God's dealings, we would not need faith.

I need no faith to see a tree when my eyes are open, or to hear the birds when my hearing is good, but to believe the things which we cannot see and cannot understand and cannot fathom—that is faith. We exercise faith when we accept the promise of Almighty God. If you are laid aside and you have been asking the question, "Why must I suffer? Why cannot I be like others?" then remember that God says, "All things work together for good to them that love God, to them who are the called according to his purpose." That is God's promise. You may not understand why, but you receive and accept His Word, and believe that what God sends to you is the best for you.
—M. R. DeHaan

*Some day He'll make it plain to me;*
*Some day when I His face shall see.*
*Some day from tears I shall be free,*
*For some day I shall understand.*

# JULY 2

*They shall perish; but thou remainest; and they all shall wax old as doth a garment . . .* — Hebrews 1:11

Most of the gifts of earth deteriorate with time and with use. The gold ring, placed so tenderly on the maiden's finger at the marriage altar, becomes thin and worn with the years. The wedding dress must be soon laid away, for its materials are so thin and frail that a little use soon destroys its usefulness. The automobile, made of steel and wood, becomes damaged by the hazards of the road, wears out with the long mileage, and must be replaced. Houses become uninhabitable by reason of the storm, the wind and the weather. Cities become buried in the sand because of the destroying winds from the desert. Ships strike hidden reefs and rocks, and flounder in the depths of the sea. Strong bodies fade and fall. Fine woods are eaten by the worms, and the best of books become powder by reason of air and dampness. Only Christ remains! The Scripture has said, "They shall fail, but Thou remainest."

—*Walter L. Wilson*

*Joy of my soul, thou Savior dear,*
*It is so sweet when Thou art near;*
*In Thy blest love all fear I hide,*
*Most gracious Lord, in me abide.*

*Keep Thou the vigil of my heart,*
*Lest from my soul Thy grace depart;*
*Oh! may Thy love fill every need,*
*For on Thy bounty I would feed.*

*Oh! may no earthly shadow fall,*
*Around my heart, Lord, keep it all;*
*Be Thou the light of Heavenly fire;*
*Thy Spirit, Lord, I so desire.*

—Joseph Swain

*But straightway Jesus spake unto them, saying, Be of good
cheer; it is I; be not afraid.* —Matthew 14:27

Christ is still able to quiet the tempest and subdue storms.
He can still work the miracle of bringing peace and quiet out
of turmoil and discord, but it is not always His will to do so.
When He permits the storm to rage, His very presence in the
lives of those who know and love Him brings peace and
confidence in the midst of the storm. It is a wonderful thing
to know the Savior, who is able to settle strife and subdue
discord and bring peace out of tumult. It is even more
wonderful, to have a Lord who can give inward peace and
confidence to His followers in the midst of the storm it is not
His divine will to subdue.

Into every life comes a time of tempest when the winds
blow and the waves beat and the seas threaten to engulf. In
such a time the very presence of the Savior is able to impart
within our souls a sense of security and calm in amazing
contrast to the tempest about us. In the midst of the storm
which He permits to rage, He comes to His own, walking on
the very waves which would become still if He should so
command. He does not address the raging elements. He speaks
instead to the frightened and storm-tossed ones. Above the
sound of the storm and the surge of the seas comes the
melody of His voice, "It is I; be not afraid," and all is quiet
and peaceful within their breasts. So amid the storms of our
lives He speaks to His own, "My peace I give unto you: not as
the world giveth, give I unto you. Let not your heart be
troubled, neither let it be afraid." —*Bob Jones, Jr.*

*Drop thy still dews of quietness till all our striving cease;*
*Take from our souls the strain and stress,*
*And let our ordered lives confess*
*The beauty of thy Peace.*

—John Greenleaf Whittier

# July 4

*Stand fast therefore in the liberty wherewith Christ hath made us free. . . .*  —Galatians 5:1

Freedom is a priceless possession. Yet it can be had as a free gift from God. God through Christ provided freedom from the law and opened the way into the marvelous liberty of the dispensation of grace. In this liberty provided through Christ we have free access, first of all, to the charter of true liberty, the Bible. All the promises of God's Word, promises like: "When thou passest through the rivers I will be with thee" and "The mountains shall depart, and the hills be removed, but my kindness shall not depart from thee" become ours. As a child of God you are a welcome guest at the bountifully spread table of promises like these. God's Word is a never-failing treasure house full of the boundless stores of grace. God's Word is the bank of Heaven from which you may draw as you please without limitation or obstacle.

This liberty also paves the way for the Christian to come in faith for the blessing of God. In the midst of trial and tribulations, in the midst of distress and sorrow, let the blessings of your Father's love freely give comfort and guide you.

In this new liberty the believer also has free access to the throne of grace. At all times, in all circumstances, God's redeemed child has access to his Heavenly Father. Whatever difficulties, whatever problems, the child of God may feel free to approach his Heavenly Father.

> *I cannot see the end,*
> *The hidden meaning of each trial sent,*
> *The pattern into which each tangled thread is bent,*
> *I cannot see the end;*
> *But I can trust,*
> *And in God's changless love I am content.*

*Why take ye thought for raiment? Consider the lilies . . .*
—Matthew 6:28

Without any toiling or spinning on their own part, God clothes the flowers in loveliness far surpassing any adornment which the most skillful human arts can provide. Flowers bloom but a day and fade. We are better than flowers. If our Father lavishes so much beauty on perishing plants, is there any danger that He will not provide raiment for His own?

We ought to study the beautiful things in nature and learn lessons from them. Here it is a lesson of contentment we are to learn. Who ever heard a lily complaining about its circumstances? It accepts life's conditions.

The lily grows from within. So ought we to grow, having within us the Divine life, to be developed in our character and spirit. The lily is an emblem of beauty; our spiritual life should unfold likewise in all lovely ways. It is a picture of perfect peace. Who ever saw wrinkles of anxiety in a lily's face? God wants us to grow into peace. The lily is fragrant; so should our lives be. The lily sometimes grows in the black bog, but it remains unspotted. Thus should we live in this world, keeping ourselves unspotted amid its evil. These are a few of the lessons from the lily.

—*J. R. Miller*

> *I do not know what may befall,*
> *Of sunshine or of rain;*
> *I do not know what may be mine,*
> *Of pleasure and of pain;*
> *But this I know—my Savior knows,*
> *And whatsoe'er it be,*
> *Still I can trust His love to give*
> *What will be best for me.*

—E. Margaret Clarkson

# July 6

The way of Christ as King, according to David's description, is like "clear shining after rain," whereby the tender grass is made to spring out of the earth. So have we often seen it. After a heavy shower of rain, or after a continued rainy season, when the sun shines, there is a delightful clearness and freshness in the air that we seldom perceive at other times. Perhaps the brightest weather is just when the rain has ceased, when the wind has driven away the clouds, and the sun peers forth from his chambers to gladden the earth with smiles.

And thus is it with the Christian's exercised heart. Sorrow does not last forever. After the pelting rain of adversity comes ever and anon the clear shining. Tried believer, consider this. After all your afflictions there remains a rest for the people of God. There is a clear shining coming to your soul when all this rain is past. When your time of rebuke is over and gone, it shall be to you as the earth when the tempest has sobbed itself to sleep, when the clouds have rent themselves to rags, and when the sun peers forth once more as a bridegroom in his glorious array. To this end, sorrow cooperates with the bliss that follows it, like rain and sunshine, to bring forth the tender blade. The tribulation and the consolation work together for our good.                    —C. H. Spurgeon

*The world's fierce winds are blowing*
*Temptations sharp and keen;*
*I feel a peace in knowing,*
*My Savior stands between.*

*For we which live are alway delivered unto death for Jesus' sake, that the life also of Jesus might be made manifest in our mortal flesh.* —2 Corinthians 4:11

What a blessed message for the afflicted soul. Oh! child of God, lift up your head for your redemption draws nigh. It is not in vain that you suffer. There can be no gold without the refiner's fire. Christ is glorified in your patience. You are bidden to count it all joy when you suffer divers testings (James 1:2). From your wounds healing streams of life— Christ's own life—are flowing. This will make for the increase and edification of Christ's body. What you suffer will deepen your "death—identification—position" with Christ. The corn of wheat must fall into the ground and die, else it abides alone.

"O thou afflicted, tossed with tempest, and not comforted, behold, I will lay thy stones with fair colors, and lay thy foundations with sapphires" (Isa. 54:11).

"For as the sufferings of Christ abound in us, so our consolation also aboundeth by Christ" (2 Cor. 1:5).

—*F. J. Huegel*

*Oh, like the air about us that we breathe,*
*As limitless and all-encompassing;*
*And like the earth beneath us that we tread*
*As strong, as solid, and unvarying;*
*And like the sky above, where sun and stars*
*In old, unalterable orbits swing;*

*So is Thy grace to us, O God of grace!*
*Pledge of Thy mercy, promise of Thy might*
*Changeless through all the sorrows of the day,*
*Changeless through all the terrors of the night,*
*A present peace, a certain comforting,*
*Sustaining joy and everlasting light.*
—Annie Johnson Flint

# July 8

*I am the vine, ye are the branches: He that abideth in me,
and I in him, the same bringeth forth much fruit: for without
me ye can do nothing.* —John 15:5

This is what our Lord would teach His disciples then. This
is what He would teach us now. What we Christians need
today more than anything else is to hear our Savior saying
once again: "Without me ye can do nothing"; and the word
which we need to emphasize in order to get the full force of
this teaching is the word nothing. Ah, perhaps in our pride we
will protest. Perhaps we will say: "Oh, I don't believe that.
Surely I can do something in myself to glorify God. If not,
why do I have all these wonderful powers and faculties—the
mind, emotions, and will?" They are only shallow and
superficial thinkers who feel that they are quite sufficient in
themselves to be good and to do good to the glory of God.
The man of sensitive conscience has discovered that when he
would do good, evil is present with him, and he can do nothing
in and of himself. He has made this discovery: apart from
Christ—helplessness; but with Christ—omnipotence; for over
against the statement—"Without me ye can do nothing," stands
the statement—"I can do all things through Christ which
strengtheneth me." —Howard W. Ferrin

*Give me Thy strength for my day, Lord,
    That wheresoe'er I go,
There shall no danger daunt me
    And I shall fear no foe . . .*

*So shall no grief o'erwhelm me,
    So shall no wave o'erflow;
Give me Thy strength for my day, Lord,
    Cover my weakness so.*
—Annie Johnson Flint

*Wherefore He is able to save them to the uttermost that come unto God by Him.*
—Hebrews 7:25

Can any of us define how far "the uttermost" is? How far from the earth, for instance, is the uttermost star in the heavens? Well, if we knew that distance and even if we could sin to the extent of getting that far away from God, Christ would still be able to save us. The blessed truth is simply this, that no one is ever beyond saving, provided that he comes to God through Christ. And there, in that qualification, lies the only reason why men die in their sins when redemption is freely offered them. They die in their sins just because they refuse to "come unto God by Him." Because they insist upon coming in their own way and thus spurning God's gift of His Son, they are lost.
— *Frank E. Gaebelein*

Most of the grand truths of God have to be learned by trouble; they must be burned into us with the hot iron of affliction, otherwise we shall not truly receive them. No man is competent to judge in matters of the kingdom, until first He has been tried; since there are many things to be learned in the depths which we can never know in the heights. He shall best meet the wants of God's people who has had those wants himself.
—*Charles H. Spurgeon*

*So many burdened lives along the way!*
*My load seems lighter than the most I see,*
*And oft I wonder if I could be brave,*
*Patient and sweet if they were laid on me.*

*But God has never said that He would give*
*Another's grace without another's thorn;*
*What matter, since for every day of mine*
*Sufficient grace for me comes with the morn?*
—Annie Johnson Flint

# JULY 10

*And ye shall find rest unto your souls.* —Matthew 11:29

Yes, it is rest that we need, for life with its drudgeries, its sin and its turmoil brings on a weariness that cannot be prevented! The burdens we bear, the thorns in the flesh which we must endure and the cross that is laid upon each of us bring about this world-weariness. We who have heeded the glorious Gospel call to "rest in the Lord" and therefore possess the earnest of better things, ought so much the more to anticipate the wondrous promise of that immortal promise: "Blessed are the dead which die in the Lord . . . (for) they may rest from their labors." After the fever of life . . . after weariness, sickness and despondency; after struggling and partially succeeding, and struggling and failing utterly; after all the change and decay of this troubled and unhealthy state at length "come the angelic messengers of peace, the Throne of God, and the beatific vision." Yes, there is an end to this earthly pilgrimage and for the saved it is bright, grand, tranquil and blessedly certain!

*—Henry G. Bosch*

*This is the hope that sustains us,*
*This is our lamp in the night,*
*This is the beacon we follow,*
*Waiting till faith becomes sight.*

*This is our pillow at night time,*
*The promise in each golden dawn;*
*This is the spur for the sluggard,*
*"Occupy while I am gone."*

*This is our heart's choicest treasure,*
*Balm for our sorrow and pain,*
*Words that are precious as rubies,*
*"Christ Jesus is coming again!"*
*—Martha Snell Nicholson*

*. . . thy love to me was wonderful . . .* —2 Samuel 1:26

Here David speaks of Jonathan's love, but today you and I are going to consider the wonderful love of, not Jonathan, but Jesus. We will not be thinking of those things we have been told—but of those things which we have ourselves experienced of the matchless and marvelous love of Christ.

When we were still wandering afar off, the love of Jesus was wonderful, restraining us from committing that sin which is unto death and withholding us from self-destruction. It was this same wonderful love of Jesus which removed from us the false assurance of self-righteousness and made us feel the true guilt of our sinful selves. This same love of Jesus comforted us in our realization of our lost condition and said, "Come unto Me and I will give you rest." Then came the wonderful assurance, "I am thine and thou art *Mine.*" This same wonderful love of Jesus comes to us moment by moment and day by day to comfort and strengthen us in our everyday problems. As we have entered our valleys and struggled over the hard places, that love has come upon us to lift us to realms of glory in contemplation of God's care. And that same love assures us even now that a mansion in the Heavenly home is being prepared for us—that we are bound for eternal bliss in the presence of Him who bought us with His precious Blood.

> *He lives to still His people's fears*
> *He lives to wipe away their tears*
> *He lives their mansions to prepare;*
> *He lives to bring them safely there.*

# JULY 12

*My voice shalt thou hear in the morning, O Lord; in the morning will I direct my prayer unto thee, and will look up.*
—Psalm 5:3

Prayer is a primary factor in our Christian lives, not a secondary one; it is fundamental, not supplemental. If we confess our prayerlessness as sin, we'll find that genuine, heartfelt repentance will bring a real blessing to our souls. Of course, Christian life is not just a life of praying all the time. No, not at all. God wants us to think and to study His Word and to serve Him. Certain blessings come only with working for the Lord. But certain blessings do come only through prayer, too.

Well, then, what is prayer?

Bunyan defines prayer as "a shield to the soul, a sacrifice to God, and a scourge for Satan." Phillips Brooks says: "A prayer, in its simplest definition, is merely a wish turned heavenward. Prayer is not conquering God's reluctance, but taking hold upon God's willingness." In simple, everyday language, prayer is talking with God—not to God, but with Him.

—*Betty Zimmerman*

*I know not by what methods rare,*
*But this I know, God answers prayer.*
*I know that He has given His Word,*
*Which tells me prayer is always heard,*
*And will be answered, soon or late.*
*And so I pray and calmly wait.*

*I know not if the blessing sought*
*Will come in just the way I thought;*
*But leave my prayers with Him alone,*
*Whose will is wiser than my own,*
*Assured that He will grant my quest,*
*Or send some answer far more blest.*
—Eliza M. Hickok

*Blessed are the pure in heart: for they shall see God.*
—Matthew 5:8

*Face to face I shall behold Him,*
*Far beyond the starry sky;*
*Face to face in all His glory,*
*I shall see Him by and by!*
—Mrs. Frank A. Breck

This is the glory of the goal of life—face to face with Him. It begins now. It is a very real thing. This is a bit of the meaning of that mountain beatitude, "the pure in heart . . . shall see God."

Yet only he who sees understands what seeing means. The subtle intensity of God's presence cannot be explained, only understood by the purified in heart. Only the opened eyes see.

But this is only a beginning. There will be the far greater glory of the final goal, as we come into His immediate presence, literally face to face. That may be when we are called away from the lower road up to the higher reaches, above the clouds and the blue, the glory-reaches, up where He now sits. It may be by that goal coming nearer, by Himself actually coming on the clouds in great glory, for His own and for the next chapter in His great world-plan. Then we shall be caught up into His presence. Then we shall be fully like Him, for we shall see Him as He is and we shall be sharers in His Glory.
—S. D. Gordon

*Face to face—and that forever;*
*Face to face, where naught can sever;*
*I shall see Him in His beauty, face to face;*
*I have caught faint glimpses here,*
*Seen through many a falling tear,*
*But—what glory when I see Him face to face!*
—Annie Johnson Flint

# JULY 14

*He that descended is the same also that ascended up far
above all heavens, that He might fill all things.*
—Ephesians 4:10

How low did He descend? He bowed from the heavens,
and came down, and darkness was under His feet. Down to
hunger and thirst, to agony and bloody sweat, to the cross and
Passion; down to death and burial even in a borrowed tomb;
down to the shadow-world of Hades, to the spirits in prison,
and if there be any lower, thither!

But He ascended from these low depths, with the keys of
Death and Hades at His girdle. He ascended on high, leading
captivity captive; and as He passed upward, He annexed each
province as He went. This same Jesus who descended is now
ascended, with no change in His nature, that He may fill all
hearts with grace and love.

Is there one person who reads this page, in loneliness,
poverty, sickness, sorrow, and pain, that can fail to get this
comfort? Read the Gospels again as the Diary and Day-Book
of the Living Savior! He that descended is the same also that
ascended; and He ascended that He might fill the lowest
depths of human need. Though ascended to the right hand of
the Majesty on high, He is the same loving, tender Savior as
when the children flocked around His knees, and His tears
brimmed over at the grave of His friend.      —F. B. Meyer

> *Now I have found a friend*
> *Jesus is mine;*
> *His love shall never end,*
> *Jesus is mine.*
> *Though earthly joys decrease,*
> *Though earthly friendships cease,*
> *Now I have everlasting peace;*
> *Jesus is mine.*
> —Henry Hope

*My God shall supply all your need according to His riches in
glory by Christ Jesus.* —Philippians 4:19

To really believe in the all-sufficiency of God means to
believe that He is actually at liberty to do for us all that we
need a God for, and that we have a right to take Him for
everything for which we are unequal and insufficient. It means
that He has promised all things necessary for life and godliness,
that He has provided all things, and that we have a right to
come to Him for all things, presenting without question the
mighty check on the bank of heaven, "My God shall supply all
your need according to His riches in glory by Christ Jesus."

It means that we have a God who is equal to our salvation
and the salvation of any sinner, however lost and however
long he has resisted the mercy and grace of God. It means
that God is equal to your sanctification and the sanctification
of any temperament, no matter how impracticable; the
counteracting of any habit no matter how confirmed; the
overcoming of any defect, infirmity and sin, no matter how
deeply rooted and aggravated; victory over any and every
temptation that may come, and a life sanctified through and
through and preserved blameless unto the coming of the Lord
Jesus Christ. —*A. B. Simpson*

*There is such strength, my soul doth ask no greater,*
*For Christ, in me, a work hath now begun*
*And I have all the strength of earth's Creator!*
*'Tis not my strength but Christ's, and we are one!*
—Connie Calenberg

# JULY 16

*The Lord is my helper, and I will not fear what man shall do unto me.*
　　　　　　　　　　　　　　　　　　　—Hebrews 13:6

The Lord is a *constant* helper. This was David's comfort in a day of distress: "God is our refuge and strength, a very present help in trouble." Our Lord is not a fairweather companion only. When the dark hour comes, when the storm beats about us, when the grievous blow falls, He is the Friend that "sticketh closer than a brother."

What is more, the Lord is a *present* helper. Turn to David's word again: "God is our refuge and strength, a very *present help* in trouble." Our Lord is not merely a distant spectator of our concerns, far removed from us in a far-off sky. He is a "present" help. How oft when we most need our human loved ones they cannot get to us! It is never thus with our heavenly Helper. Not only is our Lord a "help," and a help in "trouble," and a "present" help; He is a "very" present help—as though He would draw still closer to our hearts than even the word "present" conveys. How the Divine love heaps up these tender words of assurance!

Must we not also add that the Lord is an *individual* helper? Most certainly is He the helper of His people and their cause considered collectively: but He is more than the God of the multitude. Each of His people may boldly say, "The Lord is *my* helper." Thrice-blessed word—"*my* helper"!

　　　　　　　　　　　　　　　　　　　—J. Sidlow Baxter

*In darkest hours I hear a voice,*
　　*Which comes my saddened heart to cheer,*
*Saying in tones of love, "Rejoice!*
　　*Jesus is near!"*
　　　　　　　　　　　—Robert Cassie Waterston

*For he that is called in the Lord, being a servant, is the Lord's freeman.*
　　　　　　　　　　　　　　　　　　—1 Corinthians 7:22

Bondage for God's children? No trial can reach you without God's permission, and God's notice—or without God's way through and out. (Sometimes suffering is the only way God can get your ear.) He always hears the sighing and groaning and crying of His own. Even while you are groaning He is raising up your deliverer.

Bondage cannot hold you down unless you forget God in it. The more afflicted, the more multiplied. There always is the promise: God "will come and save." The gates of brass and bars of iron shall be broken in pieces. And there is the covenant of soul deliverance, sealed by the blood of Christ. Faith can, if it chooses, laugh at the impossible.

Bondage comes in many sorts and from many causes: illness, poverty, personality handicaps, other people, circumstances, your own spirit. But the only hopeless bondage is that of your spirit. When you submit with the soul of a slave, you lock the door of freedom from the inside. No one can set you free. Even in trouble you choose between the mount of blessing and the mount of cursing.

Life always hems in and circumscribes. If we wish, we can look at the limitations, and despair. But there are no hampering limits to the Christian who believes God. The Philippian jail is not bondage to Paul if thereby he is proving he can do all things through Christ. Prison was not prison to Madame Guyon if there her soul learned to sing in the shadows.

*But toiling in life's dusty way,*
*The Rock's blessed shadow, how sweet!*

　　　　　　　　　　　　　　　　　　*—Bertha Munro*

# JULY 18

*He went a little farther . . . and prayed.* —Matthew 26:39

What an example for prayer we have in the Lord Jesus! Whenever He was in trouble He went to His Father about it in prayer. And surely He has, in this respect, left us an example that we should follow in His steps. But in this prayer we have, perhaps, all the features of effectual prayer.

First, the Lord was alone with God. It is well not to forsake the assembling of ourselves together, for the Lord has promised to be in the midst "where two or three are gathered together in His name." But Cornelius said, "I prayed in my house," and the result of his doing so is described in Acts 10:31. And we shall do well if we frequently go "a little farther" from all our friends to get alone with God.

But this prayer was also the prayer of humility: Christ "fell on His face." It was childlike: He "prayed, saying, O My Father." It was to the point: "Let this cup pass from Me." And it was with perseverance and resignation: He "prayed the third time, saying the same words," but concluded with: "Not as I will, but as Thou wilt."

Can we possibly have a more complete lesson on prayer than this? Whatever our needs are, we may make them known to God if we do so on these Divine principles. Yes, we may even lay all our *wants* before Him if we sincerely add: "Thy will be done." Oh, to live always in the atmosphere of prayer and faith, with our will running parallel with God's! His will being done in us, by us, and through us.

> *Lord Jesus, make Thyself to me*
> *A living, bright reality;*
> *More present to faith's vision keen*
> *Than any outward object seen;*
> *More dear, more intimately nigh*
> *Than e'en the sweetest earthly tie.*
> —Author Unknown

*And hereby we know that he abideth in us, by the Spirit which he hath given us.* —1 John 3:24

Every child of God has need of the assurance of faith: the full certitude of faith that the Lord has received him and made him His child. The Holy Scripture always speaks to Christians as those who know that they are redeemed, that they are now children of God, and that they have received eternal life.

There are many Christians who think that faith in the Word is not sufficient to give full certitude: they would prefer something more. They imagine that assurance, a sure inward feeling or conviction, is what is given above or outside of faith. This is wrong. As I have need of nothing more than the word of a trustworthy man to give me complete certitude, so must the Word of God be my certitude. People err because they seek something in themselves and in their feeling. No: the whole of salvation comes from God: the soul must not be occupied with itself or its work, but with God: he who forgets himself to hear what God says, and to rely upon His promise as something worthy of credit, has in this fact the fullest assurance of faith. He does not doubt the promises, but is strong in faith, giving God the glory, and being fully assured that what He has promised God is also able to perform.

— *Andrew Murray*

*When nothing whereon to lean remains,*
*When strongholds crumble to dust;*
*When nothing is sure but that God still reigns,*
*That is just the time to trust.*

*'Tis better to walk by faith than sight,*
*In this path of yours and mine;*
*And the pitch-black night, when there's no other light,*
*Is the time for our faith to shine.*

—Clifford Lewis

# July 20

How can you lose heart when you follow such a Leader? It is said that at Waterloo, when the Duke of Wellington rode up, soldiers exposed to the hottest fire became as calm and steady as if on parade; his presence on the field of battle was worth a brigade of troops that day. And why? Because of the confidence he inspired. And shall not we have faith in the Captain of our Salvation, who singlehanded has worsted all our foes? What though that faith be tried? There is a day coming when "it shall be found to praise and honor and glory at the appearing of Jesus Christ." Let us keep our eyes on our Leader, remembering that after all the battle is not ours but God's; that it is our part to trust, and His to deliver us.

Are you tempted to plead the difficulties of your case, the peculiar character of your circumstances? Do you say that if these were altered your life would be different too? Be assured that it is not new circumstances you need, but a new apprehension of Christ in the midst of them. He is above all circumstances; nay, since He is Perfect Wisdom as well as Perfect Love, it may be that He Himself has brought you (even as He brought Joshua at this time) into these trying surroundings for the express purpose of giving you a new revelation of Himself. It is not until we are in extremity that He can appear for us. Take care how you limit His resources. If He brings you into the wilderness, He can furnish for you a table there (Ps. 78:19). The answer to all your difficulties is, "Have faith in God." "He Himself knows what He will do" (John 6:6). "Stand still and see the salvation of the Lord which He will show to you today" (Ex. 14:13).     —*E. W. Moore*

*Continue in prayer.*       —Colossians 4:2

The more praying there is in the world the better the world will be, the mightier the forces against evil everywhere. Prayer, in one phase of its operation, is a disinfectant and a preventive. It purifies the air; it destroys the contagion of evil. Prayer is no fitful, short-lived thing. It is no voice crying unheard and unheeded in the silence. It is a voice which goes into God's ear, and it lives as long as God's ear is open to holy pleas, as long as God's heart is alive to holy things.

God shapes the world by prayer. Prayers are deathless. The lips that uttered them may be closed in death, the heart that felt them may have ceased to beat, but the prayers live before God, and God's heart is set on them and prayers outlive the lives of those who uttered them; outlive a generation, outlive an age, outlive a world.

Prayer is the keynote of the most sanctified life, of the holiest ministry. He does the most for God who is the highest skilled in prayer. Jesus Christ exercised His ministry after this order.       —E. M. Bounds

> God's ear is ever open to
>  The humble cry and plea
> He takes account of each desire —
>  Helps each infirmity.
>
> Prayer must be grounded on the Word
>  Accompanied with faith
> Thus, what's according to His will
>  God answers—as He saith.
>
> God never fails to answer prayer
>  In fervency implored;
> So, let each need presented be
>  Before our gracious Lord.

*I will not leave you comfortless: I will come to you.*
—John 14:18

Christians must learn to get strength and courage from the promises and provisions of God. What if there are reverses, sufferings, hardships, disappointments, injustices here in this brief life, if the life to come is filled with joy, beauty, light, holiness, power and glory for all eternity?

John, the Apostle of love, would give us a final word concerning this. He wrote:

> *There is no fear in love; but perfect love casteth out fear: because fear hath torment. He that feareth is not made perfect in love* (1 John 4:18).

Perfect love for God casts out fear of all kinds. If our hearts are filled with love to God and man, as Jesus taught they should be, there is no room for fear, worry, resentment, hate and selfishness. And if we are filled with the Holy Spirit (Ephesians 5:18), then we will be filled with love, for love is the first fruit of the Spirit (Galatians 5:22).

God can so fill our lives that we are satisfied with Him and His provisions. Fears and worries will have to go because the things that cause them cease to matter.

—*Faris D. Whitesell*

*His faithfulness fails not; it meets each new day*
*With guidance for every new step of the way;*
*New grace for new trials, new trust for old fears,*
*New patience for bearing the wrongs of the years,*
*New strength for new burdens, new courage for old,*
*New faith for whatever the day may unfold;*
*As fresh for each need as the dew on the sod;*
*Oh, new every morning the mercies of God!*
—Annie Johnson Flint

*Jesus said unto him, If thou canst believe, all things are possible to him that believeth. And straightway the father of the child cried out, and said with tears, Lord, I believe; Help Thou mine unbelief.* — Mark 9:23, 24

Listen to this, you who are often so helpless that you do not know what to do. At times you do not even know how to pray. Your mind seems full of sin and impurity. Your mind is preoccupied with what the Bible calls, "the world." God and eternal and holy things seem so distant and foreign to you that you feel that you add sin to sin by desiring to approach God in such a state of mind. Now and then you must ask yourself the question, "Do I really desire to be set free from the lukewarmness of my heart and worldly life?"

Thus an honest soul struggles against the dishonesty of his own being. He feels himself so helplessly lost that his prayers freeze on his very lips.

Listen, my friend! Your helplessness is your best prayer. It calls from your heart to the heart of God with greater effect than all your uttered pleas. He hears it from the very moment that you are seized with helplessness, and He becomes actively engaged at once in hearing and answering the prayer of your helplessness. He hears today as He heard the helpless and wordless prayer of the palsied man. If you are a mother, you will understand very readily this phase of prayer.

Your infant child cannot formulate in words a single petition to you. Yet the little one prays the best way he knows how. All he can do is to cry, but you understand very well his pleading.

—*O. Hallesby*

*God knows, not I, the reason why*
  *His winds of storm drive through my door;*
*I am content to live or die*
  *Just knowing this, not knowing more.*
*My Father's hand appointing me*
  *My days and ways, so I am free.*
      —Margaret E. Sangster

*The Lord is thy keeper: The Lord is thy shade upon thy right hand.*
—Psalm 121:5

I remember one time my little girl was teasing her mother to get her a muff, and so one day her mother brought a muff home, and although it was storming, she very naturally wanted to go out to try her new muff. So she tried to get me to go out with her. I went out with her, and I said, "Emma, better let me take your hand." She wanted to keep her hands in her muff, and so she refused to take my hand. Well, by and by she came to an icy place, her little feet slipped, and down she went. When I helped her up she said, "Papa, you may give me your little finger," "No, my daughter, just take my hand." "No, no, papa, give me your little finger." Well, I gave my finger to her, and for a little way she got along nicely, but pretty soon we came to another icy place, and again she fell. This time she hurt herself a little, and she said, "Papa, give me your hand," and I gave her my hand, and closed my fingers about her wrist, and held her up so that she could not fall. Just so God is our keeper. He is wiser than we.

—D. L. Moody

*I'm not alone when the dawn light is breaking*
   *And westward the last mist-hung shadow has flown;*
*When from sweet slumber my soul is awaking*
   *Thou, God, art with me, I'm not alone.*

*When through the gray dawn I send my thoughts winging,*
   *Questing through prayer-laden space to the throne,*
*Stars of the morning are joyously singing,*
   *Thou, God, art with me, I'm not alone.*

*I'm not alone with the darkness around me*
   *Though the night curtains a pillow of stone;*
*A ladder of light to heaven has bound me,*
   *Thou, God, art with me, I'm not alone.*
                    —Myra Brooks Welch

*Saying, I am Alpha and Omega, the first and the last . . .*
—Revelation 1:11

Here is the neglected parable—the Cinderella of the parables! A million sermons have been preached on the parable of the prodigal son and all the rest. But here is Christ's crowning parable, a masterpiece of imagery which He left to the last and unfolded from the throne of His glory.

"I am—the Alphabet!" The Savior means that, in His redemptive fullness and splendor, He is absolutely incapable of exhaustion. The ages may draw upon His grace; the men of all nations and kindreds and peoples and tongues, a multitude which no man can number, a host which no statistician can count, may drink of His pity and pardon and peace, but they are drinking of a fountain which can never run dry.

It is the most sublime revelation ever given of the *invincibility* of Christ. He is at the beginning, that is to say, and He goes right through to the very end.

Best of all, this neglected parable is the most sublime revelation ever given of the *adaptability* of Christ. Nothing on the face of the earth is as adaptable as the alphabet. No two of us are alike, yet each can express his several individualities through the agency of the alphabet.

Just because of this remarkable quality in the alphabet, Jesus employs it as an emblem of Himself. He adapts Himself, with Divine exactitude, to the individual needs of each of us.

—*F. W. Boreham*

*Jesus, our only joy be Thou,*
*As Thou our prize wilt be;*
*In Thee be all our glory now,*
*And through eternity.*
—Bernard of Clairvaux

# JULY 26

*. . . the unsearchable riches of Christ.*        —Ephesians 3:8

My riches in Christ are beyond the measurement of mathematics, beyond the mighty dreams of imagination, and beyond the weak description of mortal words. My riches in Christ are unsearchable!

We may look and study and contemplate, but Jesus is an even greater Savior than our greatest thoughts consider Him to be. Our Lord is more abundantly able to pardon us from sin than we are able to transgress in our flesh. Our Lord is more willing to supply our needs than we are to confess our needs to Him.

My riches in Christ mean happiness today and holiness to come. In this life He may lead me to lie down in green pastures beside still waters—or through the valley of the shadow of death, and yet through it all regardless of outward circumstances I may have the comfort of His presence and nearness. There is no love like His, and neither Heaven nor earth can really reveal the depth of that love.

In Christ I am of royal lineage—I am a child of the King! My Father, the King, provides me abundant blessing not only in the life to come but in my day-by-day earthly life.

I will realize the meaning of His unsearchable riches best when I come to abide with Him forever in eternity. On my way to Heaven He supplies all I need; protection when I need it, bread when I am hungry; but it is in Heaven that I will hear the song of the redeemed and will come face to face with my Redeemer.

The unsearchable riches of Christ! Can we plumb the meaning of these words? Can we grasp their vast implications? Praise God the day will come when you and I "shall know as we are known"!

*But godliness with contentment is great gain.*

—1 Timothy 6:6

Negatively, contentment delivers from worry and fretfulness, from avarice and selfishness. Positively, it leaves us free to enjoy what God has given us.

Contentment is the product of a heart resting in God. It is the soul's enjoyment of that peace which passes all understanding. It is the outcome of my will being brought into subjection to the Divine will. It is the blessed assurance that God does all things well, and is, even now, making all things work together for my ultimate good. This experience has to be "learned" by "proving what is that good, and acceptable, and perfect, will of God" (Rom. 12:2). Contentment is possible only as we cultivate and maintain that attitude of accepting everything which enters our lives as coming from the Hand of Him who is too wise to err, and too loving to cause one of His children a needless tear.

Let our final word be this: real contentment is only possible by being much in the presence of the Lord Jesus. It is only by cultivating intimacy with that One who was never discontent that we shall be delivered from the sin of complaining. It is only by daily fellowship with Him who ever delighted in the Father's will that we shall learn the secret of contentment.

> *If the wren can cling*
> *To a spray a-swing*
> *In the mad May wind,*
> *And sing and sing,*
> *As if she'd burst for joy —*
> *Why cannot I*
> *Contented lie*
> *In His quiet arms,*
> *Beneath His sky,*
> *Unmoved by life's annoy?*

# July 28

*And it came to pass after these things, that God did tempt Abraham, and said unto him, Abraham: and he said, Behold, here I am.* —Genesis 22:1

"God did tempt (*test*, Heb. 11:17) Abraham." That is an amazing statement, full of comfort and encouragement for you and for me. If God tested the great representative believer, may I not expect Him to test me?

The life of Abraham and the experience of every true believer are similar to pursuing a course of study in school or college. There are lessons to be learned, discipline to be cultivated, and periodic tests and examinations to be passed. No one is exempt who enrolls in the school. As there are tests and examinations in school life, so there are tests and examinations in the Christian life. Abraham's spiritual experience consists of a series of such tests in which his faith was tried. This last test, when he was called upon to offer up Isaac, his "only son Isaac," was the greatest, and may fittingly be considered his *final* examination.

For this hardest test of all, however, God had graciously prepared His ancient servant, as He tenderly prepares us. He gives the easier tests first, and like a skillful teacher accommodates the examination to the maturity and advancement of the student. Faith in God is the indispensable prerequisite for passing the tests. God operates on the principle of faith. Without faith it is impossible to deal with Him or to please Him (Heb. 11:6). We shall fail miserably in the Christian life if we do not believe God. We must constantly remember that the Christian life is a life of faith, that the life of faith is tested, that obedience is the test of faith, and that God *always* rewards obedience. —*Merrill F. Unger*

*Blessed is that man that maketh the Lord his trust.*

—Psalm 40:4

There are the three keys which will let us into the innermost chambers of friendship with God—prayer, God's Word and obedience. And with them goes a *key-ring* on which these keys must be strung. It is this: *implicit trust in God.* Trust is the native air of friendship. In its native air it grows strong and beautiful. Whatever disturbs an active, abiding trust in God must be driven out of doors, and kept out. Doubt chills the air below normal. Anxiety overheats the air. A calm looking up into God's face with an unquestioning faith in *Him* under every sort of circumstance—this is trust. Faith has three elements: knowledge, belief and *trust.* Knowledge is acquaintance with certain facts. Belief is accepting these facts as true. Trust is risking something that is very precious. Trust is the life-blood of faith.

—*S. D. Gordon*

Trust God where you cannot trace Him. Do not try to penetrate the cloud He brings over you; rather look to the bow that is on it. The mystery is God's; the promise is yours.

—*John Macduff*

> *I do not know what next may come*
> *Across my pilgrim way;*
> *I do not know tomorrow's road,*
> *Nor see beyond today.*
> *But this I know—my Savior knows*
> *The path I cannot see;*
> *And I can trust His wounded hand*
> *To guide and care for me.*

—E. Margaret Clarkson

# JULY 30

*But I will bring you forth out of the midst of it.*
—Ezekiel 11:7

We need to remember that God not only leads us into valleys, but through them. God led Daniel through the den of lions, because Daniel went through with a trusting heart. The tragedy is not that we go into fires and dens but that we lose the praising heart as we go through. We must learn to trust Him implicitly anywhere, learn that when our knees shake, we should kneel on them!

We must see trials and sufferings in their eternal light; then we will see how trifling they are. "For our light affliction, which is but for a moment, worketh for us a far more exceeding and eternal weight of glory; while we look not at the things which are seen, but at the things which are not seen" (2 Cor. 4:17, 18).

We must not selfishly pray for fewer tasks, but for strength to perform the tasks God gives us. We must look beyond all human means, and understand that it is the Lord's doings. "Take my yoke upon you, and learn of me; for I am meek and lowly in heart: and ye shall find rest unto your souls" (Matt. 11:29).

It is only as our prayers lift us above the human mists and help us to see things from God's standpoint that they are truly valuable to us. *—David M. Dawson*

*All God's testings have a purpose—*
*Some day you will see the light.*
*All He asks is that you trust Him,*
*Walk by faith and not by sight.*
*Do not fear when doubts beset you,*
*Just remember—He is near;*
*He will never, never leave you,*
*He will always, always hear.*
*—John E. Zoller*

*This is a faithful saying, and worthy of all acceptation, that
Christ Jesus came into the world to save sinners.*
—1 Timothy 1:15

What source of indescribable assurance to know that in this
world of deceit and shattered promises we have one
unquestioned, rock-grounded truth! What uplifting confidence
to realize that even though human prophecies miscarry and
human promises are rudely broken, even though husbands
and wives prove unfaithful, friends unreliable, sons and
daughters ungrateful—this love of Christ will never be altered!
Your own experiences may have embittered you or made you
suspicious. The last years have taught us how promises signed
by great corporations, treaties sealed by powerful nations, are
disavowed. Yet if you have lost trust in men, find new faith in
God! Put a question mark behind any human utterances if
you must, but write "Amen" behind the faithful sayings of
God! Doubt anything if you will, when men speak, but when
God offers you grace in Christ, then with all your heart and
soul and mind accept this as the truth of all truth that it is.

— *Walter A. Maier*

*I will believe, though all my days be spent
  In ceaseless toil from morn until the night;
My Father knows, and I can rest content —
  His trusting child is precious in His sight.*

*I will believe—though faith be sorely tried,
  God's promises forever shall endure;
All needful things will surely be supplied —
  I will not doubt, but rest in Him secure.*

*I will believe—when life's last task is done,
  I know that I shall see the Christ I love;
And fellowship so sweet on earth begun
  Shall evermore endure with Him above.*
—Bessie Patten Gilmore

# AUGUST 1

*But if we walk in the light, as he is in the light, we have
fellowship one with another, and the blood of Jesus Christ
his Son cleanseth us from all sin.* —1 John 1:7

Consider what we have through the blood of Christ if we
believe.

We have salvation and safety. "For the Lord will pass
through to smite the Egyptians; and when he seeth the blood
upon the lintels, and on the two side posts, the Lord will pass
over the door and will not suffer the destroyer to come into
your house to smite you!" (Ex. 12:23). What a night was that—
in Egypt!

The blood saved them. It is God's estimate of the blood,
not of us, that counts. "When I see the blood, I will pass over
you!" That was the wondrous passover in Egypt. But Christ is
our passover. "For even Christ, our passover, sacrificed for
us!" (1 Cor. 5:7).

We have peace. "And having made *peace* through the blood
of his cross" (Col. 1:20). How little real peace there is in this
clamorous world! Behind many a smiling face is a troubled
heart. How we do need God's rest around our restlessness—
His completeness around our incompleteness! Through the
blood of the Cross, we have a peace which nothing can take
away, a joyful peace which no rust or moth" can touch.

—*Robert G. Lee*

*Jesus, Thy blood and righteousness
My beauty are, my glorious dress:
'Midst flaming worlds, in these array'd,
With joy shall I lift my head.*

*Lord, I believe Thy precious blood,
Which, at the mercy seat of God,
Forever doth for sinners plead,
For me, e'en for my soul, was shed.*
—John Wesley

*(He) is able to do exceeding abundantly above all that we ask or think, according to the power that worketh in us.*

—Ephesians 3:20

"Exceeding abundantly." Here Paul coins a word for his own peculiar use. It seems as though at times the Holy Spirit crowded such great and radiant revelations in the Apostle's mind and heart that even the rich vocabulary at his disposal was not sufficient to express them. But when ordinary language fails Paul employs his own. There was no superlative at hand which could describe his sense of the overwhelming ability of God, and so he just constructed a word of his own, the intensity of which can only be suggested in our English phrase "exceeding abundantly." The power flows up, and out, and over! It is a spring, and therefore incalculable.

We can measure the resources of a cistern; we can tell its capacity to a trifle. We can register the contents of a reservoir; at any moment we can tell how many gallons it contains. But who can measure the resources of a spring? It is to this springlike quality in the divine power, the exceeding abundance, the immeasurable quantity, that the Apostle refers.

We can bring our little vessels to the spring and take them away filled to overflowing, and the exceeding abundance remains. The "doing" of our God is an inexhaustible well.

—J. H. Jowett

*The world can neither give nor take,*
*Nor can it comprehend,*
*That peace of God, which Christ hath bought,*
*That peace which knows no end.*
—Selina, Countess of Huntington

# AUGUST 3

*Now the God of peace be with you all.* —Romans 15:33

It is in the Lord Jesus Christ, and in Him alone, that we find the knowledge, the assurance, the certitude, which create true peace within us. He brings a revelation of the Divine which is marked by a clarity, a unity, an authority, and a finality, such as we find nowhere else. In Him we see and know and possess God. We have certitude about the Divine. The God revealed in Jesus Christ is such, in His holiness and love, that we may know for certain He will never mock us in our human littleness and weakness. He loves us too dearly. He has suffered to save us. To know God thus in Jesus Christ is the first step to a true peace.

But the Lord Jesus gives us equally clear intelligence and assurance about the Beyond, about the Future, and about the Present. As for the Beyond, which has ever been a vexed question in the human heart, He tells us of "the Father's House," and assures His people that He goes to "prepare a place" for them. As for the Future, He promises, "I will come again and receive you unto Myself, that where I am there ye may be also." As for the Present, He covers all the waiting-time until His glorious reappearing by His gracious provision of the Holy Spirit, the Comforter of whom He says, "He shall abide with you"; "He shall be in you"; "He shall teach you"; "He shall guide you."

Dear Christian, these are the first things that belong to our peace. We must feed our hearts on the solid comfort of these glorious certainties which our Divine Lord gives to us. When we possess such assurance concerning God and the Beyond, and such a provision for the Future, ought not our peace, to be as a full, deep, smooth-flowing river? —*J. Sidlow Baxter*

*The heavens declare the glory of God; and the firmament sheweth his handywork.*
—Psalm 19:1

The whole creation praises God, for He it is who created all things. Everything that was made was made for His honor and for His praise. He is the One who hung the world on nothing. He is the God who reared the battlements on the hills against the sky—the One who hangs the pink curtain of the dawn in the East. He is the One who set the music in the throat of the nightingale to make beautiful the springtime. He is the One who sends the rain to wash the earth, to kiss the flowers and to anoint the green things with freshness.

He is the God who said, "Let there be light," and there was light. He is the God who commanded: "Let the dry land appear." He is the God who makes the green things burst through the sod and push into the sunlight seeking His face who is the God of heaven. He is the Lord of all creation!

There was one purpose in your coming into the world, and that was to glorify God. When He made you, He framed the foundation of bone. He fixed the joints and the marrow; He put the muscles there and gave you a brain to control the use of the muscles through the system of the nerves. He gave you power to think and eyes to see and lips to praise Him and the powers of the senses to contact the world around you. "What a piece of work is man, how noble is reason." There is no greater evidence of the power and of the existence of God than your own mortal body.
—Bob Jones, Jr.

*God is working His purpose out as year succeeds to year,*
*God is working His purpose out and the time is drawing near;*
*Nearer and nearer draws the time, the time that shall surely be,*
*When the earth shall be filled with the glory of God as the waters cover*
*the sea.*

—Arthur Campbell Ainger

> *He that believeth on me, as the scripture hath said, out of his belly shall flow rivers of living water.* —John 7:38

From the Christian's innermost being, rivers of living water flow forth to a world that sits in darkness and the shadow of death. This truth leaves one breathless with wonder and awe. The very thing all men seek so passionately, and sacrifice, only too often, all that is dear to attain—namely, abundant life—is promised to the Christian.

The great souls of the Church—Wesley, Hudson Taylor, Jessie Penn-Lewis, George Fox and a host of others were mighty fountains forever overflowing with rivers of living water. They watered and made fruitful entire continents of wasteland. They caused vast deserts to blossom like a rose. With them, it was not a question primarily of doing but of being. The doing was the result of the being, being hid with Christ in God and thus constituting themselves channels through which the life of God might flow out to a dying world. In God is life, wondrous life such as man cannot conceive, even as light is in the sun. And they who live in God and are filled with His Spirit, filled to overflowing, are necessarily like geysers from which abundant waters spring forth, mighty aqueducts through which the life of God invades the world. Jesus our Lord, in this, as in all other things that have to do with the redemption of men, was the Perfect Example of fruitfulness. He could cry out and say, "Whosoever is athirst, let him come unto Me and drink." —*F. J. Huegel*

> *I need Thee, precious Jesus!*
> *I need Thee day by day—*
> *To fill me with Thy fullness,*
> *To lead me on my way.*

*God . . . hath . . . spoken unto us by his Son, whom he hath appointed heir of all things, by whom also he made the worlds.*
—Hebrews 1:1, 2

Here in the very beginning of this marvelous epistle we are brought face to face with God. A man's word can carry weight only as his wisdom and his veracity give him standing in the community. But in this epistle One has spoken whose Word is eternal, never changing and always authoritative.

How foolish to follow the wisdom of man, even though his words are intellectual, when he speaks contrary to God's Holy Word! How foolish to build one's trust for eternity upon the sandy foundation of the empty words of unsaved men, when God has spoken. He spoke of old through the prophets but now He has spoken unto us by His Son. There is no other approach to God but through Him; no other name, no other way, no other foundation, no other hope. For this reason we ought to give the more earnest heed to His words, which are a marvelous revelation. "Faith cometh by hearing and hearing by the Word of God."
—*Charles E. Fuller*

*Have faith in God! for He who reigns on high*
*Hath borne thy grief and hears the suppliant's sigh,*
*Still to His arms, thine only refuge, fly.*
    *Have faith in God!*

*Fear not to call on Him, O soul distressed!*
*Thy sorrow's whisper woos thee to His breast;*
*He who is oftenest there is oftenest blest.*
    *Have faith in God!*

*Go tell Him all! The sigh thy bosom heaves*
*Is heard in heaven. Strength and grace He gives*
*Who gave Himself for thee. Our Jesus lives;*
    *Have faith in God.*

# AUGUST 7

*I go to prepare a place for you. And if I go and prepare a place for you, I will come again, and receive you unto Myself, that where I am, there ye may be also.* —John 14:2,3

In that passage from St. John's Gospel is this very impressive sentence, "If it were not so, I would have told you." There Christ invites us to rest all our faith in the life to come in Him and in His words. "If it were not so, I would have told you." If what were not so? Why, that there is life after death. Christ stakes His honor, His reputation, on His testimony to the life to come. By every consideration of truth and honor, if there is no future life, He was bound to have told His disciples. But He never told them that. Neither by word nor by inference, nor by His life did He ever in the least degree intimate that this life is the end of all. On the contrary, by the purity of His life, by the tone of His preaching, by His constant appeal to life to come, and by His own definite affirmation of the life after death, Christ told His disciples that this life is not the end and that there is a greater and a nobler life which is to come. —*Clarence Edward Macartney*

The joys of heaven are not the joys of passive contemplation, of dreamy remembrance, of perfect repose; but they are described thus, "They rest not day or night." "His servants serve him and see his face." —Alexander Maclaren

*We are waiting for the dawn*
  *Of that everlasting day,*
*When the night of earth shall end*
  *And the shadows flee away.*
*Morn of morns and day of days!*
  *How we wait and watch and pray*
*Till the dawn of heaven shall break,*
  *And the shadows flee away.*
                    —A. B. Simpson

*Rejoice in the Lord alway: and again I say, Rejoice.*
—Philippians 4:4

Who has more reason for genuine joy than the Christian? His springs of joy are deep and abundant because he rejoices "in the Lord." Even suffering and testing such as Paul was passing through as he writes this letter from prison cannot quench that joy. The believer will not be immune from trouble, but he has resources for every need in Christ Jesus.

The joy Christ gives is for time and eternity, for soul and body, for adversity and prosperity. His joy is rooted in the unspeakable blessedness of forgiveness, the assurance of salvation, the hope of heaven. —*William A. Swets*

*Sing all the earth, ye hills break forth with singing!*
 *Trees of the forest, clap your hands in praise!*
*Children of men, and angels voices ringing,*
 *Sing out for joy, thy glad hosannas raise—*
*Telling to all who draw this mortal breath,*
*The Son of Man hath conquered sin and death!*

*Dark was the tomb where lay the Prince of Glory,*
 *Hearts of His followers dark with despair,*
*But He arose! Oh, tell the wondrous story*
 *To every troubled soul bowed down with care.*
*The Sun of life dispels the gloom of night,*
*And in His children's hearts dawn peace and light.*

*Sing, troubled earth! Break forth with joyous singing,*
 *Waves of the ocean, shout aloud Thy praise!*
*This be the message to heav'n's portals winging—*
 *This be the anthem hearts redeemed shall*
 *raise,*
*Where is death's victory? Where, grave, thy sting?*
*Rejoice! He liveth, heaven's risen King!*
—Kathryn Blackburn Peck

# AUGUST 9

*Thou wilt show me the path of life: in thy presence is fulness of joy; at thy right hand there are pleasures for evermore.*
—Psalm 16:11

Wrapped up in these words from the Psalmist David are the past, present and future truths of the Christian life. In these few words David reveals his conception of what walking with Christ means to the Christian.

First of all, David says, "Thou wilt show me the path of life. . . ." Here David is resting upon past experience. He knows from what has happened to him in the past that God is the Christian's Guide. He knows from past experience that God personally leads the way, going with His child through the hard places as well as on the mountain peaks. David has proved God faithful. He knows from God's past performances of His promises that "He is faithful, who will not suffer us to be tempted above that we are able, but will with the temptation provide a way of escape." And on what path does God guide—it is the path of life which leads to life eternal!

David goes on to testify that "in Thy presence is fullness of joy . . ."—a witness of the fact that the Christian's present, his day-by-day life, is one of joy, a life full of joy. The only qualification for this life of joy is that it be lived "in Thy presence," in fellowship with the Heavenly Father. How glorious it is to contemplate the joys that are the Christian's portion as he walks in the center of God's will for his life. How wonderful it is to know that the present is taken care of, that God, the Great Provider, provides not only for His child's physical needs but even more importantly, his spiritual needs as well.

Looking ahead to the brightness of God's glory on high, David says, "At Thy right hand there are pleasures for evermore." At the right hand of God the Father is the throne of God the Son. And at His right hand is the place reserved for His children, the place "not made with hands" and "eternal in the Heavens." It is upon this blessed hope that the Christian gazes steadfastly, but it is this very hope that helps the Christian through what may often become a humdrum day-to-day routine. What is at the Father's right hand? Pleasures—for evermore! How restful is that word, "pleasures"—how full of promise. And to think that these pleasures will be the portion of the child of God throughout eternity—forever and ever, world without end!

How important it is for the Christian to consider all the tenses of the Christian life—past, present and future. What a warm feeling of thankfulness should course through our very beings as we realize again the abundant life and the marvelous salvation and the wonderful glory His hand has provided for us, is providing for us, and is yet to provide for us. Let us thank God for His goodness to men.

*He walks beside me every day,*
*He guides me in the things I say,*
*He stands beside me when I pray,*
  *He's all the world to me.*

*I feel His footsteps leading mine,*
*I hear His voice speak words divine,*
*His touch weaves all my life's design,*
  *His wondrous face I see.*

*His blood washed all my sins away,*
*He'll keep me in the narrow way,*
*This Savior who still lives today,*
  *The Christ of Calvary.*
                                        —Joyce Ramage

# August 10

*And Moses said unto the people, Fear ye not, stand still, and see the salvation of the Lord, which he will shew to you today: for the Egyptians whom ye have seen today, ye shall see them again no more for ever.* —Exodus 14:13

These words contain God's command to the believer when he is reduced to great straits and brought into extraordinary difficulties. He cannot retreat; he cannot go forward; he is shut up on the right hand and on the left; what is he now to do? The Master's word to him is, "Stand still." It will be well for him if at such times he listens only to his Master's word, for other and evil advisers come with their suggestions. *Despair* whispers, "Lie down and die; give it all up." But God would have us put on a cheerful courage, and even in our worst times, rejoice in His love and faithfulness. *Cowardice* says, "Retreat; go back to the worldling's way of action; you cannot play the Christian's part, it is too difficult. Relinquish your principles." But, however much Satan may urge this course upon you, you cannot follow it if you are a child of God. *Precipitancy* cries, "Do something. Stir yourself; to stand still and wait, is sheer idleness." We must be doing something at once—we must do it, so we think—instead of looking to the Lord, who will not only do something but will do everything. *Presumption* boasts, "If the sea be before you, march into it and expect a miracle." But Faith listens neither to Presumption, nor to Despair, nor to Cowardice, nor to Precipitancy, but it hears God say, "Stand still," and immovable as a rock it stands. *"Stand* still"—keep the posture of an upright man, ready for action, expecting further orders, cheerfully and patiently awaiting the directing voice; and it will not be long ere God shall say to you, as distinctly as Moses said it to the people of Israel, "Go forward." —*Charles H. Spurgeon*

*I can do all things through Christ which strengtheneth me.*
—Philippians 4:13

Bless me, Lord, and make me a blessing. To get your own doubts and fears and uncertainties settled is the best and the basic preparation for helping others. You will stand as a tower of strength in a world that is dying of fear and uncertainty. "You cannot always *do* something to help your friends, but you can always *be* something to help them if your own lamp of faith and love shines clear."

People all around us have needs that are breaking their hearts, and they look to Christ's followers for help. In a world of distress we are expected to stand in His stead. We cannot hold up unless we have superhuman resources through contact with Christ. All that is human in us will crumple, asking sympathy for ourselves.

The visionless disciples failed before a real need. Did a person ever appeal to you for soul help when you were not "prayed up" yourself? Did some younger Christian ever look to you for an example when your own steps were faltering? Suppose your big challenge or your big opportunity should come the day you were "out of touch with your Lord."

We Christians are citizens of two worlds. We must be at home in both. In the one we are receivers, in the other we are givers; in the one we are but children and learners, in the other we are to quit us like men and do exploits. We prevail below in proportion as we have learned from above.

*O use me, Lord, use even me,*
*Just as Thou wilt, and when and where.*

—Bertha Munro

# AUGUST 12

*For I reckon that the sufferings of this present time are not worthy to be compared with the glory which shall be revealed in us.* —Romans 8:18

Ah, says someone, that must have been written by a man who was a stranger to suffering, or by one acquainted with nothing more trying than the milder irritations of life. Not so. These words were penned under the direction of the Holy Spirit, and by one who drank deeply of sorrow's cup, yea, by one who suffered afflictions in their acutest forms.

But, says the writer, the Apostle Paul, one second of glory will outweigh a lifetime of suffering. What were years of toil, of sickness, of battling with poverty, of sorrow in any or every form, when compared with the glory of Immanuel's land! One draught of the river of pleasure at God's right hand, one breath of Paradise, one hour amid the blood-washed around the throne, shall more than compensate for all the tears and groans of earth. "For I reckon that the sufferings of this present time are not worthy to be compared with the glory which shall be revealed in us." May the Holy Spirit enable both writer and reader to lay hold of this with appropriating faith and live in the present possession and enjoyment of it to the praise of the glory of Divine grace. —*Arthur W. Pink*

*When the mists have rolled in splendor*
*From the beauty of the hills,*
*And the sunlight falls in gladness*
*On the river and the rills,*
*We recall our Father's promise*
*In the rainbow of the spray:*
*We shall know each other better*
*When the mists have rolled away.*

*And it shall come to pass in the day that the Lord shall give thee rest from thy sorrow, and from thy fear. . . .*
—Isaiah 14:3

There is rest for the weary, even in this world, if they will only seek it. There is repose for the weary of heart, if they will only apply for it in the *right quarter*. There is real, solid, lasting happiness to be had on this side of the grave, if people would only inquire for it where it is to be found.

Where is this rest? Where is this repose? Where is this happiness? *It is to be found in Christ.* It is given by Him to all children of mankind who will confess their need and trust Him to relieve them. It is enjoyed by all who hear Christ's voice and follow Him. "Come unto Me," He says, "all ye that labor and are heavy laden, and I will give you rest."

—*J. C. Ryle*

*When doubts or fears your pathway dim,*
   *Look up to God!*
*Let sorrow draw you close to Him,*
   *Look up to God!*
*He will banish every fear,*
*Wipe away the falling tear;*
*Trust Him now for He is near.*
   *Look up to God!*

*What's your need this very hour?*
   *Look up to God!*
*Is it peace, or joy, or power?*
   *Look up to God!*
*He will guide each thought and deed,*
*As on His Word you daily feed;*
*He supplies your every need.*
   *Look up to God!*

—Clifford Lewis

# AUGUST 14

*When thou saidst, Seek ye my face; my heart said unto thee,*
*Thy face, Lord, will I seek.* —Psalm 27:8

The Bible reminds us of a dictaphone. God has spoken into it, and as we read its pages, they transfer His living words to us. There are many things in the Bible, which, at first, we may not be able to understand, because, as the heaven is higher than the earth, so are God's thoughts higher than ours. Mr. Spurgeon used to say that when he ate fish, he did not attempt to swallow the bones, but put them aside on his plate! So when there is something beyond your understanding, put it aside, and go on to enjoy that which is easy of spiritual meditation.

The Bible contains many thousands of promises. It is God's book of signed checks. When you have found a promise which meets your need, do not ask God to keep His promise, as though He were unwilling to do so, and needed to be pressed and importuned. Present it humbly in the name of the Lord Jesus! Be sure that, so far as you know, you are fulfilling any conditions that may be attached; then look up into the face of your Heavenly Father, and tell Him that you are depending on Him to do as He has said. It is for Him to choose the time and manner of His answer; but wait quietly, be patient, and you will find that not a moment too soon, and not a moment too late, God's response will be given. "My soul, wait thou only upon God, for my expectation is from Him" (Ps. 62:5); "Blessed is she that believed: for there shall be a performance of those things that were told her from the Lord" (Luke 1:45).

Whether for the body, the soul, or spirit, there is no guide like Holy Scripture, but never read it without first looking up to its Author and Inspirer, asking that He will illuminate the page and make you wise unto salvation. —*F. B. Meyer*

*And to whom sware he that they should not enter into his
rest, but to them that believed not?* —Hebrews 3:18

Rest in expectation we may all have now if we believe in
God and know we are His children. Every taste of Him that
we have ever had becomes a prophecy of His perfect giving
of Himself to us. It is as when a pool lies far up in the dry
rocks, and hears the tide and knows that her refreshment and
replenishing is coming. How patient she is. The other pools
nearer the shore catch the sea first, and she hears them leaping
and laughing, but she waits patiently. She knows the tide will
not turn back till it has reached her. And by and by the
blessed moment comes. The last ridge of rock is overwashed.
The stream pours in; at first a trickling thread sent only at the
supreme effort of the largest wave; but by and by the great
sea in its fullness. It gives the waiting pool itself and she is
satisfied. So it will certainly be with us if we wait for the Lord,
however He delays, and refuse to let ourselves be satisfied
with any supply but Him. —*Phillips Brooks*

You have no place in which to pour your troubles except
the ear of God. Roll your burden unto God, and you have
rolled it into a great deep, out of which it will never by any
possibility rise. Cast your troubles where you cast your sins.
Never keep a trouble half an hour on your mind before you
tell it to God. As soon as the trouble comes, quick, the first
thing, tell it to your Father.

*If life, 'tis well; for though in paths of pain,
    In desert place afar, I'm led aside,
Yet here 'tis joy my Master's cup to share;
    And so I pray, O Christ, with me abide.*

*'Tis gain if death; for in that far-off land—
    No longer far—no veil of flesh will dim
For me the wondrous beauty of my King,
    As He abides with me and I with Him.*

# AUGUST 16

*Through faith we understand that the worlds were framed by the word of God, so that things which are seen were not made of things which do appear.* —Hebrews 11:3

The trust and repose of the soul on God, which is another part of the life of grace, is exceeding pleasant and quieting to the soul. To find that we stand upon a Rock, and that under us are the everlasting arms, and that we have so full security for our salvation as the promise and oath of the immutable God, what a stay, what a pleasure is this to the believer! The troubles of the godly are mostly from the remnants of their unbelief. The more they believe, the more they are comforted, and established. The life of faith is a pleasant life. Faith could not conquer so many enemies, and carry us through so much suffering and distress, as you find in that cloud of testimonies, Hebrews 11, if it were not a very comfortable work. Even we who see not the salvation ready to be revealed, may yet greatly rejoice, for all the manifold temptations, that for a season make us subject to some heaviness (1 Pet. 1:5). And we who see not Jesus Christ, yet believing can love Him, and rejoice with joy unspeakable and full of glory (v. 8). The God of hope sometimes fills His servants with all joy and peace in believing, and makes them even abound in hope through the power of the Holy Ghost (Rom. 15:13). —*Richard Baxter*

*When the tempest rages,*
*In the Rock of Ages*
*   I will safely hide;*
*Though the earth be shaking,*
*And all hearts be quaking,*
*   Christ is at my side.*
*Lightnings flash, and thunders crash;*
*Yea, though sin and hell assail me,*
*   Jesus will not fail me.*
            —Johann Franck

*When I cry unto thee, then shall mine enemies turn back:*
*this I know; for God is for me.* —Psalm 56:9

*"God is for me"*! Can we put into human speech the full meaning of this delightful phrase? Are mortal words eloquent enough to describe this glorious truth?

God was "for us" before the worlds were made, for His plan included the gift of His Son; He was "for us" despite our ruination in the fall of Adam—He loved us in spite of all; He was "for us" even when we rebelled against Him and defied Him with a high and mighty attitude; He was "for us," for He led us to humbly seek His face for forgiveness and eternal life.

He is "for us" in our daily struggles; He goes with us through the trials and temptations that beset us, He protects us through the dangers that surround us. Truly, how could we have remained unscathed and unharmed except He has been "for us"?

He is "for us" in His deity and infinity; in the omnipotence and omniscience of His love; in the infallibility of His wisdom. He is "for us" eternally. Because He is "for us" the voice of our prayer will always reach His heart and evoke His guidance and help.

"When I cry unto Thee, then shall mine enemies (be turned) back," This is no uncertain sound or hope, but a well-grounded assurance, for "this I know." I know that if I direct my prayer to Him and look up for the answer, assured that it will come, that He will defeat my enemies "for God is for me."

O, fellow believer, how happy must we be to have the King of kings at our side and the Lord of lords as our Protector. Truly, if God be for me, who can be against me?

*Great God, our Guardian, Guide and Friend!*
*O still Thy sheltering arm extend;*
*Preserved by Thee for ages past,*
*For ages let Thy kindness last!*

—William Roscoe

# AUGUST 18

*For the Lord loveth judgment, and forsaketh not His saints.*
—Psalm 37:28

All the biographers of Michael Faraday agree that he was the most transparently honest soul that the realm of science has ever known. He moved for fifty years amidst the speculations of science, whilst, in his soul, the certainties that cannot be shaken were singing their deathless song. . . . In life, as in death, he rested his soul upon certainties. And if you ask what the certainties were, his biographers will tell you they were three: *First*, he trusted implicitly in his Father's love. *Secondly*, he trusted implicitly in the redeeming work of his Savior. *Thirdly*, he trusted implicitly in the written Word. . . . In him the simplicities were always stronger than the sublimities; the child outlived the sage. As he lay dying, they tried to interview the professor, but it was the little child in him that answered. "What are your speculations?" they inquired.

"Speculations? I have none! I am resting on certainties. I know whom I have believed, and am persuaded that He is able to keep that which I have committed unto Him against that day." And, reveling like a little child in those cloudless simplicities, his great soul passed away. . . . Happy the heads that, in the soul's last straits, find themselves pillowed serenely there!
—F. W. Boreham

O for a thousand tongues to sing
 My great Redeemer's praise!
The glories of my God and King,
 The triumphs of His grace!

Jesus the name that calms my fears,
 That bids my sorrows cease;
'Tis music to my ravished ears;
 'Tis life, and health, and peace.
—Charles Wesley

*Whosoe'er will come after me; let him deny himself, and take
up his cross, and follow me.* —Mark 8:34

It is a sweet, a joyful thing to be a sharer with Christ in anything. All enjoyments wherein He is not, are bitter to a soul that loves Him, and all sufferings with Him are sweet. The worst things of Christ are more truly delightful than the best things of the world; His afflictions are sweeter than their pleasures, His *reproach* more glorious than their honors, and more rich than their treasures, as Moses accounted them (Heb. 11:26). Love delights in likeness and communion, not only in things otherwise pleasant, but in the hardest and harshest things, which have not anything in them desirable, but only that likeness. So that this thought is very sweet to a heart possessed with this love: what does the world by its hatred, and persecutions, and revilings for the sake of Christ, but make me more like Him, give me a greater share with Him, in that which He did so willingly undergo for me? And shall I shrink and creep back from what He calls me to suffer for His sake! Yea, even all my other troubles and sufferings, I will desire to have stamped thus, with this conformity to the sufferings of Christ, in the humble, obedient, cheerful endurance of them, and the giving up of my will to my Father's.

The following of Christ makes any way pleasant. His faithful followers refuse no march after Him, be it through deserts, and mountains and storms, and hazards, that will affright self-pleasing, easy spirits. Hearts kindled and actuated with the Spirit of Christ, will follow Him wheresoever He goeth.

—*Robert Leighton*

*From His high throne in bliss, He deigns
    Our every prayer to heed;
Bears with our folly, soothes our pains,
    Supplies every need.*

# AUGUST 20

*The law of thy mouth is better unto me than thousands of gold and silver.* —Psalm 119:72

How to value the Bible. The longer we live, the more wonderful we see God's gift of the Holy Scriptures to be. As life becomes more tangled and complex and we see men and women falling by the wayside, mentally unbalanced or morally wrecked because they have tried to muddle through alone, we rejoice humbly in the assurance of an infallible, unchanging revelation.

The Bible is both "law" and "testimony," that is, the character and will of God revealed and the saving grace of Jesus Christ made known. We see here God's holiness and His demand that we be holy; and here, praise God, we learn of the Calvary redemption. The Bible gives us all the knowledge necessary to salvation.

The Bible gives "statutes" and "commandments"; it tells us what is eternally right. Second only to the revelation of salvation from sin by Jesus Christ is the gift of the moral law. Here is lifted for us the immutable standard of righteousness; here are defined the everlasting principles governing the relationship of man to God and of man to man. To live by these is harmony and happiness. To disregard these is to break yourself against them.

The Bible is full of God. It exalts God as all-wise, all-powerful, all-good. This faith, this fear, is the one solid basis of enduring success and of upright character. It is safe to trust God's knowledge, God's standards, God's commissions always, and to build one's life upon them. The Bible furnishes this constantly in an unstable world. —*Bertha Munro*

*Sing them over again to me,*
*Wonderful words of life;*
*Let me more of their beauty see,*
*Wonderful words of life.*
—P. P. Bliss

*I will both lay me down in peace, and sleep: for thou, Lord,
only makest me dwell in safety.* —Psalm 4:8

*He guides our feet, He guards our way,
His morning smiles bless all the day:
He spreads the evening veil, and keeps
The silent hours while Israel sleeps.*
—Isaac Watts

We sleep in peace in the arms of God, when we yield
ourselves up to His providence, in a delightful consciousness
of His tender mercies; no more restless uncertainties, no more
anxious desires, no more impatience at the place we are in;
for it is God who has put us there, and who holds us in His
arms. Can we be unsafe where He has placed us?
—*François de La Mothe Fenelon*

One evening when Luther saw a little bird perched on a
tree, to roost there for the night, he said, "This little bird has
had its supper, and now it is getting ready to go to sleep here,
quite secure and content, never troubling itself what its food
will be, or where its lodging on the morrow. Like David, it
'abides under the shadow of the Almighty.' It sits on its little
twig content, and lets God take care."

*Give us the peace of the thought of Thy coming
'Mid raging war and the rumors of war,
Safe in the clefts of the rock do Thou hide us,
Shelter us far from the tempests' wild roar;
Under Thy wings shall no evil betide us;
In Thy strong arm shall our confidence be;
Who can make trouble when Thou givest quiet?
Peace of the world, we are trusting in Thee.*
—Annie Johnson Flint

# AUGUST 22

*And there was great joy in that city.* —Acts 8:8

The heart of a child of God has every reason to rejoice. The Christian rejoices because of what Christ has given him and because of what He has taken away. He has been given salvation. He has passed from death into life. He has been given the assurance of God's presence now and hereafter.

A day-by-day experience of God's mercy develops the Christian's joy. As he trusts his Lord for comfort in the time of sorrow and finds the comfort supplied, as he leans upon Him for strength in a moment of weakness and finds himself upheld, as he turns to Him in the hour of need and finds the need met, he cannot help rejoicing.

This joy is increased as the Lord speaks to him through His Word, the Bible. Christ Himself said to His disciples, "These things have I spoken unto you, that my joy might remain in you, and that your joy might be full" (John 15:11), and from the Word of God a joy ever new and fresh comes to the Christian as he turns the holy pages. The command to rejoice seems almost superfluous as he is told to "rejoice in the Lord alway" (Phil. 4:4). When he walks with His Father, the Christian is always filled with joy. —*Bob Jones, Jr.*

*Jesus, Thou joy of loving hearts,*
*Thou fount of life, Thou light of men,*
*From all the bliss that earth imparts*
*We turn unfilled to Thee again.*

*Thy truth unchanged hath ever stood;*
*Thou savest those that on Thee call;*
*To them that seek Thou art good,*
*To them that find Thee, all in all.*
—Bernard of Clairvaux

*He leadeth me.* —Psalm 23:2

Doesn't it sometimes feel as though we are entering a dark woods? So many tasks to be done, bills to be paid, responsibilities to meet, expectations of others, requirements to fulfill, school tests and examinations; the problem of health, of an unknown future to meet, especially for the lonely, the sorrowing, the frustrated because of unfilled hopes and longings! Sometimes it seems so hard to go on, yet we simply must. There is no turning back, nor stopping!

But look again at that little Psalm, and its hopeful note! The Lord Shepherd—*my* Shepherd—"He leadeth me"! Doesn't that spell security! "He," my heavenly Father, who cares, provides, knows, weighs, moulds and controls—He leads me. "He," Jesus, my Savior, who first Himself walked every path, "tried in all things like as are we," clearly marking the way with His own footsteps—He leads me. "He," the Holy Spirit, living in me, instructing, comforting, shedding light upon the way and its value, goal and purposes—*He* leadeth me.

But one cannot lead unless the other follows! So, if I am to enjoy the blessedness of knowing that He leads, I must willingly, gladly follow—follow where the Father, where Jesus, where the Spirit leads! —*C. M. Schoolland*

*The Lord is my Shepherd, He makes me repose*
*Where the pastures in beauty are growing;*
*He leads me afar from the world and its woes,*
*Where in peace the still waters are flowing.*
—John Knox

*Jesus wept.*                               —John 11:35

How wonderful! The Son of God groaned and wept. Let us never forget it. He, though God over all, blessed forever; though the Resurrection and the Life; though the Quickener of the dead; though the Conqueror of the grave; though on His way to deliver the body of His friend from the grasp of the enemy—sample of what He will soon do for all who belong to Him—yet, so perfectly did He enter into human sorrow, and take in all the terrible consequences of sin, all the misery and desolation of this sin-stricken world, that He groaned and wept! And those tears and groans emanated from the depths of a perfect human heart that felt as only a perfect human heart could feel—felt according to God—for every form of human sorrow and misery. Though perfectly exempt, in His own divine person, from sin and all its consequences—yes, because exempt—He could in perfect grace enter into it all and make it His own as only He could do.

"Jesus wept!" Wondrous, significant fact! He wept not for Himself, but for others. He wept with them. Mary wept. The Jews wept. All this is easily grasped and understood. But that Jesus should weep reveals a mystery which we cannot fathom. It was divine compassion weeping through human eyes over the desolation which sin had caused in this poor world, weeping in sympathy with those whose hearts had been crushed by the inexorable hand of death.

Let all who are in sorrow remember this: Jesus is the same yesterday, today and forever. His circumstances are changed, but His heart is not. His position is different, but His sympathy is the same. "We have not an high priest that cannot be touched with the feeling of our infirmities, but was in all points tempted like we are, apart from sin."

# AUGUST 25

*Take therefore no thought for the morrow: for the morrow*
*shall take thought for the things of itself.* —Matthew 6:34

To paraphrase, "Do not be anxious, therefore, about tomorrow, for tomorrow will bring its own anxieties." In nothing be anxious. Nothing is made up of nothing. It is impossible to put anything into nothing. Nothing is a circle with everything excluded. Your child's sickness; your boy's waywardness; your neighbor's meanness—all are excluded. They are but tests of your willingness to obey God rather than the promptings of human nature.

There is a reason. Worry is incompatible with a life of prayer. It prevents us from praying and God from working. Do not worry, "but—(adopt the prayer method instead)—in everything by prayer and supplication. . . ." Now we understand God's ways with us. Everything is excluded from care that it might be included in prayer. He, our Father, wants the opportunity of caring for the things that concern us.

—*Norman B. Harrison*

*The love of God has hung a veil*
  *Around tomorrow,*
*That we may not its beauty see*
  *Nor trouble borrow.*

*But, oh, 'tis sweeter far, to trust*
  *His unseen hand,*
*And know that all the path of life,*
  *His wisdom planned.*

*I know not if tomorrow's way*
  *Be steep or rough;*
*But when His hand is guiding me,*
  *That is enough.*

# AUGUST 26

*. . . the Lord shut him in.*    —Genesis 7:16

First of all, Noah was shut in away from the world by the divine hand. We as believers are not of the world any more than was our Lord Jesus of the world. We as Christians cannot enter into the sin of the world without losing our fellowship with Christ. We cannot take part in the world without losing out with Christ, for our Heavenly Father has planned to shut us in away from the world.

Noah was also shut in with his God. God told him to "come thou into the ark." That clearly shows that God Himself intended to dwell in the ark with Noah and his family. Thus all of God's children are invited to dwell in God, with God in them. How happy our case to be enclosed in the family circle with God!

Then, too, Noah was shut in so that no evil could reach him! The floods only lifted him closer to Heaven and the winds only blew him on his way. Outside of the ark was complete and utter destruction and ruin, but inside was rest and peace. Without Christ we perish, but in Christ there is complete safety and assurance.

Lastly, Noah was shut in so that he had not even the desire to come out. Those who are in Christ have complete satisfaction and lose the desire for worldly things as they become more and more attuned to the will of God for their lives. The hand of God holds them. The Master has power over every storm and in every trial. Once He has closed the door, no human hand can open it.

Here is supremest rest and confidence in Christ exemplified. We, like Noah, may find our complete satisfaction in the person of Jesus Christ.

*And ye now therefore have sorrow: but I will see you again, and your heart shall rejoice, and your joy no man taketh from you.*
—John 16:22

A father will always be eager to see his children joyful. He does all that he can to make them happy. Hence God also desires that His children should walk before Him in gladness of heart. He has promised them gladness: He will give it. He has commanded it: we must take it and walk in it at all times.

Christians, who would walk according to the will of the Lord, hear what His Word says: "Finally, my brethren, rejoice in the Lord. Rejoice in the Lord alway: again, I say, Rejoice." In the Lord Jesus there is joy unspeakable, and full of glory: believing in Him, rejoice in this. Live the life of faith: that life is salvation and glorious joy. A heart that gives itself undividedly to follow Jesus, that lives by faith in Him and His love, shall have light and gladness. Therefore, soul, only believe. Do not seek gladness; in that case you will not find it, because you are seeking feeling. But seek Jesus, follow Jesus, believe in Jesus, and gladness shall be added to you. "Not seeing, but believing, rejoice with joy unspeakable and full of glory."

—Andrew Murray

*There is joy in serving Jesus*
*As I journey on my way,*
*Joy that fills the heart with praises,*
*Ev'ry hour and ev'ry day.*

*There is joy in serving Jesus*
*As I walk alone with God;*
*'Tis the joy of Christ, my Savior,*
*Who the path of suff'ring trod.*
—Oswald J. Smith

# August 28

> *And he said, Lay not thine hand upon the lad, neither do thou any thing unto him: for now I know that thou fearest God, seeing thou hast not withheld thy son, thine only son from me.*
> —Genesis 22:12

*God rewards obedience in this life.* Isaac is spared, and in the bushes caught by his horns, Abraham sees a ram for the sacrifice. Instead of a place of unutterable woe and grief the altar of sacrifice is transformed into holy ground. Instead of "Thou Lord, hast forgotten," the mount is called "Jehovah-Jireh," "Thou Lord, dost see!" What a precious thought! In our darkest hour of testing, in our dreariest moment of trial, we can confidently know, "Thou Lord, dost see! Thou Lord, dost care!" How comforting to know in such a moment that there is no temptation taken us but such as is common to man. How unspeakably precious to prove that "God is faithful," who will not suffer us to be tempted above that we are able "but will with the temptation also make a way of escape" that we "may be able to bear it" (1 Corinthians 10:13).

When the last cherished Isaac is laid on the altar and every idol is broken at the feet of Him who is "King of kings and Lord of lords," we too shall see heaven open and hear the voice of God sweeter than music of angelic choir: "By Myself have I sworn, saith the Lord, for because thou *hast done* this thing . . . that in blessing I will bless thee . . ." (Gen. 22:16,17).

Now, to the heart of faith, the obedient heart, the yielded heart, He will give: Instead of dry land, springs of water! Instead of heaviness, the garment of praise! Instead of the thorn, the fig tree! Instead of the briar, the myrtle tree! Instead of ashes, beauty!

*God will reward obedience in the life to come.* Now, in this life, we are enrolled in the school of faith. Now is the time for discipline and study. Now is the time for submission to the divine will. Now is the time to prepare for the final examination!

Then graduation from time to eternity! Then we shall receive the diploma, "Well done, thou good and faithful servant: enter thou into the joy of thy Lord" (Matthew 25:21).

At the Judgment Seat of Christ faith and obedience will be tested and rewarded. Christian, what shall it be? Wood, hay and stubble to be burned up, or gold, silver and precious stones, to be purified and made finer to be laid at His blessed feet?

> *O for a faith that will not shrink,*
> *Tho' pressed by ev'ry foe,*
> *That will not tremble on the brink*
> *Of any earthly woe!*
>
> *That will not murmur nor complain*
> *Beneath the chastening rod,*
> *But, in the hour of grief or pain,*
> *Will lean upon its God;*
>
> *A faith that shines more bright and clear*
> *When tempests rage without;*
> *That when in danger knows no fear,*
> *In darkness feels no doubt.*
>
> —William H. Bathurst

# AUGUST 29

*In the day when I cried thou answeredest me, and strengthenedst me with strength in my soul.* —Psalm 138:3

This is a true testimony of the way in which God works in man's extremity. We do not know whether David was referring to some particular deliverance in his eventful life or whether he was thinking of a long series of deliverances. But we do know that he gives a real witness to God's method of dealing with our cries for help. First, there is the fact that God answers the prayer for help. Just how He answers is secondary; whether He immediately intervenes in a tangible way or whether He simply gives the assurance that He has heard the prayer, the fact is that He answers the heart-cry of His people. And then He did more; He strengthened them—in their souls. Many are the times when God must answer negatively some petition close to our hearts. Yet, though the thorn has to remain in our flesh, our God imparts strength to our very souls, and says to us, as He said to Paul, "My grace is sufficient for thee: for My strength is made perfect in weakness" (2 Cor. 12:9).

—*Frank E. Gaebelein*

*Child of My love, fear not the unknown morrow,*
*Dread not the new demand life makes of thee;*
*Thy ignorance doth hold no cause for sorrow*
*Since what thou knowest not is known to Me.*

*Thou canst not see today the hidden meaning*
*Of My command, but thou the light shalt gain;*
*Walk on in faith, upon My promise leaning,*
*And as thou goest all shall be made plain.*

*One step thou seest—then go forward boldly,*
*One step is far enough for faith to see;*
*Take that, and thy next duty shall be told thee,*
*For step by step thy Lord is leading thee.*

*But thanks be to God, who giveth us the victory through our*
*Lord Jesus Christ.* —1 Corinthians 15:57

We must never forget that the secret of victorious living is not the Christian struggling toward a possible but hard won victory. No. It is the Christian standing in a victory already consummated. A victory consummated for all time, one which when achieved, overcame all, the world, the flesh and the Devil. "Be of good cheer; I have overcome the world," cries the Son of God. "Behold the Lamb of God, which taketh away the sin of the world." In the agonies of the Son of Man as on Calvary's Cross He dies the death of an accursed felon, a new world is born. A new creation is forged.

No, the Christian does not struggle toward a possible victory. He is more than conqueror because his life flows from the triumphant death and resurrection of the Lord Jesus Christ. "And hath raised us up together, and made us sit together in heavenly places" (see Ephesians 2:6). Here you have the secret of the victorious Christian life. "This is the victory that overcometh the world, even our faith." That is, having received Christ as Savior, you already have victory, potentially. You need only discover all the wealth of spiritual riches (unsearchable riches) that are yours in Christ. All things are yours for you are Christ's. —F. J. Huegel

*So, let us go on with our Lord*
*To the fullness of God He has brought,*
*Unsearchable riches of Glory and good*
*Exceeding our uttermost thought;*

*Let us grow up into Christ,*
*Claiming His Life and its powers,*
*The triumphs of grace in the heavenly place*
*That our conquering Lord has made ours.*

# AUGUST 31

*Nevertheless I tell you the truth; It is expedient for you that I go away: for if I go not away, the Comforter will not come unto you; but if I depart, I will send him unto you.*

—John 16:7

God never afflicts us willingly; if He wounds, it is that He may heal; if He kills, it is that He may make alive; if He convicts, it is that He may comfort. There is comfort for those that mourn. We are reminded of the gracious utterance which seems almost to have been suggested by them. "Come unto me, all ye that labour and are heavy laden, and I will give you rest" (Matt. 11:28). Oh, yes; our God is "the God of all comfort." Christ is "the consolation of Israel," and there is no name of the Holy Ghost which speaks more peace to our hearts than the blessed name of "Comforter." —*E. W. Moore*

*Jesus, Lover of my soul,*
*Let me to Thy bosom fly,*
*While the nearer waters roll,*
*While the tempest still is high!*
*Hide me, O my Savior, Hide,*
*Till the storm of life is past;*
*Safe into the haven guide,*
*O receive my soul at last!*

*Other refuge have I none;*
*Hangs my helpless soul on Thee:*
*Leave, ah, leave me not alone,*
*Still support and comfort me!*
*All my trust on Thee is stayed,*
*All my help from Thee I bring;*
*Cover my defenseless head*
*With the shadow of Thy wing.*
—Charles Wesley

*But I know, that even now, whatsoever thou wilt ask of God,*
*God will give it thee.*
—John 11:22

Christian reader, here lies the true secret of the whole matter. Let nothing shake your confidence in the unalterable love of your Lord. Come what may—let the furnace be ever so hot; let the waters be ever so deep; let the shadows be ever so dark; let the path be ever so rough; let the pressure be ever so great—still hold fast your confidence in the perfect love and sympathy of the One who has proved His love by going down into the dust of death—down under the dark and heavy billows and waves of the wrath of God, in order to save your soul from everlasting burnings.

Be not afraid to trust Him fully—to commit yourself—without a shadow of reserve or misgiving to Him. Do not measure His love by your circumstances. If you do, you must, of necessity, reach a false conclusion. Judge not according to the outward appearance. Never reason from your surroundings. Get to the heart of Christ, and reason out from that blessed center. Never interpret His love by your circumstances; but always interpret your circumstances by His love. Let the beams of His everlasting favor shine upon your darkest surroundings, and then you will be able to answer every infidel thought, no matter from where it comes.

*At even, we shall know that the Lord hath brought us out;*
*Though the darkness deepen round us, we shall feel no fear or doubt,*
*For the fiery pillar shields us, and its burning is our light,*
*And we rest beneath its shadow while the evening brings the night.*
—Annie Johnson Flint

# September 2

*When he giveth quietness, who then can make trouble?*
—Job 34:29

These are the words of Elihu to Job, and are, perhaps, the best utterance that ever escaped his lips. Whatever Elihu might have meant by them when he spoke thus to the suffering patriarch, they are most comforting and cheering to every true saint of God today. "When He [God] giveth quietness [perfect rest and peace], who then can make trouble?" Can my circumstances? No! Can my associations? No! Can my difficulties? No! Can my enemies? No! For in all these things we are more than conquerors if God gives quietness.

But does God give to men today His quietness, this perfect rest and peace? Yes, He certainly does. But, you ask, To whom does He bestow this great blessing? Then our answer is: First, to those who are prepared to leave all and wholly follow Jesus. And then to those consecrated souls who will dare to trust God their heavenly Father to do right, and to do right for them under all circumstances and at all times. To such persons "He giveth quietness," and "who then can make trouble" for them? Not any, either on earth or in hell. Oh, to learn more and more to trust in God at all times!

—*John Roberts*

*A nation God delights to bless;*
*Can all our raging foes distress,*
*Or hurt whom they surround?*
*Hid from the general scourge we are,*
*Nor see the bloody waste of war,*
*Nor hear the trumpet's sound.*

*Thou, even thou, art Lord alone; thou hast made heaven, the heaven of heavens, with all their host, the earth, and all things that are therein, the seas, and all that is therein, and thou preservest them all. . . .* —Nehemiah 9:6

These words were spoken by companions of Nehemiah, the priestly sect of the Israelites, the Levites. In these words they are confessing God's goodness and their lack of goodness. They are reflecting upon God's power and their own weakness. The key phrase is "and Thou preservest them all."

As we meditate upon the truth contained in these words, it should renew our willingness to surrender ourselves—spirit, soul and body—to the Lord, for only when we are fully His can He use us for His glory. Not only that, but as we are surrendered to Him, He keeps us in safety and peace no matter what our surroundings—trials, temptations, difficulties and weakness.

God preserves all He has made, the earth and everything that is therein and the seas and everything that is therein. Of all His creation, man is the highest. Should we wonder then, that His deepest care and His greatest concern is His children—those who have come out from the ranks of men to stand in the light of His presence completely given over into His hands?

Yes, God "preservest them all" but most of all is His care lavished upon us, His children.

*Blest Jesus, come, and rule my heart,*
*And make me wholly Thine.*
*That I may nevermore depart*
*Nor grieve Thy love divine.*
—Benjamin Cleaveland

# SEPTEMBER 4

*My soul followeth hard after Thee: Thy right hand uphold-*
*eth me.* —Psalm 63:8

There are three notes in this Psalm which betoken the stages of the soul's growth: "My soul thirsteth for Thee"; "my soul shall be satisfied"; "my soul followeth hard after Thee." We may be passing through a wilderness of spiritual drought, the dark night of the soul, the seasons of dryness and depression which are apt to befall. In some cases, as when Elijah asked to die, or when John sent his despairing question to Christ from his prison, it is the result of physical or mental overstrain. But at such times, let us never hesitate still to speak of God as "my God." Nothing can sever you from His everlasting Love. You may not have the glad consciousness of it, but you must never surrender your belief in it. Go on blessing Him, as long as you live, and lift up your hands in prayer.

But we can never be satisfied with what we have attained. God is ever moving forward! Let us follow hard after Him.

—*F. B. Meyer*

*Not yesterday's load we are called on to bear,*
*Nor the morrow's uncertain and shadowy care;*
*Why should we look forward or back with dismay?*
*Our needs, as our mercies, are but for the day.*

*One day at a time, and the day is His day;*
*He hath numbered its hours, though they haste or delay.*
*His grace is sufficient; we walk not alone;*
*As the day, so the strength that He giveth His own.*
—Annie Johnson Flint

*Weeping may endure for a night, but joy cometh in the morning.*
— *Psalm 30:5*

Christian! If thou art in a night of trial, think of the morrow; cheer up thy heart with the thought of the coming of thy Lord. Be patient, for

> *Lo! He comes with clouds descending.*

Be patient! The Husbandman waits until He reaps His harvest. Be patient, for you know who has said, "Behold, I come quickly; and my reward is with me, to give to every man according as his work shall be." If you are feeling wretched now, remember

> *A few more rolling suns, at most,*
> *Will land thee on fair Canaan's coast.*

Thy head may be crowned with thorny troubles now, but it shall wear a starry crown ere long; thy hand may be filled with cares—it shall sweep the strings of the harp of heaven soon. Thy garments may be soiled with dust now; they shall be white by-and-by. Wait a little longer. Ah! How despicable our troubles and trials will seem when we look back upon them! Looking at them here in the prospect, they seem immense; but when we get to heaven we shall then

> *With transporting joys recount,*
> *The labors of our feet.*

Our trials will then seem light and momentary afflictions. Let us go on boldly; even though the night be dark, the morning comes, which is more than they can say who are shut up in the darkness of hell. Do you know what it is thus to live in the future—to live in expectation—to anticipate heaven? Happy believer, to have so sure, so comforting a hope.

— *Charles H. Spurgeon*

# September 6

*Thy servants are ready to do whatsoever my Lord the king shall appoint.*
—2 Samuel 15:15

*I love to think that God appoints*
  *My portion day by day;*
*Events of life are in His hand,*
  *And I would only say,*
*Appoint them in Thine own good time,*
  *And in Thine own best way.*
—A. L. Waring

If we are really, and always, and equally ready to do whatsoever the King appoints, all the trials and vexations arising from any change in His appointments, great or small, simply do not exist. If He appoints me to work there, shall I lament that I am not to work here? If He appoints me to wait indoors today, am I to be annoyed because I am not to work out-of-doors? If I meant to write His messages this morning, shall I grumble because He sends interrupting visitors, rich or poor, to whom I am to speak, or "show kindness" for His sake, or at least obey His command, "Be courteous"? If all my members are really at His disposal, why should I be put out if today's appointment is some simple work for my hands or errands for my feet, instead of some seemingly more important doing of head or tongue?
—F. R. Havergal

Receive every inward and outward trouble, every disappointment, pain, uneasiness, temptation, darkness, and desolation, with both thy hands, as a true opportunity and blessed occasion of dying to self, and entering into a fuller fellowship with thy self-denying, suffering Savior. That state is best, which exercises the highest faith in, and fullest resignation to God.
—William Law

*He leadeth me beside the still waters. He restoreth my soul:*
*He leadeth me in the paths of righteousness for His name's*
*sake.*
—Psalm 23:2, 3

*He leads me where the waters glide,*
*The waters soft and still,*
*And homeward He will gently guide*
*My wandering heart and will.*
—J. Keble

Out of obedience and devotion arises an habitual faith, which makes Him, though unseen, a part of all our life. He will guide us in a sure path, though it be a rough one: though shadows hang upon it, yet He will be with us. He will bring us home at last. Through much trial it may be, and weariness, in much fear and fainting of heart, in much sadness and loneliness, in griefs that the world never knows, and under burdens that the nearest never suspect. Yet He will suffice for all. By His eye or by His voice He will guide us, if we be docile and gentle; by His staff and by His rod, if we wander or are willful: anyhow, and by all means, He will bring us to His rest.
—*H. E. Manning*

Cheered by the presence of God, I will do at each moment, without anxiety, according to the strength which He shall give me, the work that His Providence assigns me. I will leave the rest without concern; it is not my affair. I ought to consider the duty to which I am called each day, as the work that God has given me to do, and to apply myself to it in a manner worthy of His glory, that is to say, with exactness and in peace. I must neglect nothing; I must be violent about nothing.
—*François de La Mothe Fenelon*

# SEPTEMBER 8

*Ask of me, and I shall give thee the heathen for thine inherit-*
*ance, and the uttermost parts of the earth for thy possession.*
—Psalm 2:8

The Father holds Himself in the attitude of Giver. Ask of Me, and that petition to God the Father empowers all agencies, inspires all movements. The Gospel is divinely inspired. Back of all its inspirations is prayer. Ask of Me lies back of all movements. Standing as the endowment of the enthroned Christ is the oath-bound covenant of the Father, "Ask of me, and I will give thee the nations for thine inheritance, and the uttermost parts of the earth for thy possession."

We can do all things by God's aid, and can have the whole of His aid by asking. The Gospel, in its success and power depends on our ability to pray. The dispensations of God depend on man's ability to pray. We can have all that God has. *Command ye Me.* —E. M. Bounds

How encouraging is the thought of the Redeemer's never-ceasing intercession for us. When we pray, He pleads for us; and when we are not praying, He is advocating our cause, and by His supplications shielding us from unseen dangers. We little know what we owe to our Savior's prayers. When we reach the hill-tops of heaven, and look back upon all the way whereby the Lord our God has led us, how we shall praise Him who, before the eternal throne, has pleaded our cause against our unseen enemies. "But I have prayed for thee, that thy faith fail not."

*It matters to Him about you,*
*He meaneth to see you quite through;*
*The might of His hand, no power can withstand,*
*He always is thinking of you.*

*Oh that I knew where I might find him!* —Job 23:3a.

God speaks when all the world is silent! He speaks at the new-made grave; He speaks on the battlefield; He speaks in the rough and tumble of ordinary living. He has something to say when the world about us is dumb with fear and confusion. When the soul in anguish cries out, "Oh that I knew where I might find him!" He comes strangely near. When the blackness and darkness of sin's death engulfed the whole human family, He lighted a Cross on a faraway Judean hill, and its message comes streaming down through the centuries, undimmed. God loves and cares—*and redeems!*

He does not wait for favorable circumstances or for an enlightened generation. He takes us as He finds us. For all who would follow Him He builds a highway through the desert; He makes the crooked straight and the rough places plain.

What strength there is in His arm! Strong enough to rule undismayed, but tender enough to carry the lambs of the Rock. What self-revealing love! It seeks and finds, and saves. Then He gives the redemptive message to those whom He has found. "O Zion, that bringest good tidings, get thee up into the high mountain; O Jerusalem, that bringest good tidings, lift up thy voice with strength; lift it up, be not afraid; say unto the cities of Judah, Behold your God!" (Isa. 40:9).

—*Samuel Young*

*God, who made Earth and Heaven*
*Darkness and light,*
*Who the day for toil has given,*
*For rest the night,*
*May thine angel guards defend us,*
*Slumber sweet thy mercy send us,*
*Holy dreams and hopes attend us.*
*This livelong night.*

—Reginald Heber

# SEPTEMBER 10

*He that spared not his own Son, but delivered him up for us all, how shall he not with him also freely give us all things?*
—Romans 8:32

Our text tells of the gracious character of our loving God as interpreted by the gift of His Son. And this, not merely for the instruction of our minds, but for the comfort and assurance of our hearts. The gift of His own Son is God's guarantee to His people of all needed blessings. The greater includes the less; His unspeakable spiritual gift is the pledge of all needed temporal mercies. Note in our text four things which should bring comfort to every renewed heart. The Father's costly sacrifice. Our God is a giving God and no good thing does He withhold from them that walk uprightly. The Father's gracious design. It was for us that Christ was delivered up; it was our highest and eternal interests that He had at heart. The Spirit's infallible inference. The greater includes the less; the unspeakable Gift guarantees the bestowment of all other needed favors. The comforting promise. Its sure foundation, its present and future scope, its blessed extent, are for the assuring of our hearts and the peace of our minds. May the Lord add His blessing to this little meditation.

—*Arthur W. Pink*

*He left the throne and His rightful place,*
*    The burden of sin to lift,*
*He came to this world of pain and woe,*
*    As "God's Unspeakable Gift."*

*His Kingdom is one of righteousness,*
*    And His reign shall never cease.*
*His name is "Wonderful, Counsellor,"*
*    And the blessed "Prince of Peace."*
    —Mrs. Macey P. Sealey

*But rejoice, inasmuch as ye are partakers of Christ's sufferings; that, when his glory shall be revealed, ye may be glad also with exceeding joy.* —1 Peter 4:13

If you are going to be used by God, He will take you through a multitude of experiences that are not meant for you at all, they are meant to make you useful in His hands, and to enable you to understand what transpires in other souls so that you will never be surprised at what you come across.

The sufferings of Christ are not those of ordinary men. He suffered "according to the will of God," not from the point of view we suffer from as individuals. It is only when we are related to Jesus Christ that we can understand what God is after in His dealings with us. In the history of the Christian Church the tendency has been to evade being identified with the sufferings of Jesus Christ; men have sought to procure the carrying out of God's order by a short cut of their own. God's way is always the way of suffering, the way of the "long, long trail."

Are we partakers of Christ's sufferings? We never realize at the time what God is putting us through; we go through it more or less misunderstandingly; then we come to a luminous place, and say—"Why, God has girded me, though I did not know it."

*Should all earthly friends forsake me,*
*Every grief of mine is small,*
*When I see my Savior standing*
*Mute, condemned, in Pilate's hall.*

*Oh, no cross that I may carry*
*Can be heavy when I know*
*That my Savior bore His gladly*
*Just because He loved me so.*
—Alice Mortenson

# SEPTEMBER 12

*Let Him do to me as seemeth good unto Him.*
—2 Samuel 15:26

*To have each day, the thing I wish,*
  *Lord, that seems best to me;*
*But not to have the thing I wish,*
  *Lord, that seems best to Thee.*
*Most truly, then, Thy will is done,*
  *When mine, O Lord, is crossed;*
*'Tis good to see my plans o'erthrown,*
  *My ways in Thine all lost.*
—H. Bonar

O Lord, Thou knowest what is best for us; let this or that be done, as Thou shalt please. Give what Thou wilt, and how much Thou wilt, and when Thou wilt. Deal with me as Thou thinkest good. Set me where Thou wilt, and deal with me in all things just as Thou wilt. Behold, I am Thy servant, prepared for all things: for I desire not to live unto myself, but unto Thee; and oh, that I could do it worthily and perfectly!
—*Thomas à Kempis*

Dare to look up to God, and say, "Make use of me for the future as Thou wilt. I am of the same mind; I am one with Thee. I refuse nothing which seems good to Thee. Lead me whither Thou wilt."
—*Epictetus*

How awful would be our lot, if our wishes should straightway pass into realities; if we were endowed with a power to bring about all that we desire; if the inclinations of our will were followed by fulfillment of our hasty wishes, and sudden longings were always granted. One day we shall bless Him, not more for what He has granted than for what He has denied.
—*H. E. Manning*

*For thou hast delivered my soul from death, mine eyes from tears, and my feet from falling.* —Psalm 116:8

Is God our God; and will He suffer anything to befall us for our hurt? Will He lay any more upon us, than He gives us strength to bear? Will He suffer any wind to blow upon us but for good? Doth He not set us before His face? Will a father or mother suffer a child to be wronged in their presence, if they can help it? Will a friend suffer his friend to be injured, if he may redress him? And will God, who hath put these affections into parents and friends, neglect the care of those He hath taken so near unto Himself? No surely, His eyes are open to look upon their condition; His ears are open to their prayers; a *book of remembrance*, Malachi 3:16, is written of all their good desires, speeches, and actions; He hath bottles for all their tears, their very sighs are not *hid from Him;* He hath written them upon the *palms of His hands,* and cannot but continually look upon them. Oh, let us prize the favor of so good a God, who though He dwells on high yet will regard things so low, and not neglect the mean estate of any; nay, He especially delights to be called the *Comforter of His elect,* and the God of those that are in misery, and have none to fly unto but Himself.

—*Richard Sibbes*

*Thine is the hand that is holding and leading and trying,*
*Thine is the voice that is bidding me haste or delay;*
*Who else but Thou, who seest my past and my future,*
*Who else can know how my steps should be ordered today?*
—Annie Johnson Flint

# SEPTEMBER 14

If we want to know what clouds of affliction mean and what they are sent for, we must not flee away from them in fright with closed ears and bandaged eyes. Fleeing from the cloud is fleeing from the divine love that is behind the cloud. In one of the German picture-galleries is a painting called "Cloudland"; it hangs at the end of a long gallery, and at first sight it looks like a huge repulsive daub of confused color, without form or comeliness. As you walk toward it the picture begins to take shape; it proves to be a mass of exquisite little cherub faces, like those at the head of the canvas in Raphael's "Madonna San Sisto." If you come close to the picture, you see only an innumerable company of little angels and cherubim!

How often the soul that is frightened by trial sees nothing but a confused and repulsive mass of broken expectations and crushed hopes! But if that soul, instead of fleeing away into unbelief and despair, would only draw up near to God, it would soon discover that the cloud was full of angels of mercy. In one cherub-face it would see "Whom I love I chasten." Another angel would say, "All things work together for good to them that love God." In still another sweet face the heavenly words are coming forth, "Let not your heart be troubled; you believe in God, believe also in me. In my Father's house are many mansions. . . . Where I am there shall ye be also."

No cloud can be big enough to shut out heaven if we keep the eye toward the Throne. And when we reach heaven and see the cloud from God's side, it will be blazing and beaming with the illuminations of His love. —*Theodore L. Cuyler*

*. . . whosoever drinketh of the water that I shall give him shall never thirst. . . .*
—John 4:14

Here is a blessed promise for the believer in Christ, a promise of complete and eternal satisfaction. It is a marvelous truth that if we believe in Christ as our Savior now, He gives us not only daily satisfaction but eternal contentment for evermore. The true Christian can be joyful no matter what his circumstances, because his joy comes from within and is derived from a never-ending source, his Savior. You and I as Christians need never want for comfort and cheer, for we find in Christ a veritable gushing fountain of consolation and contentment.

Our foundation is laid in that fair city "whose builder and maker is God." We do not need earthly friends for we have a "Friend that sticketh closer than a brother." No matter how we are buffeted by life, we rest upon the Rock of Ages, and "underneath are the everlasting arms."

But in one sense we will continue to thirst, that blessed thirst after Christ. No matter how often we meditate upon and drink from His Word, no matter how often we abide in His presence in prayer, we will still have that thrilling thirst after Him. All of our decisions, all of our needs, will find fruition and fulfillment in a closer, more intimate walk with our Savior. We must come continually to that fountain that never runs dry and take of the water of life which He offers freely.

*Jesus, the gift divine I know,*
*The gift divine I ask of Thee;*
*The living water now bestow,*
*Thy Spirit and Thyself, on me.*
—Charles Wesley

# SEPTEMBER 16

*For I the Lord thy God will hold thy right hand, saying unto thee, Fear not; I will help thee.* —Isaiah 41:13

*I take Thy hand, and fears grow still;*
*Behold Thy face, and doubts remove;*
*Who would not yield his wavering will*
*To perfect Truth and boundless Love?*
—S. Johnson

Do not look forward to the changes and chances of this life in fear; rather look to them with full hope that, as they arise, God, whose you are, will deliver you out of them. He has kept you hitherto—and He will lead you safely through all things; and, when you cannot stand, He will bear you in His arms. Do not look forward to what may happen tomorrow; the same everlasting Father who cares for you today, will take care of you tomorrow, and every day. Either He will shield you from suffering, or He will give you unfailing strength to bear it. Be at peace then, and put aside all anxious thoughts and imaginations. —*St. Francis de Sales*

The Shepherd knows what pastures are best for His sheep, and they must not question nor doubt, but trustingly follow Him. Perhaps He sees that the best pastures for some of us are to be found in the midst of opposition or of earthly trials. If He leads you there, you may be sure they are green for you, and you will grow and be made strong by feeding there. Perhaps He sees that the best waters for you to walk beside will be raging waves of trouble and sorrow. If this should be the case, He will make them still waters for you, and you must go and lie down beside them, and let them have all their blessed influences upon you. —*H. W. Smith*

*Blessed . . .* —Matthew 5:3

The "Blesseds" of the Scripture shine all over the inspired pages, like stars in the midnight sky. The Bible is a book of beatitudes and benedictions. God's mercy lies everywhere. Wherever we see Christ He is imparting blessings as the sun imparts light and warmth. While He was here on the earth He was always reaching out His hand to give a benediction to some life that sorely needed it. Now it was on the children's heads, now on the leper, now on the blind eyes, now on the sick, now on the dead, that He laid those gracious hands, and always He left some rich gift of blessing. Then we remember one day when those gentle hands were drawn out by cruel enemies, and with iron nails fastened back on the Cross; yet even then it was in blessing that they were extended, for it was for our sins they were transfixed thus on the wood.

Then it is a striking fact that the last glimpse we have of the Savior in this world shows Him in the attitude of blessing. He had been talking with His disciples as He led them out, and then He lifted up His hands and blessed them; and while He was blessing them He was parted from them and received up into heaven. Surely there could be no truer picture taken of Jesus at any point in His life than as He appeared in that last view of Him which this world enjoyed. In heaven now He is still a blessing Savior, holding up pierced hands before God in intercession, and reaching down gracious hands full of benedictions for our sad, sinful earth. If any life goes unblessed with such a Savior, it can be only because of unbelief and rejection.

—*J. R. Miller*

*The hands of Christ*
*Seem very frail*
*For they were broken*
*By a nail*

*But only they*
*Reach heaven at last*
*Whom these frail, broken*
*Hands hold fast.*

—John Richard Moreland

# September 18

*Having made peace through the blood of His Cross.*
—Colossians 1:20

We all need Peace! There are sources of Peace which are common to all men. The peace of a happy home; of an increasing business and enlarging influence; of the respect and love of our fellows. We can all understand a peace like that; but there is a "peace that passeth understanding." It is too deep for words. It is like the pillowed depths of the ocean, which are undisturbed by the passing storm. Here is a sufferer, almost always in acute pain, and needing constant attention, and yet so happy. Joy and Peace, like guardian angels, sit by that bedside; and Hope, not blindfolded, touches all the strings of the lyre, and sheds sunshine—how do you account for it? Let the skeptic and the scoffer answer! Here is a peace that passes understanding which comes from the God of Peace.

For the Christian soul there is a silver lining in every cloud; a blue patch in the darkest sky; a turn in the longest lane; a mountain view which shall compensate the steepest ascent. Wait on the Lord, and keep His way, and He shall exalt thee.

The peace of God is the peace of the Divine Nature—the very tranquillity which prevails in the heart of the God of Peace. It was of this that Jesus spoke when He said, "My peace I give unto you"; for His own being was filled and blessed with it during His earthly career. "The Lord of Peace Himself give you peace always."

We shall not escape life's discipline. We may expect to abound here, and to be abased there. But amid all, God's Peace, like a white-winged sentinel angel, shall come down to garrison our heart with its affections, and our mind with its thoughts.
—*F. B. Meyer*

> *But we see Jesus, who was made a little lower than the angels for the suffering of death, crowned with glory and honor; that he by the grace of God should taste death for every man.*
> —Hebrews 2:9

The suffering of Jesus is distinctive in itself, quite apart from any other suffering. It was purely voluntary: the coming down here as He did, the lowly life He led, the suffering of spirit through His life, and the great climax—the Cross. It was all done of His own free accord for us. He took our place and took what belonged to us. This reveals the real love and meaning of Jesus' suffering.

The Cross spells out two stories: one in black, ugly pot-black, the story of sin. Sin carpentered the cross, and wove the thorns, and drove the nails: our sin. And a story, too, in red, bright-flowing red, the story of love, His love, that yielded to Cross and nails and shame for us. And only the passion of His love burning within will make us hate sin, as only His blood can wash it out.
> —S. D. Gordon

*Love Divine, so great and wondrous,*
  *Deep and mighty, pure, sublime;*
*Coming from the heart of Jesus,*
  *Just the same thro' tests of time.*

*Like a dove when hunted, frightened*
  *As a wounded fawn was I;*
*Broken-hearted, yet He healed me,*
  *He will heed the sinner's cry.*

*Love Divine, so great and wondrous,*
  *All my sins He then forgave;*
*I will sing His praise forever,*
  *For His blood, His pow'r to save.*
> —Fred Blom

# September 20

*. . . and they retired from the city, every man to his tent.*
—2 Samuel 20:22

Retire, O my soul! from the busy world, and employ thyself about that for which thou wast created: the contemplation of thy God. I will hasten to my closet, or yonder solitary walk, and there hidden from a bustling world, I will not suffer a single thought of it to approach me, unless by way of pity and contempt.

How delightful is it, O my soul, for thee to enjoy this sweet communion with thy God, and thus to dwell upon divine objects. Here am I safe, and at rest in this dear place of quiet; and earnestly pity all the men of business and hurry, whose heads are full of perplexing contrivances, to procure a little happiness in a world where there is no such thing.

O blessed freedom! O charming solitude! I will grasp you, and I will hold you fast—the delight of silence and retreat! Here I can unburden my soul, and pour it out before my God. Here I can wrestle with the powers of heaven, and not let them go till 1 have obtained a blessing. Here I can confess my sins, and with hopes of comfort lay open my troubled breast before the merciful Hearer of my prayers.

—*Thomas Ken*

*I met God in the morning*
*When my day was at its best,*
*And His presence came like the sunrise—*
*Like glory in my breast.*

*All day long the Presence lingered,*
*All day long He stayed with me,*
*And we sailed in perfect calmness*
*O'er a very troubled sea . . .*

*Now I think I know the secret,*
*Learned from many a troubled way;*
*You must meet God in the morning,*
*If you would have Him through the day.*
—Ralph Spaulding Cushman

*These things have I spoken unto you, that my joy might remain in you, and that your joy might be full.* —John 15:11

If you have no joy in your religion, there's a leak in your Christianity somewhere. —*W. A. ("Billy") Sunday*

When the joy of the Lord Jesus Christ is in a man's heart his joy is always full, and there is no fullness of joy anywhere except in Christ. God has made the human heart so only He Himself can fill it. All the pleasures of the world, all the riches of earth, though they may bring a temporary thrill, leave unsatisfied the longing of the heart. "My heart and my flesh crys out for the living God," says the psalmist. The soul of man is immortal, and only God can satisfy the hunger of the soul and bring eternal joy. The immortal cannot be satisfied with the temporal, and the eternal with that which is transient. Of course, the Christian has his sorrows. He is grieved by the deaths of his loved ones, but he sorrows not "as those who have no hope," and in the midnight of his sorrow sings the nightingale of hope bringing joy to his heart with the assurance that he shall see his dear ones again.

When the man without Christ loses his wealth and his friends and his family, he has lost everything. Let the Christian see his family taken from him, his temporal possessions swept away and his friends removed—he still has the abiding presence of Christ in whom his hope is fixed and who is the Author and Source of his joy. The man whose affections are set on Christ has every reason to rejoice because he knows that all things work together for his good (Rom. 8:28). The man who lives in daily fellowship with the Lord is in contact with the Source of joy eternal. "In thy presence is fullness of joy; at thy right hand there are pleasures for evermore" (Psa. 16:11).

# SEPTEMBER 22

*That the trial of your faith, being much more precious than of gold that perisheth, though it be tried with fire, might be found unto praise and honor and glory at the appearing of Jesus Christ.* —1 Peter 1:7

*(And Job said) . . . What? shall we receive good at the hand of God, and shall we not receive evil? In all this did not Job sin with his lips.* —Job 2:10b

A few days ago I was resting quietly under one of the giant Sequoias up in the High Sierras. As I looked up through the enormous limbs to the top of the tree I noticed that the wind was swaying its branches. I said to myself, "They tell me this tree is four thousand years old. If the wind and storms had not come at various times to strengthen it, how could it have stood when the tempest in all its fury beat against it?"

And how are you, friend, going to stand unless God tests your faith? Job had to discover that truth. God allowed disaster to overtake him and he was brought to the ash heap. In the end of his testing, Job testified, "I have heard of Thee by the hearing of the ear; but now mine eye seeth Thee. Wherefore I abhor myself, and repent in dust and ashes." The whole book of Job deals with the process of the consecration of a saint. —*Charles E. Fuller*

*Make me a captive, Lord.*
*And then I shall be free;*
*Force me to render up my sword,*
*And I shall conqueror be.*
*I sink in life's alarms*
*When by myself I stand;*
*Imprison me within Thine arms,*
*And strong shall be my hand.*
—George Matheson

*But my God shall supply all your need according to his riches in glory by Christ Jesus.* —Philippians 4:19

The word "supply" in this promise means, literally, to fill full. Our need is as it were an empty vessel, and God's supply is that which fills the vessel to the brim. The thought takes our minds back to 2 Kings 4, to the account of the widow and her cruse of oil. The woman is in desperate need. The creditor has come to take her sons as bondmen. She has nothing in the house but a pot of oil. The prophet Elisha says to her, "Go, borrow thee vessels abroad of all thy neighbors, even empty vessels; borrow not a few." This is promptly done.

Elisha's further word is, "Thou shalt pour out into all those vessels, and thou shalt set aside that which is full." The woman takes her solitary cruse of oil, and begins to pour out. There would be small jars, big jars—jars of all shapes and sizes. She comes to one very large container, and thinks, as she glances again at her own small oil-pot, "Why, this will never fill that!"

Yet as she pours, there is the more to pour, until all the receptacles are filled to utmost capacity, and she calls for yet another, only to find that the supply is greater than all that which needed to be filled. Then the oil is sold; the creditor is paid; the sons are set free; and the woman's need is "filled full" even as were the oil-pots, and in a way which becomes forever a type of how God "supplies," or fills full, the needs of His people. —*J. Sidlow Baxter*

*Though troubles assail, and dangers afright;*
*Though friends should all fail, and foes all unite;*
*Yet one thing secures us, whatever betide*
*The Scripture assures us, "The Lord will provide."*

# September 24

*Unto you that fear my name shall the Sun of righteousness*
*arise with healing in his wings.* —Malachi 4:2

*As a bird in meadows fair*
*Or in lonely forest sings*
*Till it fills the summer air,*
*And the greenwood sweetly rings,*
*So my heart to Thee would raise,*
*O my God, its song of praise*
*That the gloom of night is o'er,*
*And I see the sun once more.*
—From the German, 1580

Christ, to the Christian growing older, seems to be what the sun is to the developing day, which it lightens from the morning to the evening. When the sun is in the zenith in the broad noon-day, men do their various works by his light; but they do not so often look up to him. It is the sunlight that they glory in, flooding a thousand tasks with clearness, making a million things beautiful. But as the world rolls into the evening, it is the sun itself at sunset that men gather to look at and admire and love. —*Phillips Brooks*

You know in a wheel there is one portion that never turns round, that stands steadfast—and that is the axle. So, in God's Providence there is an axle which never moves. Christian, here is a sweet thought for you! Your state is ever changing: sometimes you are exalted, and sometimes depressed; yet there is an unmoving point in your state. What is that axle? It is the axle of God's everlasting love toward His covenant people. The exterior of the wheel is changing; but the center stands forever fixed. Other things may move; but God's love never moves; it is the axle of the wheel, and will endure.

# SEPTEMBER 25

*I have called thee by thy name; thou art Mine.* —Isaiah 43:1

> *Thou art as much His care as if beside*
> *Nor man nor angel lived in heaven or earth;*
> *Thus sunbeams pour alike their glorious tide,*
> *To light up worlds, or wake an insect's mirth.*
> —J. Keble

God beholds you individually, whoever you are. "He calls thee by thy name." He sees you, and understands you. He knows what is in you, all your own peculiar feelings and thoughts, your dispositions and likings, your strength and your weakness. He views you in your day of rejoicing and your day of sorrow. He sympathizes in your hopes and in your temptations; He interests Himself in all your anxieties and your remembrances, in all the risings and fallings of your spirit. He compasses you round, and bears you in His arms; He takes you up and sets you down. You do not love yourself better than He loves you. —*J. H. Newman*

The circumstances of her life she could not alter, but she took them to the Lord, and handed them over into His management; and then she believed that He took it, and she left all the responsibility and the worry and anxiety with Him. As often as the anxieties returned she took them back; and the result was that, although the circumstances remained unchanged, her soul was kept in perfect peace in the midst of them. And the secret she found so effectual in her outward affairs, she found to be still more effectual in her inward ones, which were in truth even more utterly unmanageable. She abandoned her whole self to the Lord, with all that she was and all that she had; and, believing that He took that which she had committed to Him, she ceased to fret and worry, and her life became all sunshine in the gladness of belonging to Him. —*H. W. Smith*

# SEPTEMBER 26

*The steps of a good man are ordered by the Lord: and he delighteth in his way.* —Psalm 37:23

The God of Creation is also the God of Providence! There is as much design and purpose in the way He directs and upholds His creatures as there was, and is, in His creating of them. If there is such an abundance of wisdom evident in God's creation, we must certainly believe that this same Intelligence is operative in His providence. Particularly in the case of those who know Christ as Savior and therefore are objects of special grace can it be said that nothing in their existence is without its holy and wise design!

> *The very Law that molds a tear*
> *And bids it trickle from its source,*
> *That Law preserves the earth its sphere*
> *And guides the planets in their course.*

It is well to bear in mind when we wince beneath the rod that we cannot expect to heal the deep wound of bereavement with one small application of comfort. Sorrow is given for a more important purpose than to be thus easily erased. God's comfort, however, gives a new and blessed aspect to our trials, and, if diligently sought and applied will in time not only heal, but leave as well a cross-shaped scar of grace upon our enriched souls!

God sends the storm that we may realize that the anchor of our soul is steadfast and sure, gripping the Rock. He knows that when the waves have subsided and our moorings have proven secure, we shall sail forth toward the desired haven with new confidence and assurance. For we shall acquire steadfastness and increased courage if, having taken refuge in the Eternal God, we find that when all else failed us, underneath were still the "everlasting arms" (Deut. 33:27).

—*Henry G. Bosch*

*I would have you without carefulness.* -

*O Lord, how happy should we be*
*If we could cast our care on Thee,*
*If we from self could rest;*
*And feel at heart that One above,*
*In perfect wisdom, perfect love,*
*Is working for the best.*

—J. Anstice

Cast all your care on God. See that all your cares be such as you can cast on God, and then hold none back. Never brood over yourself; never stop short in yourself; but cast your whole self, even this very care which distresses you, upon God. Be not anxious about little things, if you would learn to trust God with your all. Act upon faith in little things; commit your daily cares and anxieties to Him; and He will strengthen your faith for any greater trials. Rather give your whole self into God's hands, and so trust Him to take care of you in all lesser things, as being His, for His own sake, whose you are.  —*E. B. Pusey*

Take courage, and turn your troubles, which are without remedy, into material for spiritual progress. Often turn to our Lord, who is watching you, poor frail little being as you are, amid your labors and distractions. He sends you help, and blesses your affliction. This thought should enable you to bear your troubles patiently and gently, for love of Him who only allows you to be tried for your own good. Raise your heart continually to God, seek His aid, and let the foundation stone of your consolation be your happiness in being His. All vexations and annoyances will be comparatively unimportant while you know that you have such a Friend, such a Stay, such a Refuge.  —*St. Francis de Sales*

*looking unto Jesus, the author and finisher of our faith. . . .*
—Hebrews 12:2

It is the Holy Spirit who turns our eyes and our thoughts entirely away from self and "unto Jesus." It is the work of Satan on the other hand to turn our eyes back upon ourselves, for it is the evil one who is constantly encouraging us to put self first. He does this in two ways: he tells us, first of all, that we are too sinful, too depraved, that we cannot have enough faith or repentance, for God to save us. He tells us that we are too weak to hold out, that the Christian life will not bring us joy. On the other hand, Satan tells us that we are too important to humble ourselves in God's sight, not bad enough to need God's forgiveness.

On the opposite side of the picture, the Holy Spirit tells us that Christ is all and we are nothing, that it is not our hold upon Christ but His hold upon us that saves us. The Holy Spirit tells us that our joy is in Christ and not dependent upon outward circumstances, that our salvation is in Christ and not in any merit of our own. "Look unto Jesus," the Holy Spirit tells us—not to ourselves, not to our surroundings, not even to our loved ones. We can never find happiness by looking for it in our feelings, in our circumstances or even in our belief in Christ. Happiness is only to be found in Christ Himself. It is not what we are but what Christ is that gives us rest unto our souls.

The only way we can overcome Satan's temptation to us to look to self is by "looking unto Jesus," keeping our eyes solely on Him. His death, His sufferings, merits and constant intercession for us at the Father's right hand should be uppermost in our thoughts. It is Christ who is our Mainstay when we lie down for the night and when we awaken at daybreak.

A famous painter of olden times made a rule that none of

those who came to learn in his studio should be allowed to paint the face of our Lord unless he were pure in heart and life. One day a young man came who was suspected of leading a wild life. The artist told him of his rule and gave him a head of Judas Iscariot to copy. He tried for some time to copy it but the face repelled him so that he came to loathe it. At last he said despairingly: "Master, I cannot reproduce this. Only give me the face of Christ and I will do my best." The artist complied with his request. As the pupil studied the sweetness and moral beauty of the face divine, its mute appeal awakened in his heart a desire to know Him. Then and there he came to hate his old life and to love goodness and purity for the sake of Him who gave His life for the world. It is only by looking unto Jesus and contemplating the love of God revealed in Him that we can see vice in its true colors and come to know the joy of walking in His steps. —*Keith L. Brooks*

*When thou wakest in the morning,*
*Ere thou tread the untried way*
*Of the lot that lies before thee,*
*Through the coming busy day,*
*Whether sunbeams promise brightness,*
*Whether dim forebodings fall,*
*Be thy dawning glad or gloomy,*
*Go to Jesus—tell Him all!*

# SEPTEMBER 29

*When thou prayest, enter into thy closet, and when thou hast shut thy door, pray to thy Father which is in secret.*
—Matthew 6:6

In our word for today we have one of our Lord's plainest and most significant instructions about the manner and the nature of prayer. The writer is speaking, not of public prayer as when the minister leads the congregation, but of personal prayer, when the child of God wants to talk to his Father of his own affairs, and lay at his feet his own individual burdens. We should seek to be alone in all such praying. Other presences about us disturb our thoughts and restrict our freedom. So we are to go into our closet and shut the door.

This shutting of the door is significant in several ways. It shuts the world out. It secures us against interruption. It ought to shut out worldly thoughts and cares and distractions, as well as worldly presences. Wandering in prayer is usually one of our sorest troubles. Then it shuts us in, and this also is important and significant. It shuts us in alone with God. No eye but His sees us as we bow in the secrecy. No ear but His hears us as we pour out our heart's feelings and desires. Thus we are helped to realize that with God alone have we to do, that He alone can help us. As we are shut up alone with God, so also are we shut up to God. There is precious comfort in the assurance that when we thus pray we are not talking into the air. There is an ear to hear, though we can see no presence, and it is the ear of our Father. This assures us of loving regard in heaven, also of prompt and gracious answer.   —*J. R. Miller*

*Away in foreign fields they wondered how their simple words had power—*
*At home the Christians, two or three had met to pray an hour.*
*Yes, we are always wondering, wondering how— Because we do not see*
*Someone—perhaps unknown and far away— On bended knee*
—Author Unknown

*For we which have believed do enter into rest . . .*

—Hebrews 4:3

Let us converse much with the glory that is to be revealed. They who by faith send their hearts and best affections before them to heaven, while they are here on this earth, may in return fetch thence some of those joys and pleasures that are at God's right hand. That which goes up in vapors of holy desire, though insensible, in "groanings which cannot be uttered," will come down again in dews of heavenly consolations, that will make the soul as a watered garden.

Let us look much to the end of our way, how glorious it will be, and that will help to make our way pleasant. This abundantly satisfies the saints, and is the fatness of God's house on earth, Psalm 36:8, 9. This makes them now to drink of the river of God's pleasures, that with Him is the fountain of life, whence all these streams come, and in His light they hope to see light—everlasting light.

By frequent meditations on that rest which remains for the people of God, Hebrews 4:3, we now enter into that rest, and partake of the comfort of it. We may have foretastes of heavenly delights, while we are here on earth—clusters from Canaan, while we are yet in this wilderness—and no pleasures are comparable to that which these afford. That is the sweetest joy within us, which is borrowed from the joy set before us; and we deprive ourselves very much of the comfort of our religion, in not having our eye more to that joy.

—*Matthew Henry*

*Oh, the rest of simply trusting!*
*Yielded to my Father's will,*
*In His loving arms enfolded,*
*Just to trust Him and be still.*
—Author Unknown

# OCTOBER 1

*And the Lord went before them by day in a pillar of a cloud,
to lead them the way. . . .* —Exodus 13:21

How perfectly safe at all times the children of Israel were, for "the Lord went before them by day in a pillar of a cloud to lead them the way, and by night in a pillar of fire to give them light." Thus they had the continual presence of the Lord God Almighty. He was with them as a guide by day, as a light by night, and as a shield or protection by both day and night. But what has that to do with me? May I expect God's presence to be with me, both for protection and direction, even as it was with the children of Israel? Yes, praise God! I may. Solomon has said: "In all thy ways acknowledge Him, and He shall direct thy paths." The Psalmist declared: "Thy word is a lamp to my feet and a light unto my path." The words of the Lord Jesus are: "The Father shall give you another Comforter, that He may abide with you for ever, even the Spirit of truth." And the apostle Paul has taught us that our "body is the temple of the Holy Ghost." Therefore, if I honor and obey Him I may with confidence expect continued guidance by God's Word, and His Holy Spirit, and His providence, both from day to day and all the days of my life.

*Captain of Israel's host and guide
    Of all who seek the land above,
Beneath Thy shadow we abide,
    The clouds of Thy protecting love.
Our strength, Thy grace—our rule, Thy Word,
    Our end, the glory of the Lord.*

—*John Roberts*

*He said unto them, Come ye yourselves apart into a desert place, and rest a while.* —Mark 6:31

How thoughtful Jesus is for the comfort of His disciples! He never wants to overwork them. He provides seasons and places of rest for them all along the way. One of these "quiet resting-places" is the night, coming after each day of toil. Then our emptied life-fountains are refilled. Another resting-place is the Lord's Day after the week of anxious battle and strife. Then it is that we should seek the renewal of our spiritual life by communing with God, by lying on our Lord's bosom. The Lord's Supper is another resting-place. The Master leads us into the upper room to sit with Him at His table, to feast our souls on the provisions of His love and grace.

Then there are many other quiet places to which our Lord invites us to come apart with Him to rest a while—the sweet hours of prayer, alone, or in the house of God, the communings with friends, the sacred hours we spend in home joys. Sometimes the Master calls us to rest a while in a sick-room, away from the noise and struggle of the busy world. It may be in pain or in suffering, and there may be no bodily rest; but our souls are resting, and we are learning lessons we never could have learned in the midst of life's exciting toil.

One thing about all these "rests" to which Jesus invites us, is that we are to rest *with Him.* He never says, "Go ye apart and rest," but ever His Word is, "Come ye apart." The resting is always to be with Him. It is His loving presence that makes the blessedness of the rest. —*J. R. Miller*

*The way is long, My Child! But it shall be*
*Not one step longer than is best for thee;*
*And thou shalt know, at last, when thou shalt stand*
*Safe at the goal, how I did take thy hand.*
—Author Unknown

# OCTOBER 3

*Ye people, pour out your heart before Him: God is a refuge for us.*
—Psalm 62:8

*Whate'er the care which breaks thy rest,*
*Whate'er the wish that swells thy breast;*
*Spread before God that wish, that care,*
*And change anxiety to prayer.*
—Jane Crewsdon

Trouble and perplexity drive us to prayer, and prayer drives away trouble and perplexity.
—*P. Melancthon*

Whatsoever it is that presses thee, go tell thy Father; put over the matter into His hand, and so thou shalt be freed from that dividing, perplexing care that the world is full of. When thou art either to do or suffer anything, when thou art about any purpose or business, go tell God of it, and acquaint Him with it; yea, burden Him with it, and thou hast done for matter of caring; no more care, but quiet, sweet diligence in thy duty, and dependence on Him for the carriage of thy matters. Roll thy cares, and thyself with them, as one burden, all on thy God.
—*R. Leighton*

As soon as we lay ourselves entirely at His feet, we have enough light given us to guide our own steps; as the foot-soldier, who hears nothing of the councils that determine the course of the great battle he is in, yet hears plainly enough the word of command which he must himself obey.
—*George Eliot*

*How strange to kneel so lonely, so afraid*
*And then to rise refreshed and undismayed!*
*You gave no outward sign that I could see,*
*And yet I felt Your love surrounding me.*

*And now my wilderness is filled with bread,*
*And I may walk as one divinely led.*
—Eugenia T. Finn

*He will give grace and glory.*                    —Psalm 84:11

Bounteous is Jehovah in His nature; to give is His delight. His gifts are beyond measure precious, and are as freely given as the light of the sun. He gives grace to His elect because He wills it, to His redeemed because of His covenant, to the called because of His promise, to believers because they seek it, to sinners because they need it. He gives grace abundantly, seasonably, constantly, readily, sovereignly; doubly enhancing the value of the boon by the manner of its bestowal. Grace in all its forms He freely renders to His people. Comforting, preserving, sanctifying, directing, instructing, assisting grace, He generously pours into their souls without ceasing, and He always will do so, whatever may occur.

Sickness may befall, but the Lord will give grace; poverty may happen to us, but grace will surely be afforded; death must come, but grace will light a candle at the darkest hour. Reader, how blessed it is as years roll round, and the leaves begin again to fall, to enjoy such an unfading promise as this, "The Lord will give grace."

The little conjunction "and" in this verse is a diamond rivet binding the present with the future; grace and glory always go together. God has married them, and none can divorce them. The Lord will never deny a soul glory to whom He has freely given grace. Glory, the glory of heaven, the glory of eternity, the glory of Jesus, the glory of the Father, the Lord will surely give to His chosen. Oh, rare promise of a faithful God!

—*Charles H. Spurgeon*

> *Amazing Grace! how sweet the sound,*
> *That saved a wretch like me;*
> *I once was lost, but now I'm found;*
> *Was blind, but now I see.*

—John Newton

# OCTOBER 5

*He is our peace. . . .*                    —Ephesians 2:14

A prize was once offered to the person who painted the best picture depicting peace. There were two that seemed superior. One depicted a summer landscape. A rivulet was noiselessly winding its way through a green meadow. Trees were undisturbed by the faintest wind. The sky was clear. Two cows grazed beneath the shadow of a great oak. A gaily colored butterfly flitted lazily from flower to flower. Birds rested in leafy boughs. This was peace.

But the prize was given to the artist who portrayed on his canvas a wild stormy ocean, beating roughly upon the crags of a rocky shore. White-capped waves beat madly against the rocky ledges. The sky was dark and heavy. Lightning blazed across the heavens. But on the side of the rock, sheltered by a little ledge, one could see a pure white sea gull brooding upon her nest. Wild and foaming waves dashed angrily against her rocky retreat, but she felt no fear. Peacefully she viewed it all, knowing she was safe in her sheltered retreat.

Christ is the believer's retreat. Seated in the heavenly places in Him, we may view all without fear.     —*Keith L. Brooks*

*Safe in the arms of Jesus, Safe on His gentle breast,*
*There by His love o'er shaded, Sweetly my soul shall rest.*
*Hark! 'tis the voice of angels, Borne in a song to me,*
*Over the fields of glory, Over the jasper sea.*

*Safe in the arms of Jesus, Safe from corroding care,*
*Safe from the world's temptations, Sin cannot harm me there,*
*Free from the blight of sorrows, Free from my doubts and fears;*
*Only a few more trials, Only a few more tears!*
                                        —Fanny J. Crosby

*Who through faith subdued kingdoms....* —Hebrews 11:33

> *She met the hosts of Sorrow with a look*
> *That altered not beneath the frown they wore,*
> *And soon the lowering brood were tamed, and took,*
> *Meekly, her gentle rule, and frowned no more.*
> *Her soft hand put aside the assaults of wrath,*
> *And calmly broke in twain*
> *The fiery shafts of pain,*
> *And rent the nets of passion from her path;*
> *By that victorious hand despair was slain;*
> *With love she vanquished hate, and overcame*
> *Evil with good, in her great Master's name.*
>
> —W. C. Bryant

As to what may befall us outwardly, in this confused state of things, shall we not trust our tender Father, and rest satisfied in His will? Shall anything hurt us? Can tribulation, distress, persecution, famine, nakedness, peril, or sword, come between the love of the Father to the child, or the child's rest, content, and delight in His love? And doth not the love, the rest, the peace, the joy felt, swallow up all the bitterness and sorrow of the outward condition? —*I. Penington*

Thou art never at any time nearer to God than when under tribulation; which He permits for the purification and beautifying of thy soul. —*M. De Molinos*

> *Why worry? Are tomorrow's skies more blue*
> *If on our beds we restless roll and toss*
> *With burning sleepless eyes until the morn,*
> *Building bridges that we may never cross?*
>
> *Does not the One who numbered every hair,*
> *And marks the little sparrow when it falls,*
> *Give ear to us in His own image made,*
> *As well as to the raven when it calls?*

# OCTOBER 7

*For in that he himself hath suffered being tempted, he is able to succor them that are tempted.* —Hebrews 2:18

Victory—how? The narrow way to the Celestial City leads straight through Vanity Fair and the Valley of the Shadow—both symbolic of fierce, insidious temptation. We cannot escape it, but we can resist the devil and be victorious.

Temptation is masterable—if we count on it and plan for victory. But we shall conquer only as Jesus did, not by strength of will or force of personality, but by claiming the commands and promises of God in living practical faith.

We overcome by the blood of the Lamb. Because Jesus won the victory in life and in death over the prince of evil, I can be assured of victory in every temptation if I claim the merits of His blood. I do not have to blunder on half-defeated. Every defeat is a reflection on Him and says that Calvary was not enough.

Jesus broke the way for me. He experienced every variety of temptation I shall ever have to meet. Thus His temptations mark the danger points and also the path to victory. If I am wise I shall study both and walk in His steps. I sang, "Where He leads me I will follow." Now is my time to prove I meant it.

Jesus settled at the outset His long-time policy. His secret can be ours: an unwavering commitment to the will of God and an unquestioning reliance on the Word of God.

—*Bertha Munro*

*How sweetly Jesus whispers,*
*"Take thy cross—thou needst not fear,*
*For I've trod the way before thee*
*And the glory lingers near."*

*For whom the Lord loveth he chasteneth, and scourgeth every son whom he receiveth.* —Hebrews 12:6

Early in my Christian ministry I was called to apprehend a man who had gone insane. After we had captured him in a field, we found that he carried a loaded revolver. I returned it to his wife, but she said, "I don't want that gun. You'd better keep it, Doctor, I don't want to see it anymore." So I took the gun, together with some of the bullets, and brought it to my home and placed it in one of the drawers of my desk and promptly forgot about it. My son, Richard, a lad of about five, was rummaging through my study one day and came upon this revolver and the bullets lying near it. "Daddy, look what I found! May I have this? May I have this?" Now, of course, you who are parents know what I did. He begged me to give him the gun, but quickly I took it away from him, after looking to see whether any bullets had been placed in the magazine. "No, no, Richard," I said, "you cannot have that gun. It's too dangerous for you."

Did my son understand? He did not!

Christian friend, are we not like that? We are only children in the faith. We plead and pray and petition for something we think we cannot do without, something we cannot live without, something which seems to be the most precious thing in all our lives. Yet, our Heavenly Father says firmly and tenderly, "No, My child, I must refuse this petition. I cannot let you have this thing that you feel you need more than everything else in your life." Although we cannot understand now, I assure you that when, by-and-by, we meet Him face to face and reach the maturity of the children of God, we shall understand.

—M. R. DeHaan

# OCTOBER 9

*Thou wilt show me the path of life: in thy presence is fulness
of joy; at thy right hand there are pleasures for evermore.*
—Psalm 16:11

*Thy presence fills my mind with peace,*
*Brightens the thoughts so dark erewhile,*
*Bids cares and sad forebodings cease,*
*Makes all things smile.*
—Charlotte Elliott

How shall we rest in God? By giving ourselves wholly to
Him. If you give yourself by halves, you cannot find full rest;
there will ever be a lurking disquiet in that hail which is
withheld. Martyrs, confessors and saints have tasted this rest,
and "counted themselves happy in that they endured." A
countless host of God's faithful servants have drunk deeply of
it under the daily burden of a weary life—dull, commonplace,
painful, or desolate. All that God has been to them he is ready
to be to you. Your heart once fairly given to God, with a clear
conscience, a fitting rule of life, and a steadfast purpose of
obedience, you will find a wonderful sense of rest coming
over you.                              —*Jean Nicolas Grou*

Resignation to the will of God is the whole of piety; it
includes in it all that is good; and is a source of the most
settled quiet and composure of mind. Our resignation to the
will of God may be said to be perfect, when our will is lost
and resolved up into His; when we rest in His will as our end,
as being itself most just, and right, and good.

—*Joseph Butler*

There are no disappointments to those whose wills are
buried in the will of God.                    —*F. W. Faber*

*When through the deep waters I call thee to go,*
*The rivers of sorrow shall not thee overflow;*
*For I will be with thee thy troubles to bless,*
*And sanctify to thee thy deepest distress.*

*Thou art my portion, O Lord . . .* —Psalm 119:57

There are times, fellow Christian, when we lose sight of our Savior to the extent that we gaze upon those about us who are perhaps more richly blessed with this earth's goods than we are. Perhaps our ungodly neighbor lives in a bigger, more luxurious home, or drives a bigger car than we do. Perhaps his fields yield a greater harvest than do ours. But, what is his harvest compared to our God who is the God of harvests? What is gold compared to God? Rich harvests and vast wealth cannot sustain us spiritually. Our spiritual lives would starve if they depended upon earthly food and wealth for sustenance. What good is wealth to bring comfort to a despondent or troubled heart? What good is the applause of men to bring consolation to the bereaved? There are griefs in life and trials which wealth cannot alleviate or solve. There is the deepest need at the dying hour which wealth cannot supply.

But we, as God's children, have God more than all else put together. In Him every need is provided for whether in life or death. In Him is adequate comfort for sorrow and ample provision for every need. In Christ we are indeed more wealthy than the richest man on earth. In God we have a Guide whose services no amount of earthly wealth could command. In Christ we have a Comforter whose blessed services could not be purchased with any amount of wealth.

It was Esau, the worldly man, who said, "I have enough." But it was Jacob, the man whom God named Israel, who said, "I have all things." That degree of supply is beyond the understanding of worldly men, but it is our portion for with the Psalmist we can say, "Thou art my portion, O Lord."

> *Yesterday, today, forever,*
> *Jesus is the same;*
> *All may change, but Jesus never,*
> *Glory to His Name.*

# OCTOBER 11

*God hath not cast away his people which he foreknew . . .*
—Romans 11:2

He will in no wise cast you out. He will never leave you or forsake you. His eye, before which the night shineth as the day, will watch over you with unceasing care; and His hand, which nothing can resist or escape, will guard you with infinite tenderness. In every sorrow He will comfort; in every danger He will deliver. The bed of death He will spread with down; the passage into eternity He will illumine with the light of His own countenance. In the judgment He will acquit you of all your guilt; and in His own house, the mansion of eternal light, and peace, and joy, He will present you to His Father as trophies of His cross, the monuments of His boundless love.

—*Timothy Dwight*

*Majestic sweetness sits enthroned*
*Upon the Savior's brow;*
*His head with radiant glories crowned,*
*His lips with grace o'erflow.*

*No mortal can with Him compare,*
*Among the sons of men;*
*Fairer is He than all the fair*
*That fill the heavenly train.*

*To Him I owe my life and breath,*
*And all the joys I have;*
*He makes me triumph over death,*
*He saves me from the grave.*

*Since from His bounty I receive*
*Such proofs of love divine,*
*Had I a thousand hearts to give,*
*Lord! they should all be Thine.*

—Stennett

*He maketh the storm a calm, so that the waves thereof are still.*
—Psalm 107:29

In all lives there are periods of tumult and storm. We are whirled about by angry billows, and it seems as though we shall never reach the harbor of peace and rest. Some give themselves up to such experiences as a fact which they cannot avoid, or attempt to drown their fears and dull their senses to suffering and danger. But faith cleaves its way through the murky mists and driving cloud-wrack, and establishes a sure connection with the throne of the Eternal Father. This is what the New Testament calls the anchorage of the soul, and however severe the storm that sweeps over the earth, the soul that shelters there is safe. "Then they cried unto the Lord in their trouble, and He delivered them out of their distresses."

At this moment you may be passing through a storm of outward trouble. Wave after wave beats upon you, as one calamity is followed by another, until it seems as though the little vessel of your life must be overwhelmed. Look up to God and cry to Him. He sees you, and will not allow you to be engulfed.

Or you may be experiencing inward sorrow. Your affections have been misplaced; the one you love has deceived and failed you, and the sky is now dark and stormy. The one resort of the soul when it is hard driven, is to look up to Him who holds the winds in His fist, the waters in the hollow of His hand, and who cannot forget or forsake those who cry to Him.
—F. B. Meyer

*Then cast all your care upon Him,*
*For He careth night and day!*
*You have never far to seek Him—*
*He's beside you! Yes, alway.*
—Rose Benn

# October 13

*In whom we have redemption through His blood, the for-giveness of sins, according to the riches of His grace.*
—Ephesians 1:7

The Apostle uses an expression some eleven times in this epistle which suggests the measure of God's ability "to do." The expression is "according to." We will not mention the entire number, but call your attention to only a few. In the first chapter of Ephesians he writes: "According to the good pleasure of His will" (v. 5); "according to the riches of his grace" (v. 7); "according to His good pleasure" (v. 9); "according to the purpose of Him who worketh all things after the counsel of His will" (v. 11); and in the third chapter, "according to the riches of His glory" (v. 16); and "according to the power that worketh in us" (v. 20).

A beloved friend of mine rejoiced my heart by pointing out the significance of this expression. He said there was a vast difference between God giving us "out of" His riches, and His giving us "according to" His riches. Then he illustrated it after this manner. If Henry Ford gave me something out of his riches, he might give me ten dollars or one hundred dollars or even one thousand dollars, or he might give me only ten cents. On the other hand, if Henry Ford gave me according to his riches, who can estimate the largeness of the gift he might bestow upon me? God measures His gifts to us not by your puny scale of measurement but "according to" the riches which He possesses in Himself, and in which He has abounded toward us through Jesus Christ our Lord. Surely, if He does something through Christ, it will not be a scanty doing—it will be "exceeding abundantly."                    —*Howard W. Ferrin*

*Whoso trusteth in the Lord, happy is he.* —Proverbs 16:20

*The heart that trusts forever sings,*
*And feels as light as it had wings,*
*A well of peace within it springs,—*
  *Come good or ill,*
*Whate'er today, tomorrow brings,*
  *It is His will.*

—I. Williams

He who believes in God is not careful for the morrow, but labors joyfully and with a great heart. "For he giveth his beloved, as in sleep." They must work and watch, yet never be careful or anxious, but commit all to Him, and live in serene tranquillity; with a quiet heart, as one who sleeps safely and quietly. —*Martin Luther*

If we wished to gain contentment, we might try such rules as these:

1. Allow ourselves to complain of nothing, not even the weather.
2. Never picture ourselves under any circumstances in which we are not.
3. Never compare our own lot with that of another.
4. Never allow ourselves to dwell on the wish that this or that had been, or were, otherwise than it was, or is. God Almighty loves us better and more wisely than we do ourselves.
5. Never dwell on the morrow. Remember that it is God's, not ours. The heaviest part of sorrow often is the looking forward to it. "The Lord will provide." —*E. B. Pusey*

*He sees, and that is quite enough,*
  *I would not ask to see;*
*But listening through the darkness hear,*
  *His loving "Follow Me."*

—M. E. Rae

# OCTOBER 15

*Wherefore have thy servants set my field on fire?*
—2 Samuel 14:31

Count up all the worldly losses you have had, and see if you are not the gainer, if these losses have not drawn you closer to your Savior. You have less money, perhaps, but more enjoyment of the treasures you found at the Cross. You are richer toward God. Perhaps there is a child the less in that crib now empty, but there is a child the more in glory; and when the Shepherd took your lamb He drew you nearer to Him and to the fold on high. Our loving God has a purpose in every trial. If any heart-broken reader of these lines is crying out, like Joab, "Wherefore hast thou set my field on fire?" I beseech you not to flee away from God in petulant despair. He is only burning up your barley to bring you closer to Himself. Let the flames light you to the mercy-seat. The promises will read the brighter. It is better to lose the barley than to lose the blessing.                        —*John Roberts*

> *I've found a joy in sorrow,*
> *A secret balm for pain,*
> *A beautiful tomorrow*
> *Of sunshine after rain.*
> *I've found a branch of healing*
> *Near every bitter spring;*
> *A whispered promise stealing*
> *O'er every broken string.*
>
> *My Savior! Thee possessing*
> *I have the joy, the balm,*
> *The healing and the blessing,*
> *The sunshine and the psalm;*
> *The promise for the fearful,*
> *The Elim for the faint,*
> *The rainbow for the tearful,*
> *The glory for the saint.*
> —Jane Crewsdon

*Take therefore no thought for the morrow: for the morrow shall take thought for the things of itself. Sufficient unto the day is the evil thereof.* —Matthew 6:34

This reason our Lord gives against anxiety for the future is that we have nothing to do with the future. God gives us life by days, little single days. Each day has its own duties, its own needs, its own trials and temptations, its own griefs and sorrows. God always gives us strength enough for the day as He gives it, with all that He puts into it. But if we insist on dragging back tomorrow's cares and piling them on top of today's, the strength will not be enough for the load. God will not add strength just to humor our whims of anxiety and distrust.

So the lesson is that we should keep each day distinct and attend strictly to what it brings us. Charles Kingsley says: "Do today's duty, fight today's temptation, and do not weaken and distract yourself by looking forward to things which you cannot see, and could not understand if you saw them." We really have nothing at all to do with the future, save to prepare for it by doing with fidelity the duties of today.

No one was ever crushed by the burdens of one day. We can always get along with our heaviest load till the sun goes down; well, that is all we ever have to do. Tomorrow? Oh, you may have no tomorrow; you may be in heaven. If you are here God will be here too, and you will receive new strength sufficient for the new day.

*One day at a time—but a single day,*
*Whatever its load, whatever its length;*
*And there's a bit of precious Scripture to say*
*That according to each shall be our strength.*

—J. R. Miller

# OCTOBER 17

*Be not afraid . . . for I am with thee to deliver thee, saith the Lord.* —Jeremiah 1:8

Life is a journey. It is a trip through a strange land where you have never been before, and you never know a moment ahead where you are going next. Strange languages, strange scenes, strange dilemmas; new tangles, new experiences, and some old ones with new faces, so that you do not know them. It is just as chock-full of pleasure and enjoyment as it can be, if you could only make some provision for the drudgery and hard things that seem to crowd in so thick and fast sometimes, as to make people forget the gladness of it.

Now I have something to tell you that seems too utterly good to be believed, and yet keeps getting better all the way along. It is this: the Master has planned that your life journey shall be a personally conducted one on this ideal plan. He has arranged with His best friend, who is an experienced traveler, to go with you and devote Himself wholly to your interests.

—S. D. Gordon

*No distant Lord have I, loving afar to be;*
*Made flesh for me—He cannot rest, until He rests in me.*
*Brother in joy or pain; Bone of my bone was He,*
*Now with me closer still—He dwells Himself in me.*

*I need not journey far this distant Friend to see;*
*Companionship is always mine, He makes His home with me.*
*I envy not the twelve; nearer to me is He,*
*The life He once lived here on earth, He lives again in me.*
—Maltbie Babcock

*Is there some battle you must face?*
*Be not dismayed, nor yet afraid,*
*Thy God hath power, might and grace,*
*So let your heart on Him be stayed.*
—Grace B. Renfrow

*The Lord shall preserve thee from all evil: He shall preserve thy soul.*
                                              —Psalm 121:7

*Under Thy wings, my God, I rest,*
  *Under Thy shadow safely lie;*
*By Thy own strength in peace possessed,*
  *While dreaded evils pass me by.*
                                              —A. L. Waring

A heart rejoicing in God delights in all His will, and is surely provided with the most firm joy in all estates; for if nothing can come to pass beside or against His will, then cannot that soul be vexed which delights in Him and has no will but His, but follows Him in all times, in all estates; not only when He shines bright on them, but when they are clouded. That flower which follows the sun does so even in dark and cloudy days; when it does not shine forth, yet it follows the hidden course and motion of it. So the soul that moves after God keeps that course when He hides His face; is content, yea, even glad at His will in all estates or conditions or events.                                    —R. Leighton

Neither go back in fear and misgiving to the past, nor in anxiety and forecasting to the future; but lie quiet under His hand, having no will but His.             —H. E. Manning

I saw a delicate flower that had grown up two feet high, between the horses' path and the wheeltrack. An inch higher and it would have been crushed; and yet it lives to flourish as much as if it had a thousand acres of untrodden space around it, and never knew the danger it incurred. It did not borrow trouble, nor invite an evil fate by apprehending it.
                                              —Henry D. Thoreau

# OCTOBER 19

*Blessed are all they that put their trust in Him.* —Psalm 2:12

The second Psalm is such a marvelous condensation of Messianic prophecy that the beatitude with which it closes may have been neglected by many readers. Yet of all the Scripture beatitudes none is more comforting than this one: "Blessed are all they that put their trust in Him." What a wealth of assurance lies in that word "all"! It states a great principle of the spiritual life—that trusting is the sure prelude to blessing. It shows that there are no exceptions in God's faithfulness. Look trustingly to the Lord and you will be blessed. The sequence is rooted in the divine logic. And that wonderful word "all" transcends time and outward circumstance. "All," both now and in the past and in the future, "all" who possess the single qualification of putting their trust in God, will be blessed.

Let us, however, be careful to avoid a low view of the qualifying clause in the beatitude. Christians who really know what it means to put their trust in the Lord are all too uncommon. For trusting God, which is the precursor of blessedness, means committal of everything to Him.

—*Frank E. Gaebelein*

*I know—my firm foundation this,*
*    The Rock amid the shifting sand,*
*I know that Jesus is the Christ,*
*    And builded here my house shall stand;*
*I know, though all my hand hath wrought*
*    By fire and flood be swept away,*
*This corner stone of faith shall rest*
*    Unshaken in the last great day.*
—Annie Johnson Flint

*Looking unto Jesus the author and finisher of our faith; who for the joy that was set before him endured the cross, despising the shame, and is set down at the right hand of the throne of God.*
—Hebrews 12:2

Great and wonderful is the *consolation* that such a life of faith affords. In all the vicissitudes of life and horrors of death, nothing can cheer and fortify the mind like this. By faith in an unseen world we can endure injuries without revenge, afflictions without fainting, and losses without despair. Let the nations of the earth dash, one against another; yea, let nature herself approach toward her final dissolution; let her groan as being ready to expire, and sink into her primitive nothing; still the believer lives! His all is not on board that vessel! His chief inheritance lies in another soil!

Believers venture their all in the hands of Christ, persuaded that He is able to keep that which they have committed to Him against that day. To find at last that they have not confided in Him in vain—yea, that their expectations are not only answered, but infinitely outdone—will surely enhance the bliss of heaven. The remembrance of our dangers, fear and sorrows will enable us to enjoy the heavenly state with a degree of happiness impossible to have been felt, if those dangers, fears and sorrows had never existed.
—*Andrew Fuller*

*O Friend of souls! how blest the time*
*When in Thy love I rest!*
*When from my weariness I climb*
*E'en to Thy tender breast!*
*The night of sorrow endeth there,*
*Thy rays outshine the sun;*
*And in Thy pardon and Thy care*
*The heaven of heavens is won.*

# October 21

*My presence shall go with thee, and I will give thee rest.*
—Exodus 33:14

How wonderful are these promises of the Divine Presence! They constitute one of the most comforting and edifying studies in the Bible. The merest glance at some of them is enough to fill the desponding heart with fresh courage and gladness. Still more, when we ponder them carefully, examining their terms and considering the circumstances in which they were given, do we discover indeed the "exceeding great" riches which we possess in them. As a specimen, let us take the promise given to Moses: "My presence shall go with thee, and I will give thee rest." This promise in particular commends itself because it lays even added stress upon the fact of the divine presence, in that precious pronoun "My"—"My presence shall go with thee, and I will give thee rest."

The promise is a benediction in itself: but it is when we take it with its context that its fuller graciousness and glory break upon us. However beautiful a jewel may be in itself, its beauty is enhanced by an appropriate setting. However lovely a full-blown rose may be in isolation, it has its loveliest look and fullest fragrance when it blooms in its native bower. So is it with this promise. In the context we find that Moses was a *discouraged* and *disappointed* man. Our God offers His presence to us in our extremity!           —*J. Sidlow Baxter*

Lord, what a change within us one short hour
  Spent in Thy presence will avail to make!
  What heavy burdens from our bosoms take!
What parched grounds refresh as with a shower!
We kneel, and all around us seems to lower;
  We rise, and all, the distant and the near,
  Stands forth in sunny outline, brave and clear;
We kneel, how weak; we rise, how full of power!
      —Richard Chenevix Trench

*The Lord preserveth the simple.* —Psalm 116:6

*Thy home is with the humble, Lord!*
*The simple are Thy rest;*
*Thy lodging is in childlike hearts;*
*Thou makest there Thy nest.*

—F. W. Faber

This deliverance of the soul from all useless and selfish and unquiet cares, brings to it an unspeakable peace and freedom; this is true simplicity. This state of entire resignation and perpetual acquiescence produces true liberty; and this liberty brings perfect simplicity. The soul which knows no self-seeking, no interested ends, is thoroughly candid; it goes straight forward without hindrance; its path opens daily more and more to "perfect day," in proportion as its self-renunciation and its self-forgetfulness increase; and its peace, amid whatever troubles beset it, will be as boundless as the depths of the sea.

—*François de La Mothe Fenelon*

Beware of letting your care degenerate into anxiety and unrest; tossed as you are amid the winds and waves of sundry troubles, keep your eyes fixed on the Lord, and say, "Oh, my God, I look to Thee alone; be Thou my Guide, my Pilot"; and then be comforted. When the shore is gained, who will heed the toil and the storm? And we shall steer safely through every storm, so long as our trust is fixed on God.

—*St. Francis de Sales*

*Stand still and wait! Nor count the waiting vain*
*If thou hast caught a glimpse of His dear face;*
*Thy waiting hours will bring far greater gain*
*If thou hast learned the wonders of His grace.*
—Avis B. Christiansen

# OCTOBER 23

*Lo, I am with you alway, even unto the end of the world.*
—Matthew 28:20

"Lo, I am with you alway," Christ declares. And souls today, many and many of our souls, my friends, have found the rich fulfillment of His promise. Sometimes it comes to us with a strange surprise. When we are living on as if we lived alone, when we are sitting working silently in some still room which we think is empty but for our own presence, when we are busy in some work which seems as if it were our work, to be done as we should please; slowly, sweetly, surely we become aware of a richer presence which is truly with us, of a love which enfolds us, and an authority which controls us. We are not alone. The work is not our work but His. The strength to do it with is not to be called up out of the depths of ourselves, but taken down from the heights of Him. The room is full, the world is full of Jesus. He is doing what He said He would do. He is with us as He said He would be.   —*Phillips Brooks*

*"Lo, I am with you always."*
 *Softly the promise steals*
*Like sunlight into my shadows,*
 *And brightens and warms and heals;*
*Heals my anguish of spirit*
 *And horror of loneliness,*
*Flooding my heart's dark chambers—*
 *Words that comfort and bless.*

*And always He goes before me*
 *On my thorn-strewn paths of pain;*
*Never will He forsake me*
 *Nor leave me alone again.*
*Sweet is His voice in the twilight*
 *As the evening shadows blend,*
*"Lo, I am with you always,*
 *Even unto the end!"*
—Martha Snell Nicholson

*Commit thy works unto the Lord, and thy thoughts shall be established.*
—Proverbs 16:3

It is one thing to work for God; it is another to have God work through us. We are often eager for the former; God is always desirous of doing the latter. One of the important facts in the surrender of the life is that it is the attitude which gives God the chance to work His perfect will through us. For it is God who is working to evangelize the world; it is God who has laid the plans for it; it is God who has the power to successfully execute them. Now the God who is the Ruler of the universe does not want us to plan, and worry, and work for Him. For while He appreciates our purposes toward Him, yet they may be all athwart His purposes for and through us. What He wants is not our plans, but our lives, that He may work His plans through us. —*James H. McConkey*

*Cease your thinking, troubled Christian,*
*What avails your anxious cares?*
*God is ever thinking for you,*
*Jesus every burden bears.*
*Casting all your care upon Him,*
*Sink into His blessed will;*
*While He folds you to His bosom,*
*Sweetly whispering, "Peace, be still."*

*Jesus knows the way He leads me,*
*I have but to hold His hand;*
*Nothing from His thought is hidden,*
*Why need I to understand?*
*Let me, like the loved disciple,*
*Hide my head upon His breast;*
*Till upon His faithful bosom,*
*All my cares are hushed to rest.*
—A. B. Simpson

# OCTOBER 25

*Behold, He cometh with clouds.* —Revelation 1:7

In the Bible clouds are always connected with God. Clouds are those sorrows or sufferings or providences, within or without our personal lives, which seem to dispute the rule of God. It is by those very clouds that the Spirit of God is teaching us how to walk by faith. If there were no clouds, we should have no faith. "The clouds are but the dust of our Father's feet." The clouds are a sign that He is there. What a revelation it is to know that sorrow and bereavement and suffering are the clouds that come along with God! God cannot come near without clouds, He does not come in clear shining.

It is not true to say that God wants to teach us something in our trials: through every cloud He brings, He wants us to unlearn something. His purpose in the cloud is to simplify our belief until our relationship to Him is exactly that of a child—God and my own soul, only, other people are shadows. Until other people become shadows, clouds and darkness will be mine ever now and again. Is the relationship between myself and God getting simpler than ever it has been?

There is a connection between the strange providences of God and what we know of Him, and we have to learn to interpret the mysteries of life in the light of our knowledge of God. Unless we can look the darkest, blackest fact full in the face without damaging God's character, we do not yet know Him.

"They feared as they entered the cloud. . . ." Is there anyone "save Jesus only" in your cloud? If so, it will get darker; you must get to the place where there is "no one any more save Jesus only." —*Oswald Chambers*

# OCTOBER 26

*For the Lord shall be thine everlasting light, and the days of thy mourning shall be ended.* —Isaiah 60:20

The man who follows Christ never walks in darkness. He may walk in the midst of darkness, but his steps are lighted by the presence of the Savior whom he follows, just as a man who walks on a dark night behind a guide with a lantern finds, in the midst of the darkness, light in the spot where he walks. The man who follows Christ has the light of divine wisdom cast upon the problems which confront him, and in this light he is able to solve them. He may not be able to see the future or view the long way stretching ahead, but there is light where he needs it, when he needs it, in the very spot where he finds himself. In the night of great sorrow the man who follows Christ finds the light of hope to cheer his way. Christ proves Himself the true light to all who follow Him. —*Bob Jones, Jr.*

*Christ, whose glory fills the skies,*
*    Christ the true, the only light,*
*Sun of Righteousness, arise,*
*    Triumph o'er the shades of night;*
*Dayspring from on high, be near;*
*Daystar, in my heart appear.*
*Dark and cheerless is the morn*
*    Unaccompanied by Thee;*
*Joyless is the day's return,*
*    Till Thy mercy's beams I see,*
*Till Thy inward light impart,*
*Glad my eyes and warm my heart.*
                —Charles Wesley

# OCTOBER 27

*He shall feed his flock like a shepherd: he shall gather his lambs with his arm, and carry them in his bosom....*
—Isaiah 40:11

Our Savior is called by many names throughout His Word, but perhaps the most pleasant to contemplate is the name, "the Good Shepherd." It is He of whom these words are spoken. It is He who feeds and cares for His flock; it is He who gathers His lambs lovingly in His arms and carries them safely in His bosom.

Here is a beautiful picture of His Shepherdship, His tenderness and love toward His children. The heart hunger of His flock meets with His gracious provision; the weakness of the little ones, His lambs, meets with His strength.

Why does the Shepherd have this interest in His people? He has purchased them with His blood, they are His property. He has numbered the very hairs of their heads. He is preparing for them a home in glory. He is waiting to welcome them at the Father's right hand.

He carries them—sometimes by keeping them from trial and testing. Sometimes He "carries" them by giving to His child a clear-cut simple faith which stands fast in spite of buffeting from without. And what a blessed thought it is to consider where He carries His child—in His very bosom. O what love! What tenderness! What a place of perfect safety! No one can hurt the child in his place in the Father's bosom without first hurting the Shepherd. What perfect "rest" and all-sufficient peace is our portion as one of His lambs!

*I know mine own: their doubts and tears,*
*Their burdens and their load of care;*
*I give them comfort, strength and grace,*
*And for their rest my folds prepare.*

*A bruised reed shall He not break.* —Isaiah 42:3

*All my life I still have found,*
*And I will forget it never;*
*Every sorrow hath its bound,*
*And no cross endures forever.*
*All things else have but their day,*
*God's love only lasts for aye.*
—P. Gerhardt

We never have more than we can bear. The present hour we are always able to endure. As our day, so is our strength. If the trials of many years were gathered into one, they would overwhelm us; therefore, in pity to our little strength, He sends first one, and then another, then removes both, and lays on a third, heavier, perhaps, than either; but all is so wisely measured to our strength that the bruised reed is never broken. We do not enough look at our trials in this continuous and successive view. Each one is sent to teach us something, and altogether they have a lesson which is beyond the power of any to teach alone. —*H. E. Manning*

Your external circumstances may change, toil may take the place of rest, sickness of health, trials may thicken within and without. Externally, you are the prey of such circumstances; but if your heart is stayed on God, no changes or chances can touch it, and all that may befall you will but draw you closer to Him. Whatever the present moment may bring, your knowledge that it is His will, and that your future heavenly life will be influenced by it, will make all not only tolerable, but welcome to you, while no circumstances can affect you greatly, knowing that He who holds you in His powerful hand cannot change, but abideth forever. —*Jean Nicolas Grou*

# OCTOBER 29

*. . . to know the love of Christ, which passeth knowledge.*
—Ephesians 3:19

The dimensions of the Love of Christ! It is broad as humanity, "for God so loved the world"; the *length*—God's love had no date of origin, and shall have none of conclusion. God *is* Love, it continueth ever, indissoluble, unchangeable, a perpetual present tense. Its *height* as the Flood out-topped the highest mountains, so that Love covers our highest sins. It is as high as the heaven above the earth. Its *depth*—Christ our Lord descended into the lowest before He rose to the highest. He has touched the bottomless pit of our sin and misery, sorrow and need. However low your fall, or lowly your lot, the everlasting arms of His love are always underneath.

As Christ's love through you broadens, lengthens, deepens, heightens, you will know the love of Christ, not intellectually, but experimentally (1 John 4:11, 12, 20, 21).

But you say, "There are people in my life whom I cannot love." Granted, but you must distinguish between love and the emotion or feeling of love. You may not be able to feel love at the outset, but you can be willing to be the channel of Christ's love. I cannot love, but Christ is in me, and *He* can. Is it too much to ask that all this should be realized in ourselves and in others? No, because God is already at work within us by His Holy Spirit, and He is able to do infinitely beyond all our highest requests or thoughts. Ask your furthest, think your highest, and the Divine Love is always infinitely in advance. —*F. B. Meyer*

*Love ever gives,*
*Forgives, outlives,*
*And ever stands with open hands,*
*And while it lives it gives.*
*For this is Love's preogative*
*To give—and give—and give.*

—Author Unknown

*My presence shall go with thee.* —Exodus 33:14

Moses had seen the impossibility of going forward happily or successfully, unaccompanied by the presence of God, and as he pleaded for the divine presence, he received an answer which to him was most assuring and satisfactory, for the Lord said: "My presence shall go with thee, and I will give thee rest." And these are the assuring words I desire from God on the threshold of this new day. I need His guiding presence so as to have rest from all undue anxieties and embarrassments. I need His protecting presence so as to have rest from fear of all dangers that may be awaiting me. I need His bountiful presence so as to be assured that all my needs will be met and supplied by Him. And I need His comforting presence so as to have rest from sorrow if called upon to pass through trial. His presence is what I need, and His presence is what I may have, for if I yield myself up fully to His claims he will speak to me as clearly as He did to Moses. "My presence shall go with thee, and I will give thee rest." —*John Roberts*

*I need Thee every hour;*
*Stay Thou near by.*
*Temptations lose their power*
*When Thou art nigh.*

*I need Thee every hour,*
*In joy or pain;*
*Come quickly and abide,*
*Or life is vain.*

*I need Thee every hour.*
*Teach me Thy will;*
*And Thy rich promises*
*In me fulfill.*

# OCTOBER 31

*The Lord shall give thee rest from thy sorrow, and from thy fear, and from the hard bondage wherein thou wast made to serve.*
—Isaiah 14:3

*Today, beneath Thy chastening eye,*
*I crave alone for peace and rest;*
*Submissive in Thy hand to lie,*
  *And feel that it is best.*
—J. G. Whittier

O Lord, who art as the Shadow of a great Rock in a weary land, who beholdest Thy weak creatures, weary of labor, weary of pleasure, weary of hope deferred, weary of self; in Thine abundant compassion, and unutterable tenderness, bring us, I pray Thee, unto Thy rest. Amen. *—Christina G. Rossetti*

Grant to me above all things that can be desired, to rest in Thee, and in Thee to have my heart at peace. Thou art the true peace of the heart, Thou its only rest; out of Thee all things are hard and restless. In this very peace, that is, in Thee, the One Chiefest Eternal Good, I will sleep and rest. Amen. *—Thomas à Kempis*

Thou has made us for Thyself, O Lord; and our heart is restless until it rests in Thee. *—St. Augustine*

I have learned to see a need of everything God gives me, and want nothing that He denies me. Whether it be taken from or not given me, sooner or later God quiets me in Himself without it. I cast all my concerns on the Lord, and live securely on the care and wisdom of my Heavenly Father. *—Joseph Eliot, 1664*

*Wait on the Lord: be of good courage, and he shall strength-
en thine heart: wait, I say, on the Lord.* —Psalm 27:14

The favorite word for listening in the Bible is the word
waiting. It is a great word full of simple yet wondrous meaning
. . . . It means the turning of the face full up to God so as to
know by a look what He would suggest; it means hearing
through the eyes. It is exquisitely put in the Psalms. God
assures us that He is ever keeping His eye upon us so that by
our looking up we can catch His eye and so know what to do.

It means on our side watching God's slightest movement as
intensely as a slave in those old times watched for the first and
last suggestion of the master's desire. As the watch-guard on
night duty upon the city wall in old Judea kept his eyes keenly
toward the East to see the first gleam of the coming day that
would relieve his long, lonely vigil—so intensely and keenly
we are to look toward God to get the first inkling of His will.
The life is to be lived with its face always turned to God.

—*S. D. Gordon*

*When hope deferred brings thy heart nigh to breaking,*
*With upward looking thine eyes seem to fail;*
*When thy poor heart has grown weary with aching*
*And powers of evil thy spirit assail;*

*Still then thy heart for the voice that would guide thee,*
*Hush every thought that His word you may hear.*
*Fear not the way for whate'er may betide thee,*
*He will be with thee to help and to cheer.*

*Be silent to God! Still the voice of thy grieving,*
*Turn from thy thinking and agonizing prayer,*
*Patiently wait, in His loving hands leaving*
*All of thy hopes, and thy burdens and care.*

—H. D. Winant

# November 2

*. . . for unto thee will I pray.* —Psalm 5:2

*And they . . . said one to another, What manner of man is this, that even the wind and the sea obey him?* —Mark 4:41

D. L. Moody used to tell a story of a little child whose father and mother had died, and who was taken into another family. The first night she asked whether she could pray as she used to do. They said: "Oh yes!" So she knelt down and prayed as her mother had taught her; and when that was ended, she added a little prayer of her own: "O God, make these people as kind to me as father and mother were." Then she paused and looked up, as if expecting the answer, and then added: "Of course You will." How sweetly simple was that little one's faith! She expected God to answer and "do," and "of course" she got her request, and that is the spirit in which God invites us to approach Him.

Robert Louis Stevenson tells a vivid story of a storm at sea. The passengers below were greatly alarmed, as the waves dashed over the vessel. At last one of them, against orders, crept to the deck, and came to the pilot, who was lashed to the wheel which he was turning without flinching. The pilot caught sight of the terror-stricken man, and gave him a reassuring smile. Below went the passenger, and comforted the others by saying, "I have seen the face of the pilot, and he smiled. All is well."

That is how we feel when through the gateway of prayer we find our way into the Father's presence. We see His face, and we know that all is well, since His hand is on the helm of events, and "even the winds and the waves obey Him." When we live in fellowship with Him, we come with confidence into His presence, asking in the full confidence of receiving and meeting with the justification of our faith. —E. M. Bounds

# NOVEMBER 3

*He hath set me in dark places .*  —Lamentations 3:6

When we reach heaven, we may discover that the richest and deepest and most profitable experiences we had in this world were those which were gained in the very roads from which we shrank back with dread. The bitter cups we tried to push away contained the medicines we most needed. The hardest lessons that we learn are those which teach us the most and best fit us for service here and glory hereafter. It is the easiest thing in the world to obey God when He commands us to do what we like, and to trust Him when the path is all sunshine. The real victory of faith is to trust God in the dark and through the dark.

To all my readers who are wondering why a loving God has subjected them so often to the furnace, my only answer is, that *God owns you and me,* and He has a right to do with us just as He pleases. If He wants to keep His silver over a hot flame until He can see His own countenance reflected in the metal, then He has a right to do so. It is the Lord, it is my loving Teacher, it is my Heavenly Father; let Him do what seemeth Him good. He will not lay on one stroke in cruelty, or a single one that He cannot give me grace to bear. Life's school days and nights will soon be over. Pruning-time will soon be ended. The crucibles will not be needed in heaven.

—*Theodore L. Cuyler*

*"Peace" cries the world of men today,*
*But Christ alone can peace convey.*
*And strife and sin shall ever reign,*
*Till Christ the Lord shall come again.*
—Ernest Douthit

# November 4

*And the Lord shall guide thee continually, and satisfy thy soul in drought.* —Isaiah 58:11

*Wherever He may guide me,*
*No want shall turn me back;*
*My Shepherd is beside me,*
*And nothing can I lack.*
—A. L. Waring

Abandon yourself to His care and guidance, as a sheep in the care of a shepherd, and trust Him utterly. No matter though you may seem to yourself to be in the very midst of a desert, with nothing green about you, inwardly or outwardly, and may think you will have to make a long journey before you can get into the green pastures. Our Shepherd will turn that very place where you are into green pastures, for He has power to make the desert rejoice and blossom as a rose.
—H. W. Smith

*I am so glad! It is such rest to know*
*That Thou hast ordered and appointed all,*
*And wilt yet order and appoint my lot.*
*For though so much I cannot understand,*
*And would not choose, has been, and yet may be,*
*Thou choosest, Thou performest, Thou, my lord.*
*This is enough for me.*
—F. R. Havergal

We mustn't be in a hurry to fix and choose our own lot; and we must wait to be guided. We are led on, like the little children, by a way that we know not. It is a vain thought to flee from the work that God appoints us to, for the sake of finding a greater blessing to our own souls; as if we could choose for ourselves where we shall find the fullness of the Divine Presence, instead of seeking it where alone it is to be found, in loving obedience.
—George Eliot

*And He saw them toiling in rowing; for the wind was contrary unto them. . . . .*
—Mark 6:48

*And when we [Paul and Luke] had launched from thence, we sailed under Cyprus, because the winds were contrary.*
—Acts 27:4

It is pleasant for us, dear reader, when life goes smoothly without the contrary winds of circumstances blowing against us. But God in His omnipotent wisdom sometimes permits "contrary" winds, for no obstacles are overcome, no waves surmounted on a smooth and glassy sea. It is in the midst of obstacle and storm that victories are won for Christ, that the greatest revelations come from the Heavenly Father.

More than that, meditate upon the first three words of our text—"He saw *them*." We as His consecrated children need never fear winds, no matter how contrary, for we have His assurance that He sees us. His all-seeing eye is always upon us and when we look up to Him, He is ready to help. Whatever our difficulty, "He is always near." He speaks to our listening ears amidst the roar of contrary winds and we can hear Him as distinctly as if in the quiet of our private prayer. There is nothing to fear if we are in the presence of Jesus—and we need never be out of His presence, for He has said, "I will never leave thee nor forsake thee." We need never be out of His sight, for He sees us no matter how turbulent our testing, no matter how severe our trial.

> *How sweet the name of Jesus sounds*
> *In the believer's ears;*
> *It soothes his sorrows, heals his wounds*
> *And drives away his fears.*
>
> *It makes the wounded spirit whole*
> *And calms the troubled breast;*
> *'Tis manna to the hungry soul,*
> *And to the weary rest.*

# NOVEMBER 6

> *And Joses, who by the apostles was surnamed Barnabas,(which is, being interpreted, The son of consolation,) a Levite, and of the country of Cyprus, Having land, sold it, and brought the money, and laid it at the apostles' feet.* —Acts 4:36, 37

What genius a man has who has the genius of comforting and consoling the people! Christianity is vigorous consolation. Christianity means comfort to the people. Christianity is not an oppressive thing, taking the heart and the hope and the life and the peace out of men. No, it is just the opposite. It is to hearten and to inspire and to uplift the sons of men. What a genius, then, a good man has when he has the genius of consolation!

The man with the genius for consoling in the noblest sense, how much such a man means in the affairs of Church! Mr. Spurgeon said he had one blind man in his church, and now and then spells came over his church, as come over many a church, when the people's lips hung down and when they whined and cried and groaned. Spurgeon said that on such occasions the blind man got up and said just the thing that went through his church like an electric shock, and brought them back to their senses. One day the blind man asked them if God was dead; he would like to know. One day he asked if Jesus had vacated the world and let Satan have it; he wanted to know. And with words like that, with a genius always for saying the right thing, he put heart and hope and spirit into the great church. Now, Barnabas had that same genius, after the noblest sort of fashion. Christianity is vigorous comfort. Barnabas teaches us here a lesson of priceless moment.

We cannot all be great men like Paul. None of us can. But we can be good men like Barnabas. We can be good men.

—*George W. Truett*

*God is faithful.* —1 Corinthians 1:9

Yes, we know that God is faithful, but what a comfort it is just to be reminded of the blessed fact. Let friends fail and relatives forsake us, our God is faithful. But to what is He faithful? Two words give the answer—His promises. Therefore, if we would really appreciate His faithfulness, we must first know His promises. There is no surer way to grow spiritually than to search the Word for God's promises, to rest upon them when you have found them, and then to praise Him for His faithfulness to them. A promise a day, treasured in the heart and really believed, will give you a grip on God's faithfulness that you will never lose.

Hudson Taylor of China used to say: "It is not so much great faith that we need as faith in a great God." The distinction may seem subtle, yet it is vastly important. Answered prayer depends upon God's inexhaustible power whereby He is abundantly able to be faithful to His pledged Word. It is our privilege simply to reckon upon the unchangeable reliability of our omnipotent God, believing that He not only can, but also will do all that He has promised. But surely "privileged" is too weak a word. For the Lord Jesus used the verb form which expresses a command. "Have faith in God" (Mark 11:22), He said. So He is telling us Christian believers that we have an imperative obligation to be just what our name implied—believers. Will you not be enough of a believer to "hold fast God's faithfulness" in everything that faces you this day?

—*Frank E. Gaebelein*

*I cannot doubt Thy hand of love,*
*E'en though my heart be torn;*
*Thy hands and feet for me were pierced,*
*Thy dear brow crowned with thorn.*

—Avis B. Christiansen

# NOVEMBER 8

*Fret not thyself . . .*                                —Psalm 37:1

Fret not thyself. Do not get into a perilous heat about things. And yet, if ever heat were justified, it was surely justified in the circumstances outlined in the Psalm. Evil-doers were moving about clothed in purple and fine linen, and faring sumptuously every day. "Workers of iniquity" were climbing into the supreme places of power, and were tyrannizing their less fortunate brethren. Sinful men and women were stalking through the land in the pride of life, and basking in the light and comfort of great prosperity. And good men were becoming heated and fretful. "Fret not thyself." Do not get unduly heated! Keep cool! Even in a good cause fretfulness is not a wise helpmeet. Fretting only heats the bearings, it does not generate the steam.

—J. H. Jowett

*When I'm afraid of times before,*
  *What coming days will bring;*
*When life's omissions I deplore,*
  *And earth-mists round me cling;*
*O Lord of love, my weakness see —*
*When I'm afraid I'll trust in Thee.*

*When I'm afraid of wily foes,*
  *Their flattery and hate —*
*Who seek my progress to oppose,*
  *My joys to dissipate;*
*O Lord of hosts, my weakness see —*
*When I'm afraid I'll trust in Thee.*

*When I'm afraid of dangers near,*
  *Foreboding future ills;*
*When rocks and shoals and deeps I fear,*
  *And gloom my spirit fills;*
*O Lord of might, my weakness see,*
*When I'm afraid I'll trust in Thee.*

—A. Gardner

*And he awoke.* —Mark 4:39

Our Savior hears the prayers of His children. The roar of the storm He did not hear in His sound sleep; but the moment there was a cry from His disciples for help He instantly awoke. What a revelation of heart have we here! He is never asleep to His people when they call upon Him. Amid the wildest tumults of this world He ever hears the faintest cry of prayer. Nor is He ever too weary to listen to His children in distress.

We have another illustration of this same quickness to hear prayer in the hours of our Lord's sufferings on the Cross. His life was fast ebbing away. His own agony was intense beyond description. Around Him surged a storm of human passion. Curses fell upon His ear. But amid all this tempest of hate He was silent. To all these bitter insults and keen reproaches He answered not a word. Then amid the derisions and jeers of the multitude there broke a voice of prayer. It came from one of the crosses beside Him. It was the penitential cry of a soul— "Lord, remember me." And in all the tumult of the hour He heard this feeble supplication. In His own agony He gave instant answer. Doubt not that this Jesus always hears prayer. His love is ever on the watch, ready to catch the faintest note of human distress.

Though aroused so suddenly in the midst of such scenes of terror, Jesus awoke calm and peaceful. Dean Trench says: "It is such cases as these—cases of sudden, unexpected terror, met without a moment of preparation—which test a man what spirit he is of, which show not only his nerve, but the grandeur and purity of his whole nature." Here we have an illustration of what Christ's peace was, and of what He meant when He said, "My peace I give unto you." It was thus He lived.

—*J. R. Miller*

# NOVEMBER 10

*. . . We are journeying. . . .* —Numbers 10:29

These were the words of Moses to his brother-in-law. They contain, in the first place, the experience of all true followers of the Lord Jesus: "We are journeying unto the place of which the Lord said, I will give it you." There is no uncertain sound about that ringing testimony. In the most positive and emphatic, and, we might add, triumphant manner he exclaimed: "We are journeying." And is it not God's will today that all His children should be possessed of this full assurance of faith? It is the privilege of everyone to say with Moses, "We are journeying," or with the apostle John, "We know that we have passed from death unto life," or with the apostle Paul, "We know that if our earthly house of this tabernacle were dissolved we have a building of God, an house not made with hands, eternal in the heavens."

But how can we be possessed of this wonderful assurance? Listen to Moses: "The Lord said I will give it you." The origin of Moses' assurance was divine, and that is the only assurance worth possessing. When the Holy Spirit bears witness with our spirit that we are the children of God, then the Lord Jesus whispers in our heart: "I go to prepare a place for you, and . . . I will come again and receive you unto Myself." Thus our experience is one full of assurance, and the origin of it is—divine. —*John Roberts*

> *I dare not pray for any gift*
> *Upon my pilgrim path to Heaven;*
> *I only ask one thing of Thee;*
> *Give Thou Thyself and all is given.*
> *I am not strong nor brave nor wise;*
> *Be Thou with me—it shall suffice.*
> —Annie Johnson Flint

*The power of an endless life.* —Hebrews 7:16

> *Believ'st thou in eternal things?*
>    *Thou knowest, in thy inmost heart,*
> *Thou are not clay; thy soul hath wings,*
>    *And what thou seest is but part.*
> *Make this thy med'cine for the smart*
>    *Of every day's distress; be dumb,*
> *In each new loss thou truly art*
>    *Tasting the power of things that come.*
>          —T. W. Parsons

Every contradiction of our will, every little ailment, every petty disappointment, will, if we take it patiently, become a blessing. So, walking on earth, we may be in heaven; the ill-tempers of others, the slights and rudenesses of the world, ill-health, the daily accidents with which God has mercifully strewed our paths, instead of ruffling or disturbing our peace, may cause His peace to be shed abroad in our hearts abundantly. —E. B. Pusey

The very least and the very greatest sorrows that God ever suffers to befall you, proceed from the depths of His unspeakable love; and such great love were better for you than the highest and best gift besides that He has given you, or ever could give you, if you could but see it in this light. —J. Tauler

> *Every sorrow, every smart,*
> *That the Eternal Father's heart*
> *Hath appointed me of yore,*
> *Or hath yet for me in store,*
> *As my life flows on, I'll take*
> *Calmly, gladly, for His sake,*
> *No more faithless murmurs make.*
>          —P. Gerhardt

# November 12

*For we see through a glass, darkly; but then face to face: now I know in part; but then shall I know even as also I am known.* —1 Corinthians 13:12

God is working out a pattern in our lives. We see only the present and the immediate, but God sees the whole picture of one's life as it will appear when the last stroke of the brush has completed the picture. In this pattern of our lives there are bright spots and dark backgrounds, all of them necessary for the complete portrait. As we pass through the dark experiences resemble a jigsaw puzzle. Here is a black piece, which seems to fit nowhere at all. It does not make sense. Here is a little brighter piece, and other sections of the jigsaw puzzle are dark, and some pitch black, and we cry and moan in these black moments. But by-and-by the Master will take all the pieces, which look so disconnected to us now, and carefully arrange each piece in its proper place, and then we shall see the completed work of Him who makes no mistakes.

Listen, when it is all ready, we shall find that the dark pieces of the puzzle were as important in the completion of the full beauty of the pattern as the bright sections. The dark background will only bring out in bolder and more gorgeous relief the figures in the picture, in the center of which will be His lovely face, and around it the experiences of life over which we mourn now but for which we will praise Him then.

—M. R. DeHaan

*God knows the way, He holds the key,*
*He guides us with unerring hand;*
*Some time with tearless eyes we'll see;*
*Yes, there, up there, we'll understand.*
—Maxwell N. Cornelius

*To guide our feet into the way of peace.* —Luke 1:79

There never would have been a path of peace had not Jesus Himself made it. All ways in life save that one which He has opened for us are full of pain and trouble, and lead only to sorrow, despair and death. But Christ prepared a highway that is beautiful and blessed, and that leads to eternal joy and glory. It was not easy work building this road. In the construction of some of this world's great thoroughfares thousands of human lives were sacrificed. We forget sometimes, as we move on in the highway of redemption, amid peaceful scenes, with soft music in our ears, and rich comforts in our hearts, and heavenly hopes to woo us forward, what it cost our blessed Lord, what toil and tears and blood, to prepare the way for us, to bridge over the chasms and level down the mountains. But now the way is open, and from beginning to end it is a way of peace.

A great many people think that the Christian life is hard and unpleasant, that it is a rough and steep road; but truly it is a way of pleasantness and peace. The only really happy people in this world are those who are following Christ along the way of redemption. They have their share of troubles, disappointments, sorrows; but all the time in the midst of these they have a secret peace of which the world knows nothing. There are paths in the low valleys, among the great mountains, which are sweet pictures of the Christian's way of peace. High up among the peaks and crags the storms sweep in wild fury, but on these valley paths no breath of tempest ever blows. Flowers bloom and springs of water gurgle along the wayside, and trees cast their graceful shadow, and bird-songs fill the air. Such is Christ's "way of peace" in this world.

—*J. R. Miller*

*The joy of the Lord is our strength.* —Nehemiah 8:10

Some forty thousand Jews, the remnant that stayed with Nehemiah and assisted in the work of building their temple in the ruins of Jerusalem and resumed worship in the Lord's house, are among the wonder people of history. They were few, oppressed, and in terrible circumstances. They were under the tyranny of Persian satraps. The neighboring Samaritans pillaged their barns and fields. Bandits over-ran their country and made it desolate, but these Jewish believers prayed it through and astounded a world with their success. Their secret—"The joy of the Lord was their strength." They had God with them, and that was sufficient. His presence was sufficient then, and it is now. But when we break fellowship with God we go down in defeat.

What is it that obtains the great favor of God? What is it that bears one up in the time of storm? We have it here: it is a full and complete surrender to the will of God. That is your privilege and my privilege now.

—C. E. Matthews

*No resting-place we seek on earth,*
*    No loveliness we see;*
*Our eye is on the royal crown*
*    Prepared for us and Thee.*

*But, dearest Lord, however bright*
*    That crown of joy above,*
*What is it to the brighter hope*
*    Of dwelling in Thy love?*

*What to the joy—the deeper joy,*
*    Unmingled, pure, and free—*
*Of union with our Living Head,*
*    Of fellowship with Thee?*
                    —Sir Edward Denny

*Whatsoever He saith unto you, do it.* —John 2:5

The Spirit of prayer would teach us that we should disregard the question as to whether the fulfillment of our prayer is hard or easy for God. What we think or do not think about this has no bearing on the hearing and answering of prayer. Not only that; it has a blighting and destructive effect upon our prayer life, because we waste our strength on something which is not our concern and which our Lord has never asked us to be concerned about.

This secret of prayer became very plain to me once many years ago as I was reading the delightful little account of the wedding in Cana of Galilee (John 2:1-11).

Jesus, His mother, and His disciples were bidden to the wedding. In all likelihood the family was closely related to, or very friendly toward, the family of Jesus. At least, we notice that the host and hostess had acquainted the mother of Jesus with the embarrassing situation which had arisen when the wine had given out.

Whereupon the mother of Jesus reveals herself as a tried and true woman of prayer.

In the first place, she goes to the right place with the need with which she has become acquainted. She goes to Jesus and tells Him everything.

In the next place, notice what she says to Jesus. Just these few, simple words, "They have no wine." Note here what prayer is. To pray is to tell Jesus what we lack. Intercession is to tell Jesus what we see that others lack.

She knew also that she did not have to influence Him or persuade Him to give these friends a helping hand. No one is so willing to help as He is!

—O. Hallesby

# November 16

*In your patience possess ye your souls.*     —Luke 21:19

> *What though thy way be dark, and earth*
> *With ceaseless care do cark, till mirth*
>    *To thee no sweet strain singeth;*
> *Still hide thy life above, and still*
> *Believe that God is love; Fulfill*
>    *Whatever lot He bringeth.*
>                 —Albert E. Evans

The chief pang of most trials is not so much the actual suffering itself, as our own spirit of resistance to it.
                                  —*Jean Nicolas Grou*

The mind never puts forth greater power over itself than when, in great trials, it yields up calmly its desires, affections, interests to God. There are seasons when to be *still* demands immeasurably higher strength than to act. Composure is often the highest result of power. Do you think it demands no power to calm the stormy elements of passion, to moderate the vehemence of desire, to throw off the load of dejection, to suppress every repining thought, when the dearest hopes are withered, and to turn the wounded spirit from dangerous reveries and wasting grief, to the quiet discharge of ordinary duties? Is there no power put forth, when a man, stripped of his property, of the fruits of a life's labors, quells discontent and gloomy forebodings, and serenely and patiently returns to the tasks which Providence assigns?     —*Wm. E. Channing*

> *When obstacles and trials seem*
>    *Like prison-walls to be,*
> *I do the little I can do,*
>    *And leave the rest to Thee.*
>                 —F. W. Faber

*He Himself hath suffered being tempted.* —Hebrews 2:18

It is a common-place thought, and yet it tastes like nectar to the weary heart—Jesus was tempted as I am. You have heard that truth many times: have you grasped it? He was tempted to the very same sins into which we fall. Do not dissociate Jesus from our common manhood. It is a dark room which you are going through, but Jesus went through it before. It is a sharp fight which you are waging, but Jesus has stood foot to foot with the same enemy. Let us be of good cheer, Christ has borne the load before us, and the blood-stained footsteps of the King of glory may be seen along the road which we traverse at this hour.

There is something sweeter yet—Jesus was tempted, but Jesus never sinned. Then, my soul, it is not needful for you to sin, for Jesus was a man, and if one man endured these temptations and sinned not, then in His power His members may also cease from sin.

Some beginners in the divine life think that they cannot be tempted without sinning, but they mistake; there is no sin in being tempted, but there is sin in yielding to temptation. Herein is comfort for the sorely tempted ones. There is still more to encourage them if they reflect that the Lord Jesus, though tempted, gloriously triumphed, and as He overcame, so surely shall His followers also, for Jesus is the representative man for His people; the Head has triumphed, and the members share in the victory. Fears are needless, for Christ is with us, armed for our defense. Our place of safety is the bosom of the Savior. Perhaps we are tempted just now, in order to drive us nearer to Him. Blessed be any wind that blows us into the port of our Savior's love! Happy wounds, which make us seek the beloved Physician.

—*Charles H. Spurgeon*

# NOVEMBER 18

*Giving thanks always for all things unto God and the Father.*
—Ephesians 5:20

"Forget not all his benefits." Not all supposedly good things prove to be blessings; and some very uncomfortable experiences have brought us great riches. Count your blessings, yes; but count as blessing only what springs from Him as its source.

Give thanks for the way God has dealt with your sins. Past sins are forgiven and buried forever; deeper than the stain, the cleansing. Present shortcomings, confessed, are covered by the Blood. And for the future, keeping in the hour of temptation and presenting faultless in glory is the program. Can you think of it without a shout!

Give thanks for the satisfaction He has given you in living, the eternal youth He has put in your spirit, the exhilarations of grace and glory. The body still wearies and decays, but "the Spirit is life because of righteousness." God's children need never really grow old.

Thank Him for the inner zest He gives you to enjoy the simple things of life: His handiwork in nature, the sweet interchanges of common family ways, the satisfaction of sound thinking, of work well done, and of clean recreation. Work, worship, love and play all come as pure gifts from His hand.

Count in the differences between what you might have been and what by His grace you have become. Those young people who started with you but refused to walk with God— where are they? O how thankful we should be for God's great goodness to His children. God treats His people well.

*Bless Jehovah, and forget not*
*All His mercies to proclaim.*

*Take therefore no thought for the morrow: for the morrow shall take thought for the things of itself. Sufficient unto the day is the evil thereof.*
—Matthew 6:34

I am glad that as a child of God I do not have to plan my own future. I am quite content to leave it in the hand of Him who knows the end from the beginning. That which looks very wise to me today may, in the light of tomorrow's now unborn moments, prove to have been foolish in the extreme. The man who trusts God completely and who accepts with unquestioning obedience the will and commands of God will always find that those things which happen to him today, though they may seem today unfortunate, will tomorrow be golden links in a chain of blessing. Illness may be God's way of putting His child in the place where special blessing awaits him. The bitter waters of sorrow forced to my lips may cause me to cry out for relief to God and in new reliance upon Him I shall find crystal streams of abundant joy.

No man knows what tomorrow will bring forth. The Christian does not need to know, for whatever it brings forth will prove a blessing for him. The darkness of sorrow brings to the ear of the Christian the melody of songs which were drowned by the laughter of the day, and the flames of a martyr's death become the wings of a fiery chariot bearing a victorious saint to glory. How wise to leave our tomorrows with Him who orders all our ways!

*I have nothing to do with tomorrow,*
*My Savior will make that His care;*
*Its grace and its strength I can't borrow,*
*So why should I borrow its care?*

—Bob Jones, Jr.

*. . . stand every morning to thank and praise the Lord. . . .*
—1 Chronicles 23:30

In Old Testament times it was the office of the Levites, the priestly tribe of the Israelites, to stand up in public and express the praise of the people to their God Jehovah. It was the task of the Levites to "stand every morning to thank and praise the Lord." Today, however, in this dispensation of grace, it is the privilege of every child of God to stand in the presence of the Father "to thank and praise the Lord." Bringing praise to the Father in the morning before entering into the heat of the day is truly "getting off on the right foot." It is those who begin the day in the presence of the Lord who are most likely to continue and end the day in His presence. It was Daniel who loved to kneel in the presence of his God three times a day to praise and give Him thanks. The Psalmist David did the same and, we are told, in the New Testament, Peter and John as well as others of Christ's disciples had set times during the day which were set apart for communion in prayer with the Heavenly Father.

During His earthly ministry Jesus taught that "Man ought always to pray." And the Apostle Paul instructed his fellow Christians to "Pray without ceasing," and "In everything give thanks. . . ."

On the basis of these examples from God's Word we as God's children should be instructed to make prayer and praise a happy habit of our daily living so that we can know from experience what it means to "bless the Lord at all times" with "His praise . . . continually in our mouth."

*Now thank we all our God,*
*With heart and hand and voices*
*Who wondrous things hath done,*
*In whom His world rejoices.*
—Catherine Winkworth: Tr. of Johann Crüger

*Forget not all His benefits.* —Psalm 103:2

It is a delightful and profitable occupation to mark the hand of God in the lives of ancient saints, and to observe His goodness in delivering them, His mercy in pardoning them, and His faithfulness in keeping His covenant with them. But would it not be even more interesting and profitable for us to notice the hand of God in our own lives? Ought we not to look upon our own history as being at least as full of God, as full of His goodness and of His truth, as much a proof of His faithfulness and veracity, as the lives of any of the saints who have gone before? We do our Lord an injustice when we suppose that He wrought all His mighty acts, and showed Himself strong for those in the early time, but does not perform wonders or lay bare His arm for the saints who are now upon the earth.

Let us review our own lives. Surely in these we may discover some happy incidents, refreshing to ourselves and glorifying to our God. Have you had no deliverances? Have you passed through no rivers, supported by the divine presence? Have you walked through no fires unharmed? Have you had no manifestations? Have you had no choice favors? The God who gave Solomon the desire of his heart, has He never listened to you and answered your requests? Have you never been made to lie down in green pastures? Have you never been led by the still waters?

Surely the goodness of God has been the same to us as to the saints of old. Let us, then, weave His mercies into a song. Let us take the pure gold of thankfulness, and the jewels of praise and make them into another crown for the head of Jesus. —*Charles H. Spurgeon*

# NOVEMBER 22

*My presence shall go with thee.* —Exodus 33:14

Dear Christian, can you not believe it?—this wondrous consciousness of your Lord's continual presence is meant for you. It is in no sense the exclusive portion of a privileged class. God does not deal with us in that way. Nor is it only possible to those whose circumstances allow hours of protracted retirement each day. True prayer is a bigger thing than can be confined to forms and times and places—though this by no means belittles the importance of our having regular and set times for prayer each day. Well does God know that most of us must give hours daily to other things; yet, nonetheless, He is with us, and we may develop such an uninterrupted consciousness of His presence as shall transfigure all our daily work, making life's dullest places bloom and smile.

Moses, Joseph, Daniel, were all "men of affairs," having their hands full of what we call "non-religious" matters; yet how vivid was the nearness of God to them! The same could be said of a host whose names are not so familiar to us. Do some of us feel ourselves too small for God to think specially upon us? It is an enemy who has suggested this. Will He whose watchful eye loses not sight of the falling sparrow turn His eye away from His own children? Will He who paints the wayside bower, as well as lights the evening star, be unmindful of those whom He has redeemed with the precious blood of Christ? However mean our earthly circumstances may be, we are "heirs of God, and joint-heirs with Christ"; and shall God forget His very elect? —*J. Sidlow Baxter*

*Holding a beggar's child*
*Against my heart,*
*Through blinding tears I see*
*That as I love the tiny, pietous thing,*
*So God loves me!*

—Toyohiko Kagawa

*Hold thou me up, and I shall be safe:* —Psalm 119:117

*Fear not, little flock, He goeth ahead,*
*    Your Shepherd selecteth the path you must tread;*
*The waters of Marah He'll sweeten for thee,*
*    He drank all the bitter in Gethsemane.*

*Fear not, little flock, whatever your lot,*
*    He enters all rooms, "the doors being shut";*
*He never forsakes, He never is gone,*
*    So count on His presence in darkness and dawn.*
                                        —Paul Rader

Not only a Christ to stand outside and support with the strong hands of His forgiveness, but a Christ to come in and strengthen by the power of His incorporated life. Christ is the Staff we lean on, the Rock on which we stand, the Light that leads us, the Master on whose breast we lie; but He is also the Bread of Life. He is many things outside of us—Wisdom, Righteousness, Redemption. He says, "Lean on Me, stand on Me, take hold of Me and walk." But when He takes up His deepest word it is this—"Feed on Me; unless you feed on Me you have no life in you." He says, "Look and see how good God is; touch Me and feel God's mercy; hear Me and I will tell you how He loves you." But at the last this comes as a commandment of the deepest faith, the promise of the highest mercy—"O taste and see that the Lord is gracious."

                                        —*Phillips Brooks*

*No more I ask the reason why,*
*    Although I may not see*
*The path ahead, His way I go;*
*For tho' I know not, He doth know,*
*    And He will choose safe paths for me.*
                        —Author Unknown

*How long wilt thou mourn? . . . fill thy horn with oil, and go,*
*I will send thee . . . I have provided. . . .* —1 Samuel 16:1

Yes, human sorrow must flow on until the heart finds rest in the rich resources of the blessed God. The varied blanks which human events leave in the heart can only be filled up by the power of faith in the precious word, "I have provided." This really settles everything. This dries the tear, alleviates the sorrow, fills the blank. The moment the spirit rests in the provision of God's love, there is a period put to all our sorrows. May we all know the power and varied application of this truth; may we know what it is to have our tears dried up, and our horn filled by the conviction of our Father's wise and merciful provision.

*The veil is rent:—our souls draw near*
    *Unto a throne of grace;*
*The merits of the Lord appear,*
    *They fill the holy place.*

*His precious blood has spoken there,*
    *Before and on the throne:*
*And His own wounds in heaven declare,*
    *The atoning work is done.*

*'Tis finished!—here our souls have rest,*
    *His work can never fail:*
*By Him, our Sacrifice and Priest,*
    *We pass within the veil.*

*Boldly the heart and voice we raise,*
    *His blood, His name, our plea:*
*Assured our prayers and songs of praise*
    *Ascend, by Christ, to Thee.*
                                        —J. G. Deck

*What time I am afraid, I will trust in Thee.* —Psalm 56:3

The crosses of the present moment always bring their own special grace and consequent comfort with them; we see the hand of God in them when it is laid upon us. But the crosses of anxious foreboding are seen out of the dispensation of God; we see them without grace to bear them; we see them indeed through a faithless spirit which banishes grace. So, everything in them is bitter and unendurable; all seems dark and helpless. Let us throw self aside; no more self-interest, and then God's will, unfolding every moment in everything, will console us also every moment for all that He shall do around us, or within us, for our discipline.

—*François de La Mothe Fenelon*

Nothing does so much establish the mind amidst the rollings and turbulency of present things, as both a look above them, and a look beyond them; above them to the good and steady Hand by which they are ruled, and beyond them to the sweet and beautiful end to which by that Hand, they shall be brought.

—*R. Leighton*

*I have a loving Savior,*
*My Shepherd-Guide is He;*
*With tend'rest love and mercy*
*He watches over me.*

*His grace is freely given*
*For ev'ry unknown way;*
*I have His peace within my heart;*
*His rod and staff, my stay.*
—Helen A. Lewis

# November 26

*A bright cloud overshadowed them.* —Matthew 17:5

The cloud was a symbol of the Divine presence. One of the writers says the disciples were afraid as they saw the cloud come down over the Master and the heavenly visitants. God still comes to us often in thick clouds, and we are afraid, too. But the cloud meant no harm to the disciples. No cloud means any harm to a disciple when God is in the cloud; and always, if we only listen, we may hear words of love.

> *Sorrow touched by love grows bright*
> *With more than rapture's ray;*
> *And darkness shows us worlds of light*
> *We never saw by day.*

There are times when God's ways with us seem very hard, and we think disaster is coming to every fair prospect in our life. In all such hours we should remember that He who rules over all is the Son of God, our Friend and Savior; and our trust in Him should never doubt nor fear. What so staggered the disciples then we now see to have been the most glorious and loving wisdom. So in our sorest trials there are the truest wisdom and the richest love. Hereafter we shall know. It was out of the cloud that this voice came. Out of the clouds that hang over us come often the tenderest voices of Divine love, the most precious disclosures of Divine grace.  —*J. R. Miller*

Most of us know what it is to be overwhelmed in heart. Disappointments and heartbreaks will do this when billow after billow rolls over us. But higher than we are is He, His mercy higher than our sins, His love higher than our thoughts. A rock He is since He changes not, and a high rock, because the tempests which overwhelm us roll far beneath at His feet. O Lord, our God, by the Holy Spirit, teach us Thy way of faith, lead us unto Thy rest.

*The eternal God is your refuge, and underneath are the everlasting arms.*
—Deuteronomy 33:27 NIV

One of the sweetest passages in the Bible is this one: "Underneath are the everlasting arms."

We often sink low under the weight of sorrows. Sudden disappointments can carry us, in an hour, from the heights down to the very depths. Props that we leaned upon are stricken away. What God means by it very often is just to bring us down to "the everlasting arms." We did not feel our need of them before. We were "making flesh our arm," and relying on human comforts or resources.

There is something about deep sorrow that tends to wake up the child-feeling in all of us. A man of giant intellect becomes like a little child when a great grief smites him, or when a grave opens beneath his fireside.

One great purpose in all affliction is to bring us down to the everlasting arms. What new strength and peace it gives us to feel them underneath us! We know that, far as we may have sunk, we cannot go any farther. Those mighty arms cannot only hold us, they can lift us up. They can carry us along. Faith, in its essence, is simply a resting on the everlasting arms. It is trusting them, and not our own weakness. The sublime act of Jesus as our Redeemer was to descend to the lowest depths of human depravity and guilt, and to bring up His redeemed ones from that horrible pit in His loving arms. Faith is just the clinging to those arms, and nothing more.

—*Theodore L. Cuyler*

*What a fellowship, what a joy divine,*
*Leaning on the everlasting arms;*
*What a blessedness, what a peace is mine,*
*Leaning on the everlasting arms.*
—E. A. Hoffman

# November 28

*God is with thee in all that thou doest. . . .* —Genesis 21:22

Oh, think that He, in all your sorrows, pities you! Yes, your God feels for you. Your sufferings go to His heart. There is One in heaven who, from that exaltation, looks down upon you; and the eye that watches over you wept for you once, and would, if it had tears, weep for you again. He knows your frame. He remembers that you are dust. He will not break the bruised reed, nor quench the smoking flax. It was He who, when His disciples had nothing to say for themselves, made that kind apology for them, "The spirit is willing but the flesh is weak." He can be touched with the feeling of all your infirmities. You may cast all your cares on Him, for He cares for you. All through this vale of tears, you may rest assured of His sympathy, and when the vale of tears declines into the valley of the shadow of death, not His sympathy only will you have, but His inspiring presence and His timely succor. And after that, what will not His bounty be whose pity has been so great? When there is no longer any occasion for pity when misery is no more, and sighing has ceased, and God's hand has for the last time passed across your weeping eyes, and wiped away the final tear, what then will be the riches of His munificence? —*William Nevins*

*We cannot buy God's treasures*
*Our poverty to bless,*
*But Christ exchangeth with us*
*And giveth more for less;*
*The oil of joy for mourning*
*And praise for heaviness,*
*More grace for little thorn pricks,*
*Much fruit for purging light,*
*For earth's brief tribulation*
*Eternal glory bright.*
—Annie Johnson Flint

# NOVEMBER 29

*My beloved is mine, and I am His. . . .*

—Song of Solomon 2:16

So full of contentment and joy is this assured statement of fact that it might well have been written by the same hand which penned the beloved 23rd Psalm. Surely, this is one of the happiest verses in Scripture, so peaceful and over-running with happiness is this striking statement of assurance.

But if we read on in this chapter we find that life is not without shadows, for verse 17 reads, "Until the day break and the shadows flee away. . . ." Yes, fellow Christian, even a life lived in the center of God's will may not be free from trouble and testing, clouds and disappointments. And often, in the midst of testing we, as Christians, lose sight of the fact that "My beloved is mine and I am His. . . ." We doubt our salvation, we forget that Christ is our Savior. We neglect coming to Him for His sufficiency. In the midst of trial and testing is the time when we need most to come before His presence praying "Until the day break, and the shadows flee away. . . ."

What blessed fellowship can be ours if we are walking in His will side by side with our blessed Savior. What wonderful assurance can be ours if we are casting our cares upon Him, confident that He can assume our heavy burden, presenting us spotless before His presence through His shed blood. Meditate upon these words, fellow Christian, and take them with you today. What blessed assurance can be ours if we walk this pilgrim way!

> *Blessed assurance, Jesus is mine!*
> *Oh, what a foretaste of glory divine!*
> *Heir of salvation, purchase of God,*
> *Born of His Spirit, washed in His blood.*

# November 30

*Under whose wings thou art come to trust.* —Ruth 2:12

This was the result of Ruth's noble decision: "Thy people shall be my people, and thy God my God." Having chosen the God of Israel to be her God, she was able to put her entire trust and confidence in Him. And just as the little chick feels perfectly safe when under the wings of the mother hen, so Ruth felt at peace and at rest under the protecting care of God.

Trust is always the result of knowledge. We dare not trust those we do not know, but those we know and love we easily trust. Ruth was brought to know God, then to love Him and then to trust Him. We are here reminded of David's declaration: "My soul trusteth in Thee, yea, in the shadow of Thy wings will I make my refuge," and again: "Because Thou hast been my help, therefore in the shadow of Thy wings will I rejoice." So there is both safety and enjoyment under the shadow of God's wings.

Well might the same writer say, "How excellent is Thy loving-kindness, therefore the children of men put their trust under the shadow of Thy wings," and even "when the noisome pestilence" is raging, if we are dwelling "in the secret place of the Most High," we need not fear, for "He shall cover thee with His feathers, and under His wings shalt thou trust." Our God loves to be trusted. It is impossible to trust Him overmuch; neither Ruth, nor Daniel, nor David, nor any other warrior ever did. Let me, then, join hands with Ruth and get under God's wings or into God's presence, and then at all times trust alone in Him.

—*John Roberts*

# DECEMBER 1

*And I have also given thee that which thou hast not asked.*
*—1 Kings 3:13*

*No voice of prayer to Thee can rise,*
*But swift as light Thy Love replies;*
*Not always what we ask, indeed,*
*But, O most Kind! what most we need.*
*—H. M. Kimball*

If you have any trial which seems intolerable, pray—pray that it be relieved or changed. There is no harm in that. We may pray for anything, not wrong in itself, with perfect freedom, if we do not pray selfishly. One disabled from duty by sickness may pray for health, that he may do his work; or one hemmed in by internal impediments may pray for utterance, that he may serve better the truth and the right. Or, if we have a besetting sin, we may pray to be delivered from it, in order to serve God and man, and not be ourselves Satans to mislead and destroy. But the answer to the prayer may be, as it was to Paul, not the removal of the thorn, but, instead, a growing insight into its meaning and value. The voice of God in our soul may show us, as we look up to Him, that His strength is enough to enable us to bear it.
*—J. F. Clarke*

All who call on God in true faith, earnestly from the heart, will certainly be heard, and will receive what they have asked and desired, although not in the hour or in the measure, or the very thing which they ask; yet they will obtain something greater and more glorious than they had dared to ask.
*—Martin Luther*

# DECEMBER 2

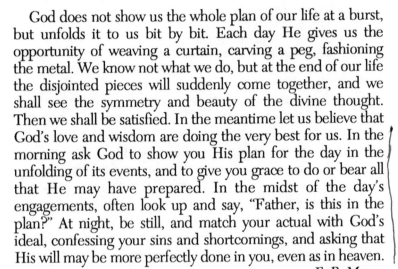

*Show me Thy ways, O Lord; teach me Thy paths. Lead me in Thy truth, and teach me.* —Psalm 25:4, 5

God does not show us the whole plan of our life at a burst, but unfolds it to us bit by bit. Each day He gives us the opportunity of weaving a curtain, carving a peg, fashioning the metal. We know not what we do, but at the end of our life the disjointed pieces will suddenly come together, and we shall see the symmetry and beauty of the divine thought. Then we shall be satisfied. In the meantime let us believe that God's love and wisdom are doing the very best for us. In the morning ask God to show you His plan for the day in the unfolding of its events, and to give you grace to do or bear all that He may have prepared. In the midst of the day's engagements, often look up and say, "Father, is this in the plan?" At night, be still, and match your actual with God's ideal, confessing your sins and shortcomings, and asking that His will may be more perfectly done in you, even as in heaven.

—F. B. Meyer

*His way! I fain would learn it;*
 *His meek and gentle way.*
*The worldly wise may spurn it,*
 *But teach me, Lord, Thy way.*

*We have Thy promise—plead it,*
 *Oh, waiting, longing heart,*
*Thy teaching, Lord, I need it;*
 *The lesson now impart.*

*I would be meek and lowly,*
 *So would I learn each day.*
*Made gentle, true, and holy,*
 *Made wise in Thine own way.*
—William Luff

*Caleb, the son of Jephunneh . . .*　　　　　—Joshua 14:6

You search in vain in the life story of Caleb to find a single instance where he was pessimistic, or cheerless, or dejected at all, but rather, the opposite shines out from his life story all along. He is one of the sunniest characters in all the Bible. Caleb had the New Testament spirit, enjoined long afterwards by Paul, when Paul urged: "Rejoice evermore." And when again he said: "Rejoice in the Lord alway, and again I say, rejoice," Caleb had caught that spirit most graciously, and throughout his eventful life he was the man whose disposition was one of uniform and glorious cheerfulness. It is a most valuable lesson to learn, dear friends. "The joy of the Lord is your strength." The dejected, moping, cheerless Christian, the one without joy, the one whose face indicates sorrow forever, is not the one who makes a gracious impression upon an unbelieving world. Caleb is a man, with all that hearty, cheerful, sunshiny life, to give men to understand how healthy and happy a thing it is for one to be a genuine Christian.

Caleb "wholly followed the Lord his God." That is what the Scriptures say again and again about him. And that is the secret, the sublime secret, of all the other wonderful elements of his character. Caleb wholly followed the Lord his God. Whenever a man does that, what does he care for anything except the "Well done" of the God whom he serves? Caleb wholly followed the Lord his God. Caleb said that for himself: "I have wholly followed Him." And Moses said it about Caleb. And God Himself said: "My servant, Caleb, has wholly followed Me." So that he had the overwhelming testimony of the reality of his devotion to God. Now, in that fact resides the sublime secret of Caleb's marvelous power for God.

—*George W. Truett*

# DECEMBER 4

*And the Lord shall guide thee continually, and satisfy thy soul in drought, and make fat thy bones. . . .* —Isaiah 58:11

Little do self-willed souls know what they miss when they refuse to be guided. The worrying and the fretting, the anxious planning and plotting for the future, the carving out for ourselves our pathway in the world, all this is spared to those who are willing to be guided. Perfect confidence in your guide brings rest. And where rest reigns, the worry which kills men must depart.

Let us rejoice in the assurance that this guidance is perpetual. The promise covers the whole range of our life and being. "The Lord shall guide thee continually . . ." not merely for a day, or week, or year, but all your days; and everywhere: in the busy roadway of the world, and amid the quiet duties of home. We need never lose our way. There are to be no gaps, no intervals during which we must be left to plod our weary way alone. "Lo, I am with you all the days, even to the end of the age" are the cheery words with which our unbelief is chided.

—*E. W. Moore*

*When shall I doubt? Not yet,*
*   Till God forgets*
*And my soul an hungered goes—*
*   No manna gets!*
*Not till my God cares not!*
*   When will that be?*
*When time is not, nor e'en*
*   Eternity!*

—George W. Tuttle

*Jesus himself drew near. "I will never forsake thee."*
                                                    —Luke 24:15

"I will never forsake thee." Sometimes it seems to us, in the hour of trial or bereavement, that He has forgotten His promise, but He has not. The trial is only designed to make us more conscious of our helplessness in order that we may call upon Him. He loves to bear our burdens. "His yoke is easy and His burden is light." He invited us to exchange our yoke for His yoke. Our yoke is irksome; His is restful. But we cannot take His yoke until we give up our own yoke, our own way, and learn to walk in step with Him. If He seems to have gone away it is probably because we are out of step with Him.
                                                    —*J. Elwin Wright*

*I prayed for relief from my burden,*
    *Asked the Lord to take it away,*
*But I grew unsettled and doubtful,*
    *For the burden grew harder each day;*
*Then I changed the note of my praying,*
    *And asked for the Master alone,*
*Then turned to take up my burden*
    *But lo! my burden was gone.*

*So now, if I'm burdened or doubtful,*
    *Or weary with overmuch care,*
*I go at once to my Savior,*
    *Ask Him the burden to share;*
*And I find Him ever so willing,*
    *For He walks by my side, on the road,*
*Now, wonder of wonders, I'm telling,*
    *He takes from my heart all the load!*
                                                    —Agnes K. King

# DECEMBER 6

*Let not your heart be troubled.* —John 14:1

Jesus always loved to comfort. He loves to put little candles in the darkened chambers of sorrow. He loves to dry tears and change grief into joy. Then He is able to give comfort, because He has the comfort in Himself. We cannot give what we have not to give. Standing on the ship in the midst of a wild sea, Jesus said, "Peace!" and the winds and waves instantly became a calm. He had the peace in Himself, and could give peace to the sea. It is the same with His comfort: His words of consolation are not like so many of ours; they have power to quiet the troubled heart.

It was a time of the deepest grief and the sorest sorrow for the disciples when Jesus said, "Let not your heart be troubled." Not only were they to lose their best Friend, but they were to lose Him in the saddest way—by death in the shame of the cross. Nor was that all of their sorrow. They had hoped He was the Messiah; now that hope was gone. They were in utter desolation—in a starless midnight. Surely there could be no comfort for such grief as theirs, they thought that night, as with breaking hearts they sat there in the darkness.

Yet right into the midst of this despairing grief came the words, "Let not your heart be troubled." Let us never say, therefore, that there is any, even the bitterest grief, for which there is no possible comfort. No matter how dark the night is, Christ can put stars into our sky, and bring a glorious morning after the darkness. There is comfort for Christ's disciples in the most hopeless grief. We have but to look forward a few days to see the sorrow of these men turned to blessed joy. So it always is. However we may grieve, there is never any reason why we should lose our peace. —*J. R. Miller*

*Every day will I bless Thee.* —Psalm 145:2

It is a step forward in the Christian life when one definitely decides to seek to have fellowship with God in His Word each day without fail. His perseverance will be crowned with success, if he is really in earnest. His experiences may be somewhat as follows:

On waking in the morning, God will be his first thought. He must set apart a time for prayer, and resolve to give God time to hear his requests, and to reveal Himself to him. Then he may speak out all his desires to God, and expect an answer.

Later on in the day, even if only for a few minutes, he will take time to keep up the fellowship with God. And again in the evening, a quiet period is necessary to review the day's work, and with confession of sin receive the assurance of forgiveness, and dedicate himself afresh to God and His service.

Such a one will gradually get an insight into what is lacking in his life, and will be ready to say: Not only "every day" but "all the day." He will realize that the Holy Spirit is in him unceasingly, just as his breathing is continuous. In the inner chamber he will make it his aim to gain the assurance through faith that the Holy Spirit, and the Lord Jesus, and the Father Himself will grant His presence and help all through the day.

All the day! Christian, the Holy Spirit says: "Today." "Behold, now is the accepted time!" A man who had undergone a serious operation, asked his doctor, "How long will I have to lie here?" And the answer came: "Only a day at a time." And that is the law of the Christian life. —*Andrew Murray*

*O God of the impossible,*
*    When we no hope can see,*
*Grant us the faith that still believes*
*    ALL possible to Thee!*

# DECEMBER 8

*And therefore will the Lord wait, that he may be gracious unto you ... blessed are all they that wait for him.*
                                                              —Isaiah 30:18

God's delays are not denials; they are not neglectful nor unkind. He is waiting with watchful eye and intent for the precise moment to strike, when I can give a blessing which will be without alloy, and will flood all after life with blessings so royal, so plenteous, so divine that eternity will be too short to utter all our praise.                    —*F. B. Meyer*

A truth that all of us need to learn, dear fellow Christian, is that God often delays in answering prayer. There are several instances illustrating this Scriptural truth in His Word. For instance, Jacob had to wrestle all night before he received the blessing from the angel. In the New Testament, the Apostle Paul besought the Lord three times that the thorn in his flesh might be removed, and received no assurance that it would be taken away, but rather God's promise that His grace should be sufficient.

Perhaps you are wondering why He does not answer your petition. Well, fellow pilgrim, God has reasons peculiar to Himself for keeping us waiting. Sometimes it is to show His power and might, that men may know that He has the right to give or withhold the answer.

Perhaps, too, there is some lesson we need to learn that will cause us to be drawn even closer to our Father. Comfort yourself with this thought, as well, that all of your prayers are heard if they are presented in faith believing. The answer may be delayed, but be assured that your Heavenly Father has not forgotten.

*And she shall bring forth a son, and thou shalt call His name Jesus; for he shall save his people from their sins.*

—Matthew 1:21

If Jesus had not come, no carols; for no song of salvation to sing. No hymns of praise; for no deliverance. Go through your hymnal and count the sacred songs you must lose if Jesus had not come: "Joy to the World," "Hark! the Herald Angels Sing," "Rock of Ages," "Jesus Lover of My Soul"—but why begin? His coming set earth's joybells ringing. He keeps a song singing in my heart.

*No Savior.* However self-confident men are, they cannot lift themselves to God by their own bootstraps. Sin is real and it is too strong for us. But since He came there is a path clear between the Cross and every seeking sinner. He came to save.

*No Lamb* slain, no atoning Blood, no cleansing fountain. Suppose I could not sing:

*There is a fountain filled with blood*
*Drawn from Immanuel's veins,*
*And sinners plunged beneath that flood*
*Lose all their guilty stains.*

*No Prince of Peace.* War is the Devil's schedule: for nations, for families, for human hearts. I choose Christ's better way of conquering by love.

*No victory over Satan.* I can always put the enemy to flight if I call on the name of Jesus.

*The soul that on Jesus hath leaned for repose*
*I will not, I will not desert to his foes.*

—*Bertha Munro*

# DECEMBER 10

*Likewise the Spirit also helpeth our infirmities: for we know not what we should pray for as we ought: but the Spirit itself maketh intercession for us with groanings which cannot be uttered.* —Romans 8:26

Notice how graciously prayer has been designed. To pray is nothing more involved than to let Jesus into our needs. To pray is to ask Jesus to employ His powers in the alleviation of our distress. To pray is to let Jesus glorify His name in the midst of our needs.

The results of prayer are, therefore, not dependent upon the powers of the one who prays. His intense will, his fervent emotions, or his clear comprehension of what he is praying for are not the reasons why his prayers will be heard and answered. Nay, God be praised, the results of prayer are not dependent upon these things!

To pray is nothing more involved than to open the door, giving Jesus access to exercise His own power in dealing with our needs.

He who gave us the privilege of prayer knows us very well. He knows our frame; He remembers that we are dust.

That is why He designed prayer in such a way that the most impotent can make use of it. For to pray is to open the door unto Jesus. And that requires no strength. Will we give Jesus access to our needs? That is the one great and fundamental question in connection with prayer.

—O. Hallesby

*Prayer is the simplest form of speech*
*That infant lips can try;*
*Prayer the sublimest strains that reach*
*The Majesty on high.*
—James Montgomery

*... Out of weakness were made strong. ...* —Hebrews 11:34

God's strength is "made perfect in our weakness." This means that the divine power is most conspicuous when our weakness is the most thoroughly felt. We must first be emptied of all self-conceit and self-confidence. A bucket cannot hold air and water at the same time. As the water comes in the air must go out. The meaning of some hard trials is to get the accursed spirit of self out of our hearts. When we have been emptied of self-trust, we are in the condition to be filled with might in the inner man by the power of the Holy Spirit. When Isaiah felt that he was but a child, and an unclean one at that, he received the touch of celestial fire. Peter had immense confidence in Peter when he boasted of his own strength; but after pride receives its fall, Peter is endued with power from on high, and then the apostle who was frightened by a servant-girl could face a Sanhedrin. A Christian must not only realize his own utter feebleness, but he must give up what worldlings rely on, and admit that "vain is the help of man."

One great purpose in all afflictions is to bring us down to the everlasting arms. We had become presumptuous, and had made flesh our arm. We were trying to go alone, and then came a fall. Trouble, and even bereavement, may be a great blessing, if it sends us home to Jesus. A boy often forgets that he has a home until a cut or a bruise sends him crying to his mother's side for the bandage or the medicine. God often strikes away our props to bring us down upon His mighty arms.                          —*Theodore L. Cuyler*

> *Lead me higher, nothing dreading,*
> *In the race to never stop;*
> *In Thy footsteps keep me treading,*
> *Give me grace to reach the top.*

—Author Unknown

# DECEMBER 12

*But when the fulness of the time was come, God sent forth his Son.* —Galatians 4:4

Jesus came in the fullness of time. God's timing of His dispensations is exact. We grow panicky and say, "How long?" An infinitely wise God has His eye on world conditions. His Son is coming again—not too late, nor too soon.

The fullness of time did not mean the easy time. God did not smooth the way; He prepared it. There is a difference. It was the most effective moment, not the simplest. I would rather have God's calendar than mine always. I would rather do my errands for Him at the right time than at the easy time. Like Jesus I would say, "I delight to do thy will, O my God."

Situation unfavorable? Circumstances against you? Opportunities lacking? All this seems to matter little to Jesus. He seems to live by the firm faith that for the man who has chosen the will of God any situation can be manipulated by divine power, irradiated by divine energy, turned into a divine victory, made to shout the praise of God. To modify Chesterton: "(God's) man is not the creature of circumstances; circumstances may be the creature of (God's) man."

Our world is one as never before—what does it mean? Newspapers and radio are a-tingle with electric transpirings; everyday events are big with possibilities. Let us utilize the new opportunities as Jesus' first disciples did till He comes to stand on Olivet again. —*Bertha Munro*

*Ah, what a life is theirs who live in Christ;*
  *How vast the mystery!*
*Reaching in height to heaven, and in its depth*
  *The unfathomed sea!*
—Elizabeth Payson Prentiss

*And he said unto them, Why are ye troubled? and why do
thoughts arise in your hearts?* —Luke 24:38

With these words our Lord shows His concern for the very
smallest incidents in the lives of His children. The Lord cares
for all things, great and small, but His particular care is for
His children—and He is concerned even for their "thoughts"!
The marvelous truth of this fact should cause every child of
God to rejoice.

"The angel of the Lord encampeth round about them that
fear him." "The very hairs of your head are all numbered."
Let the thought of His *special* care for you be a comfort and
blessing day by day. "I will never leave *thee*, nor forsake *thee*."
Our Lord means that as much for us today as He did to the
saints of old.

It is only too true that we as individual Christians lose
much of the joy of our salvation by habitually reading His
promises as though they only applied to the Christian church
as a whole, rather than directly applying them to ourselves.
Join with Spurgeon in saying, "Jesus whispers consolation; I
cannot refuse it; I will sit under His shadow with great delight."
Apply the promises of God to yourself, personally, and revel
in the sheer wonder of His personal interest in everything
that affects you. Even your thoughts warrant the Lord's care
and concern. What a marvelous indication of His love for you!

*The weary ones had rest, the sad had joy
    That day, and wondered "how?"
A ploughman singing at his work, had prayed,
    "Lord, help them now."*

*Yes, we are always wondering, wondering "how,"
    Because we do not see
Someone, unknown perhaps, and far away,
    On bended knee.*

# DECEMBER 14

*And this is the victory that overcometh the world, even our*
*faith.*                                                    —1 John 5:4

This word of the Apostle expresses the victorious mood in
which victory was achieved. The early believers in the Lord Jesus
won the victory in their hearts before they won it on the field. In
Christ Jesus they anticipated triumph, and their anticipations
made the triumph possible. And this mood is one of the secrets
of victory in every kingdom. Is there any record of an army
winning a battle when the soldiers entered the conflict believing
they would fail? Such a gloomy lack of confidence would breed a
dismal progeny of wants, and the army would be sapped of its
vital resources before the battle began.

And surely this victorious mood is needed today. Our tasks
are tremendous. To lose confidence is to lose everything. The
devil always wins when he breaks our assurance. To be sure
in Christ Jesus is the beginning of victory. Nay, it is victory!
"This is the victory which overcometh the world, even our
faith."                                                   —J. H. Jowett

> Commit your way unto the Lord,
>   Let all thy soul in Him delight;
> Trust thou in Him, believe His Word,
>   And you shall know His arm of might.
> When you have asked, in patience wait,
>   Till answer shall from heav'n come through,
> In confidence anticipate,
>   And see what wonders God will do.
>
> He that within you doth abide,
>   Is mightier than any foe;
> He notes how sorely you are tried,
>   The way ahead doth fully know.
> Delays are not denials, child,
>   When you have asked that which is right,
> But oftentimes, God's mercy mild,
>   To lead you on to higher height.
>                           —Grace B. Renfrow

*Therefore the Lord Himself shall give you a sign; Behold, a virgin shall conceive, and bear a Son, and shall call His Name Immanuel.* —Isaiah 7:14

This is the traditional season for remembering the birth of One who came into the world long ago. And there is probably no single statement that more clearly demonstrates the uniqueness of that birth than this verse. The world venerates the anniversaries of the greatest of the past. But there is no other whose birth can be recalled with a statement written over seven hundred years in advance of the event. Yes, our verse for today is often quoted, but it is none the less a miracle. Every time it appears on a Christmas card it witnesses to the supernatural birth of the Babe of Bethlehem.

"Immanuel"! His divinely pre-written Name gives His divinely appointed message, "Immanuel—God with us." How sad that from the very beginning men had no room for Immanuel. How tragic that today there is still no room for Him. Room for war, room for sin, room for pleasure and lust—but no room for Immanuel. —*Frank E. Gaebelein*

*Lo, God, our God, has come!*
  *To us a Child is born,*
*To us a Son is given;*
  *Bless, bless the blessed morn,*
*O Happy, lowly, lofty birth,*
*Now God, our God, has come to earth.*

*Rejoice, our God has come!*
  *In love and lowliness.*
*The Son of God has come,*
  *The sons of men to bless.*
*God with us now descends to dwell,*
*God in our flesh, Immanuel.*
—Horatius Bonar

# DECEMBER 16

*Perserve me, O God: for in thee do I put my trust.*
—Psalm 16:1

Still another meditation upon the blessedness of trusting in the Lord! Oh, the times we have had to consider this subject during our daily reading in God's precious truth. The fact is, God's Word is just full of counsels and directions for faith and trust and confidence in Him, together with examples of holy men who have dared, under all circumstances, to put their trust in the Living God.

Today we hear the Psalmist, in his private devotions, saying: "Preserve me, O God, for in Thee do I put my trust." And it is the privilege of every child of God to put their trust in Him. See how the Lord Jesus teaches us to do this in Matthew 6:25-33, "Therefore I say unto you, Take no thought (no anxiety) for your life, what ye shall eat, or what ye shall drink . . . for your heavenly Father knoweth that ye have need of these things." Therefore, trust Him.

See how the same truth was exemplified in the apostle in the first chapter of Philippians. He was prevented from preaching the Gospel by being imprisoned. But did he complain? Not at all. He simply said: "I know that this shall turn to my salvation." And so it did, for "many of the brethren in the Lord, waxing confident by his bonds, were much more bold to speak the Word without fear." So that when the enemy was permitted to shut one man's mouth, God opened many others, which was the purpose for which Paul wished to live and die.                    —*John Roberts*

*"I believe"—ay, do I! I believe*
*He will never fail me, never leave;*
*I believe He holds me, and I know*
*His strong hand will never let me go.*
—Annie Johnson Flint

*He that spared not his own Son, but delivered him up for us all, how shall he not with him also freely give us all things?*
—Romans 8:32

In the Lord Jesus Christ every believer has a treasure which cannot be described in terms of material wealth and possessions. We are members of the wealthiest and happiest family in all the universe, for God is our Father, the One who made the heavens and the earth, the sea and all that in it is, the One who is the Creator of all things. The gold and the silver are His, and the cattle upon a thousand hills. He is the Father of every believer, and we are heirs of all things which are His. The Son is ours, and we are His, the Son who gave His life and shed His blood upon Calvary's Cross. But He broke the bands of death and arose, and is today seated at the right hand of God the Father in heaven. And He is soon coming again to put down all rule and authority and power, and reign upon this earth in perfect righteousness and justice. And we shall reign with Him. It is only a little while and He will come.

Salvation is ours; sanctification is ours; glorification is ours. All the promises of the Book are ours. We wait for that glad day when Jesus shall come and we shall receive new bodies like the body of our Lord, painless, deathless, sinless bodies in which we shall be able to enjoy to the full all the blessings of the new heavens and the new earth forever and ever. There will be no more weariness, sickness, pain, sorrow, parting, dying or sinning, but through all eternity, on and on and on and on, forever and ever, we shall enjoy in infinite capacity the "things which God hath prepared for them that love him."
—*M. R. DeHaan*

# DECEMBER 18

*My brethren, count it all joy when ye fall into divers temptations.*
—James 1:2

"What kind of a Christian will God use?" is the great question. That is not difficult to answer. He will use the same kind He has always used. Just turn through the Bible and see whom He used in times past. Look at Joseph in the Old Testament. Who was tried more than this son of Jacob? He was abused by his brethren, sold into slavery, imprisoned on false charges, but he was patient and forebearing. It was Joseph who saved the Jewish race in that terrible famine. It was Joseph who won the favor of a pagan king and thereby obtained a home for his father and brethren. He could say, "Count it all joy when you fall into divers trials." The way to face every trial and every temptation is with a smile on your face and a song in your heart. Jesus said, "Blessed are they that have been persecuted for righteousness' sake."

Trial lets down a blazing torch into human nature and helps one to see many things which he little expected to see. One of the marvels of modern science is the use of electric light by divers at the bottom of the sea to take pictures of sea life. It is this biological conception that James has in mind in order to reveal spiritual truth. What do we learn by trials and temptations? We learn patience. Patience is the product of trial. Happiness is found also by enduring ill for the sake of Jesus.
—*C. E. Matthews*

*Set apart—no reputation*
*On this earth had He.*
*For thy sake reproach fell on Him,*
*For His sake on thee.*

*And the Word was made flesh, and dwelt among us, (and we beheld his glory, the glory as of the only begotten of the Father,) full of grace and truth.* —John 1:14

As we are looking forward, today, dear reader, to the happy celebration of our King's birthday, it is well for us to consider for a few moments the nature of our Savior King as revealed in the titles given Him in the first chapter of John's gospel.

Some of the glory of Christ is revealed in the first verse of John 1, for here our Savior is spoken of as the Word. The psalmist tells us that the heavens declare the glory of God and that the firmament reveals His handiwork, but nothing in nature can match the presentation of God as we have Him in His Son, Jesus. John says that Jesus is God Himself, that Jesus is God's revealed Word to men.

In the second and third verses Jesus is declared to be the Creator. For, says John, Jesus was present when the earth was created. Even stronger than that John says, "All things were made by Him . . ." (verse 3). The wood from which the Cross of Jesus Christ was fashioned was made by Jesus Himself as were the thorns which formed His crown. Even the iron from which the piercing nails were formed was created by Him.

In verse 4 and following verses Christ is called the Life and the Light. Then, in verses 10 and 11 Christ is referred to as the Promised Messiah, but "He came unto His own, and His own received Him not."

Then, because Christ is the only begotten Son of God we may also become sons of God through His shed blood. Even though He *is* THE SON, He is not ashamed to call us His brethren. How wonderful that truth is and how thankful we should be for our wonderful privilege of sonship.

# December 20

*And thine ears shall hear a word behind thee, saying, This is the way, walk ye in it, when ye turn to the right hand, and when ye turn to the left.* —Isaiah 30:21

There is a tender awe in knowing that there is Someone at your side guiding every step, restraining here, leading on there. He knows the way better than the oldest Swiss guide knows the mountain trail. He has love's concern that all shall go well with you. There is a great peace for us in that, and with it a tender awe to think who He is, and that He is close by your side. When you come to the splitting of the road into two, with a third path forking off from the others, there is peace in just holding steady and very quiet while you put out your hand and say, "Jesus, Master, guide here." And then to hear a Voice so soft that only in great quiet is it heard, softer than faintest breath on your cheek or slightest touch on your arm, telling the way in fewest words or syllables—that makes the peace unspeakable. —*S. D. Gordon*

*The way was rocky, rough, and steep;*
*My feet were weary, sore;*
*I stumbled oft and almost fell;*
*How could I bear much more?*
*'Twas then I felt a great strong hand*
*Close o'er my little one;*
*New strength, new courage, came to me.*
*Oh, this must be God's Son!*

*A voice was speaking, "Fear thou not,*
*For I am with thee still;*
*I'll never leave thee, nor forsake;*
*I'll help thee up the hill.*
*Be not dismayed, for I'm thy God,*
*The God of Canaan land,*
*I'll strengthen thee with righteousness,*
*Uphold thee by My hand."*
—Grace B. Renfrow

> *. . . Let us now go even unto Bethlehem, and see this thing*
> *which is come to pass, which the Lord hath made known*
> *unto us.*                                    —Luke 2:15

God's answer to the problems of the world when tyranny reigned triumphant and when idolatry, slavery and immorality were rampant on every hand, was this Babe of Bethlehem. We think we are lost in the unsolvable problems of our day: the conflict between East and West; the slavery of half the world; the drive of totalitarianism; the sin that destroys heart and home; the stubborn refusal to repent and turn to God. What shall we do and to whom shall we go? The star of Bethlehem leads the way. The prophet Micah points out the road. God in heaven answers from the skies. The virgin-born Babe in the manger, God with us in the flesh, Prince Immanuel, He is our ultimate answer to every problem and the final, all-sufficient Savior of the world.    —*W. A. Criswell*

*Over a scarred and war-torn world,*
  *The message, still sweet and clear,*
*Is ringing with hope and triumph for those*
  *Whose hearts are attuned to hear:*

*"Peace upon earth, the Savior is born,"*
  *Yes born, and He still lives today,*
*With love that is strong and steadfast and sure,*
  *Though evil may seem to hold sway.*

*The din of no battle can ever drown out*
  *The song that still rings through the ages,*
*Nor fire extinguish the dear Word of God,*
  *Or scoffer obscure its pages;*

*For the Bethlehem Star shines on through the night—*
  *Through war, with its anguish and sorrow,*
*With peace for the heart and strength for today,*
  *And a glorious hope for tomorrow!*

—Alice Mortenson

# DECEMBER 22

*Now on whom dost thou trust?* —Isaiah 36:5

Reader, this is an important question. Listen to the Christian's answer, and see if it is yours. "On whom dost thou trust?" "I trust," says the Christian, "in a triune God. I trust the Father, believing that He has chosen me from before the foundations of the world; I trust Him to provide for me in providence, to teach me, to guide me, to correct me if need be, and to bring me home to His own house where the many mansions are. I trust the Son. Very God of very God is He— the man Christ Jesus. I trust in Him to take away all my sins by His own sacrifice, and to adorn me with His perfect righteousness. I trust Him to be my Intercessor, to present my prayers and desires before His Father's throne, and I trust Him to be my Advocate at the last great day, to plead my cause, and to justify me. I trust Him for what He is, for what He has done, and for what He has promised yet to do. And I trust the Holy Spirit. I trust Him to drive out all my sins; I trust Him to curb my temper, to subdue my will, to enlighten my understanding, to check my passions, to comfort my despondency, to help my weakness, to illuminate my darkness; I trust Him to dwell in me as my life, to reign in me as my King, to sanctify me wholly, spirit, soul and body, and then to take me up to dwell with the saints in light for ever."

Oh, blessed trust! To trust Him whose power will never be exhausted, whose love will never wane, whose kindness will never change, whose faithfulness will never fail, whose wisdom will never be nonplussed, and whose perfect goodness can never know a diminution! Happy art thou, reader, if this trust is thine! So trusting, thou shalt enjoy sweet peace now, and glory hereafter, and the foundation of thy trust shall never be removed. —*Charles H. Spurgeon*

# DECEMBER 23

*. . . an angel touched him, and said unto him, arise and eat.*
—1 Kings 19:5

What an infinite comfort it is to realize that God knows how easily our nature may become jangled and out of tune! He can attribute our doubts and fears to their right source. He knows the bow is bent to the point of breaking, and the string strained to its utmost tension. He does not rebuke His servants when they cast themselves under juniper bushes, and ask to die, but provides them food and sleep. And when they send from their prisons, saying, "Art Thou He?" there is no word of rebuke, but tender encouragement and instruction.

Our Lord deals with us as we with children. The dearly loved child may have its passionate outbursts, but what mother would judge the child by that transient manifestation? She knows that it is a mood, perhaps traceable in part to physical conditions; she realizes that beyond the passing cloud there is the blue sky of disposition. She says to herself, "The mood will pass, but the disposition will remain. Let me wait patiently, and help the child to regain its true balance." It is not otherwise with us. This is the human side of the great doctrine of imputed righteousness. The Apostle says that God looks on us arrayed in the righteousness of Christ. He sees what we shall be, when in the meridian of eternity we are perfectly conformed to the image of His Son.

We may go to God and say, "I have not been myself today, but Thou knowest what I would be. I come back to myself, to Thine ideal, to the Christ ideal, and I stand before Thee 'accepted in the beloved.'" Even when we seem most feeble and unstable, the Lord believes in our essential self, which lies beneath all these moods, in the very depths of our being, until He shall call it forth. —*F. B. Meyer*

# DECEMBER 24

*Ye shall find the babe wrapped in swaddling clothes, lying in a manger.* —Luke 2:12

When God in the person of the Lord Jesus Christ was incarnate among men, it was a complete identification of the deity and humanity: God in Christ became man, in all points like unto man, except that He only of all the sons of man was completely free from sin. The Lord of glory became a child of earth. How great a mystery! The tiny Babe lying in the manger of Bethlehem was the One without whom "was not any thing made that was made." The tiny, chubby hand upon the cheek of the Virgin Mother was the hand of Him who holds the universe in the hollow of His hand. The baby arm about the mother's neck was the arm of the One whose everlasting arms are underneath all things.

The whole wonder of the incarnation is this: it was for us, for you and for me, that God became flesh and dwelt among us. The personal application of His shed blood to our sinful hearts cleanses us; faith in Him imparts salvation to us. How wonderful that God should take upon Himself the form of man, become an inheritor of the "ills that flesh is heir to," suffer the ignominy of the Cross! But how much more wonderful that He did this for us! —*Bob Jones, Jr.*

*Hark, the glad sound! the Savior comes,*
*The Savior promised long:*
*Let every heart prepare a throne,*
*And every voice a song.*

*He comes, the broken heart to bind,*
*The wounded soul to cure,*
*And, with the treasures of His grace,*
*To enrich the humble poor.*

*Our glad hosannas, Prince of Peace,*
*Thy welcome shall proclaim;*
*And heaven's eternal arches ring*
*With Thy beloved name.*

—Philip Doddridge

# DECEMBER 25

What a blessed experience it is, dear fellow Christian, to reflect upon this wonderfully simple birth announcement. What a blessed expression of God's love to us—this gift of His Son, the Lord Jesus. What a blessed expectancy is ours if we reflect upon the Person and Presence of our wonderful Savior.

On this Christmas Day, we cannot help but be filled with joy and gratitude—for the complete salvation we have in Christ, for the rich contentment we have in contemplating Him. To us as Christians, Christmas means "Christ with us." And truly He is with us, not only on this Christmas Day, but every day of our lives as we walk in His will.

We enjoy not only the Presence of Christ in our daily walk, but we also feel a certain partnership with the countless scores of our fellow Christians who are also remembering the birth of Christ in the midst of a "perverse and unbelieving generation." Our fellowship is not with the world—our fellowship is heavenly, with Christ, and with all believers through Him.

The good news in our verse for the day is for the very personal "you." Our Savior brings with Him "good tidings of great joy" (Luke 2:10). These "good tidings" are in essence the Gospel of Jesus Christ. As this "good news" comes to us, we are to transmit it to others—through a consecrated life, a dedicated testimony, looking for the "blessed hope" of His coming again. Yes, "this same Jesus" is the One who gave Himself on Calvary's Cross for our sins, the One who has opened the way to Heaven for every believer. This is the good news for this Christmas Day!

# DECEMBER 26

*And they came with haste, and found Mary, and Joseph, and the babe lying in a manger.* —Luke 2:16

Nothing more fitting than the manger. Indeed we can see the Hand of God at work here. The Savior's majesty and glory are such that no earthly tinsel could add to them. Had His kingship been of a purely human order, the stable would have been infinitely incongruous. We discover as we look deeply into the mystery of the manger that however shocking to human concepts, such a birth lays a perfect foundation for the very work the Redeemer came to do. . . . Bethlehem's Manger is found on the divine highway to Calvary's Cross. Indeed the colors do blend. Nothing is more in tune with the song of the angels which the shepherds heard as they kept watch by night over their flocks. Nothing is more attuned to Bethlehem's Star than Bethlehem's Manger. Of course, we will need to have our eyes anointed with the Oil of the Spirit to see it, for the natural man cannot understand the things of God.

—F. J. Huegel

*We worship Thee, O Son of God,*
*On this most holy day,*
*Who came to earth a little Babe*
*And in a manger lay;*
*Thou who didst leave Thy heavenly home*
*To break earth's chains of night,*
*Whose advent brought a world new hope,*
*Changed darkness into light.*
—Julia Benson Parker

*But unto the Son he saith, Thy throne, O God, is for ever and ever: a scepter of righteousness is the scepter of thy kingdom.* —Hebrews 1:8

*Our infinite source of joy.* Jesus' coming was God shining through into our dark world. The brightness of His glory—that is, Himself—we cannot conceive; our human gaze could not endure it. But we caught a glimpse when He came veiled in flesh. And that glimpse brought us the good news of a better world, a world of light, an eternal brightness beyond. Nothing can rob us of that knowledge. His coming told us of heaven.

Jesus' coming showed us "the express image of His (God's) person." He brought us the good news of a holy God. Other gods of the nations are cruel, vile, hateful and retaliative; He is kind, morally spotless, all love. Others are arbitrary; He is just. And because He is holy, we see that we too should be holy.

Jesus' errand was salvation. He Himself "purged our sins." And that makes Christianity a singing religion instead of a sinning religion, a praising religion instead of a wailing religion. The Christless religions have a sense of sin, but no sense of a Savior. They know they are wrong, but they have no dynamic to make them right. Let me not mock my mighty Savior by naming His name, then living in sin. —*Bertha Munro*

*Hark! the herald angels sing,*
*Glory to the newborn King:*
*Peace on earth, and mercy mild,*
*God and sinners reconciled.*
        —Charles Wesley

# December 28

*Teach me Thy way, O Lord, and lead me in a plain path.*
—Psalm 27:11

*Lead, kindly Light, amid the encircling gloom,*
  *Lead Thou me on!*
*The night is dark, and I am far from home,*
  *Lead Thou me on!*
*Keep Thou my feet; I do not ask to see*
*The distant scene; one step enough for me.*
—J. H. Newman

God only is holy; He alone knows how to lead His children in the paths of holiness. He knows every aspect of your soul, every thought of your heart, every secret of your character, its difficulties and hindrances; He knows how to mold you to His will, and lead you onwards; He knows exactly how each event, each trial, each temptation, will tell upon you, and He disposes all things accordingly. The consequences of this belief, if fully grasped, will influence your whole life. You will seek to give yourself up to God more and more unreservedly, asking nothing, refusing nothing, wishing nothing, but what He wills; not seeking to bring things about for yourself, taking all He sends joyfully, and believing the "one step" set before you to be enough for you. You will be satisfied that even though there are clouds around, and your way seems dark, He is directing all, and that which seems a hindrance will prove a blessing, since He wills it. —*Jean Nicolas Grou*

*Leave God to order all thy ways,*
  *And hope in Him, whate'er betide,*
*Thou'lt find in Him, in evil days,*
  *Thy all-sufficient strength and guide.*
*Who trusts in God's unchanging love*
*Builds on the rock that naught can move.*

# DECEMBER 29

*Cast thy burden upon the Lord, and He shall sustain thee.*
—Psalm 55:22

Excessive care about *any* thing is contrary to God's will as expressed in this verse—and is, therefore, sin! Have you ever thought that your anxiety concerning your problems was actually sin? Would you ever stop to think that anxious care is actually setting yourself up as wiser than God and putting yourself in His place? Here you are with your burden, loaded down and staggering beneath the heavy load—simply because you do not accept God's out-spoken promise to "sustain thee."

You would never knowingly doubt God. You would never knowingly lose confidence in God. Yet in your anxiety you are guilty of just these acts.

Why not rest unquestionably upon His promise? Why not "cast thy burden upon the Lord . . ."? Why not put your complete confidence and trust in Him? "In all thy ways acknowledge Him, and He shall direct thy paths." Could any promise be plainer?

Christian reader, this Lord of rest is interested in *you!* The thousands and thousands of promises in His Word are for *you.* This is only one of them. He is the answer to all care and anxiety, the solution to every problem.

> *If we would please our blessed Lord,*
> *Our faith in Him would prove,*
> *We'd lean upon His promises,*
> *And rest in His great love.*
>
> *Whate'er our lot or circumstance*
> *We would not fret or doubt,*
> *But just commit our path to Him,*
> *For good He works things out.*
>
> *Nor would we try to hurry Him,*
> *To please our restless will;*
> *But trusting Him, we'd bide His time,*
> *His promise to fulfill.*

# DECEMBER 30

*By faith Moses, when he was come to years, refused to be called the son of Pharaoh's daughter.* —Hebrews 11:24

*I do not ask for earthly store*
*Beyond a day's supply;*
*I only covet more and more*
*The clear and single eye.*
*To see my duty face to face*
*And trust the Lord for daily grace.*
—J. Maxfield

Moses fed daily on the promises of God, pleading them in prayer, and leaning his whole weight upon them. And he often knew what it was to leave behind him the familiar and tried, for the strange and new; at the bidding of God, he stepped out, though there seemed nothing to tread upon, launching himself and three million people absolutely on the care of God, assured that God's faithfulness could not fail.

Are you willing to die to your own strength; to forsake your own plans for God's; to seek out and do His will absolutely; to take up the attitude of entire and absolute surrender to His purposes; to feed daily on the promises of God; to step out in faith, reckoning, without emotion of any kind, on the faithfulness of God, only fully persuaded that He will perform all that He has promised? Then surely through you God will, here or hereafter, work as in the times of old, of which our fathers have told us. —F. B. Meyer

*Faith came singing into my room,*
*And other guests took flight;*
*Fear and anxiety, grief and gloom*
*Sped out into the night.*
*I wondered that such peace could be;*
*But Faith said gently, "Don't you see,*
*They really cannot live with me."*

*This spake he, signifying by what death he should glorify God. And when he had spoken this, he saith unto him, Follow me.* —John 21:19

*Has the year brought sadness?*
*Joy is yet in store.*
*Has it given gladness?*
*Next year giveth more.*
*Let your Father measure*
*All your pain and care,*
*Let Him weigh the burden*
*That your heart must bear,*
*Sending light or shadow*
*As He deemeth best,*
*For in His sure wisdom*
*You can safely rest.*
*Peace for all the morrows,*
*Strength for all the days,*
*These shall be your portion*
*Through the New Year's ways.*
—Annie Johnson Flint

We have come now to the last day of the year. For a whole year in these daily readings we have been walking with Christ. Is there any better word with which to close this book and close the year than this last invitation of Jesus—"Follow me"?

To follow Christ is to go where He leads, without questioning or demurring. It may be to a life of trial, suffering, or sacrifice—but no matter; we have nothing whatever to do with the kind of life to which our Lord calls us. Our only simple duty is to obey and follow. We know that Jesus will lead us only in right paths, and that the way He takes slopes upward and ends at the feet of God. —*J. R. Miller*

# SCRIPTURE INDEX

# SCRIPTURE INDEX

# CONTRIBUTOR INDEX

# CONTRIBUTING POETS